CANADA IN QUESTION

Federalism in the Seventies

mcgraw-hill series in canadian politics

Paul W. Fox, *General Editor*

CANADA IN QUESTION
Federalism in the Seventies

DONALD V. SMILEY

Professor of Political Science
Erindale College
University of Toronto

Toronto
McGraw-Hill Ryerson Limited
Montreal
New York
London
Sydney
Johannesburg
Mexico
Panama
Düsseldorf
Singapore
Rio de Janeiro
Kuala Lumpur
New Delhi

CANADA IN QUESTION
Federalism in the Seventies

Library of Congress Catalog Card Number 72-2783

ISBN 0-07-077363-7

3 4 5 6 7 8 9 10   D-72   10 9 8 7 6 5 4

Printed and bound in Canada

CONTENTS

This book is dedicated to Henry Angus, Dean Emeritus of Graduate Studies of the University of British Columbia, whose study of the Canadian Confederation extends for over sixty years of its history. His lucidity in analysis and exactness in expression are standards which I should like sometime to meet.

Foreword

Students of Canadian politics have been badly in need of a sound review and stimulating analysis of the contemporary course of federalism in our country. So much has happened in this core area in the past few years that it has been difficult to keep up with the pace of events, let alone to distinguish new departures and significant developments amidst the welter of proposals, competing interests, divergent ideas, contradictory opinions and arguments that have bedizened the field.

It was with great pleasure, therefore, that I received from Professor Donald Smiley the manuscript of a book which not only summarizes recent developments in Canadian federalism but analyzes them and assesses their direction. It was also with keen anticipation that I sat down to read what he had to say since no one is better qualified than Donald Smiley to comment on the subject of Canadian federalism. For more than a decade Professor Smiley has been studying the topic intensively. He has published some of his findings and thinking on various aspects of the subject in a number of leading articles in scholarly journals, in studies for the Canadian Tax Foundation and the Royal Commission on Bilingualism and Biculturalism, and in an earlier book.

What would such an authority say at this juncture about the prickly problems that have arisen lately in Canadian federalism and what hope — if any — would he see for their solution? Has the thorny path we have been treading led up or down? Have we been progressing or regressing as we have tinkered with our basic constitutional structure? To put the question in fundamental extremes, is Canada evolving towards a "higher," more complex organic form of federalism or degenerating into a rudimentary kind of parochialism?

These are the sorts of questions that have been troubling Canadians as they have watched with bewilderment and apprehension the succession of events and crises that have befallen federalism in the past decade. There certainly has been no shortage of such traumas. Probably no period in Canadian history has been so concerned with federal problems; to mention only a few, for example, deadlock over rival Canadian and Quebec pension plans, continual confrontation at federal-provincial conferences, hard-nosed bargaining in renewing taxation and fiscal agreements, Quebec's plea for "special status," the "two nation theory," threats of separatism, appeals to alleviate regional economic disparities, and arguments about cultural duality and multi-culturalism.

Professor Smiley deals with virtually all such important issues. He does a masterly job in threading a way for the reader through the maze of complicated problems that have beset Canadian federalism in the past decade. His chapter on the political economy of federalism, for instance, is a *tour de force*. He manages at one and the same time to explain clearly and in detail the very complicated developments that have occurred in federal-provincial financial arrangements recently, without ever losing sight of his major objective, which is to discuss how they affect the balance of power between Ottawa and the provinces. His chapter on executive federalism is written with similar finesse. Professor Smiley conveys all the relevant facts to show how a fine but resilient web of inter-governmental executive and administrative relations has emerged beneath the surface of the constitution — in numerous conferences of officials, ministers, and prime ministers, for instance — to provide a sort of cybernetics system undergirding federation. He has his own opinions, of course, about the utility and potentiality of some of these recent developments in executive federalism, just as he has his own views about the wisdom of some of the steps taken in federal-provincial financial relations.

It is this skilful blending of sound scholarship and informed opinion that is characteristic of Professor Smiley and always makes his work so worth reading. One not only learns but is provoked to think. I suspect, for example, that when some readers get to his chapter on cultural duality, they will be inclined to disagree with his views. But all to the good. I imagine Donald Smiley is the last person who would believe that every one would agree with him.

I will be frank to say that I found his chapter on political parties and their role in federalism the most captivating in the book. Here Professor Smiley breaks new and extremely important gound. Bringing his habitual clear-sighted powers of analysis to bear, he examines the question of whether our political parties assist in integrating the country or are disintegrative forces. Without giving away his conclusions, I would say that his findings are sobering. In any case, this chapter opens up a significant topic for the study of contemporary Canadian federalism and makes Professor Smiley's book, in my opinion, even more essential for students and stimulating to general readers.

Professor Smiley has produced a superlative brief, descriptive, critical, and provocative analysis of Canadian federalism at a vitally important point in its existence. Need I say more, except to thank him for contributing to our knowledge and to our Series — and to advise readers to conclude this Foreword as quickly as possible and to get into the meat of his book.

University of Toronto, April 5, 1972.

PAUL W. FOX,
GENERAL EDITOR.

Introduction

There is no end to writings on Canadian federalism. This is attested by my crowded files and library shelves. It remains a matter of contention whether the century-old preoccupation of Canadians with federal institutions is worthy. John Porter wrote in 1965, "... it may be speculated that (Canadian) federalism as such has meaning only for politicians and senior civil servants who work with the complex machinery they have set up as well as for the scholars who provide a continuing commentary on it, but that it has very little meaning for the bulk of the population."[1] So far as Porter is concerned, federal institutions in Canada are for the most part dysfunctional, and when a sociologist of this methodological bent calls something "dysfunctional" that is the worst he can say of it.

As I understand it, one of the most distinctive contributions of the political scientist as such is to relate the institutions and processes of government with the substantive public issues dealt with by governmental authorities. Daniel Elazar in his distinguished study of American federalism proceeds in a way very similar to that attempted in this book, "In the United States the very existence of federalism requires that virtually all political issues be considered with two questions in mind: What kinds of issues are raised in American politics because the states (and their cities) exist as they do? and How are these issues developed and resolved in the American political system because of the existence of the states (and their cities) in their present form?"[2] Several directions in contemporary political analysis deny the validity of the perspective which posits the interrelation of institutions and issues. The disposition of radical thought is of course to regard the forms and procedures of government as nothing more than a superstructure erected on basic constellations of social class and economic power. From a different perspective, behavioural analysis also downgrades the importance of institutions as Claude E. Forget has recently written:

> The modern development of social sciences has given prominence to behavioural factors based on values, choices, and motivations at the expense of institutional factors based on history and expressed through a legal system of constraints. Modern social science all but dismisses most formal institutions as lagging reflections of past attitudes, values, and technology. It is generally assumed that the set of institutional constraints found at any time will eventually wear down wherever present attitudes and objectives which conflict with it and that these attitudes and objectives constitute what is important and needs to be understood."[3]

Those concerned primarily with substantive issues often proceed in complete neglect of the structures and processes of public authority. And there still linger kinds of formalistic analysis which deal with structures and sometimes processes of government without reference to how these shape, and are shaped by, the context of public activity.

The synthetic approach to political analysis imposes demands upon the scholar which I am painfully aware I cannot meet. The developed nation-state is the most inclusive of human organizations; with the possible exception of the Roman Catholic Church, international and supranational organizations serve much more fragmentary purposes. To describe these national institutions and processes involves the political scientist in other people's specialized scholarly territory — in this book in the territory of the constitutional historian and constitutional lawyer, the economist and the political sociologist. In writing this study I have sometimes felt like Goethe's Dr. Faust:

> You sit forever, gluing, patching,
> You cook the scraps from others' fare,
> And from your heaps of ashes hatching
> A starveling flame, ye blow it bare!

So far as Canadian federalism is concerned, the "scraps from others' fare" sometimes provide an over-generous repast and sometimes not. In respect, for example, to judicial review of the constitution and some aspects of fiscal policy the literature is vast and I can hope to do no more than to deal with these matters with a degree of lucidity. Other crucial areas of investigation such as the relations between federal and provincial political parties have been almost entirely neglected by scholars.

The other demand made upon the contemporary student of politics is methodological. In comparison with other areas of political science, the fields of Canadian federalism and comparative federalism are not characterized by analytical rigor and this book does nothing to remedy the deficiency. Harold Kaplan in his able analysis of the institutions of Metropolitan Toronto has given a demonstration of how functional analysis can fruitfully be used to investigate and describe federalism at the local level.[4] I have not the wits to take up Kaplan's standing challenge. In a broad and haphazard sense, I recognize and try to describe the inter-relationships between what may loosely be described as the sub-systems of Canadian federalism — and in particular those of the formal/constitutional, the partisan/political and the executive systems. Further than this, I do not go.

The completion of this short book has been delayed by two periods in which I ceased work because of the judgment that the federation would not last as long as it would take to finish the manuscript. I have neither the prophetic capacity nor the tools of analysis to tell whether Confederation will survive in recognizable form or, if it does not, whether it will end with a whimper or a bang. Whatever happens, Canadians in the future will have been shaped partly by their previous experience with federal institutions. Perhaps the only other certainty is that whether Canadian federalism survives or collapses scholars will be found to demonstrate that things could not possibly have turned out any other way. However, while Confederation persists it deserves continuing study. As others have examined it in its more particularized dimensions, I try to analyze it as a working system.

One of the hazards of this kind of study is that it is quickly overtaken by new commentaries and investigations. Since the last chapter was completed D. W. Carr's *Recovering Canada's Nationhood*[5], a comprehensive blueprint for new national economic policies, has been published. While Carr's book is, I think, marred by the author's regrettable tendency to regard those who disagree with him as unpatriotic, he has gone much further than anyone else in relating a specific economic strategy for national survival to cultural duality and to the institutions and processes of Canadian federalism. In late. 1971 *One Country or Two?*[6] was published under the editorship of R. M. Burns. This is a collection of essays by English-Canadian scholars focused on the probable consequences of the disintegration of Confederation for particular parts of Canada. These analyses are on the whole free of the sentimentalization of Quebec nationalism and the apologetic stance toward the federal experience which characterizes a good deal of recent English-Canadian scholarship. If a constructive debate between Canada's two historic communities is still possible, it might well begin from the sane formulations of this book. Yet another study is soon to be released with the imminent publication of the Report of the Special Joint Committee of the Senate and House of Commons on the Constitution of Canada. This Report is unlikely to have any importance in reviving the process of constitutional reform broken off in mid-1971, and will no doubt take its place on academic book-shelves as yet another demonstration of the continuing dissatisfaction of right-thinking Canadians with the constitutional arrange-ments under which they seem destined to be governed. And the reported lack of agreement on important aspects of the Report among members of the Committee indicates to me at least the improbability of Canadians being able to come together on comprehensive constitutional changes.

I had intended to publish a select bibliography on contemporary Canadian federalism in this book. However, an excellent bibliography is contained in *Canadian Federalism: Myth or Reality*, Second Edition, J. Peter Meekison, Editor, Methuen of Canada, Toronto, 1971 and those interested may refer to this. For students of comparative federalism there is a useful bibliography *Federalism and Intergovernmental Relations in Australia, Canada, the United States and other Countries*, Institute of Intergovernmental Relations, Queen's University, Kingston, 1967.

Several intellectual debts must be acknowledged. During my years at the University of British Columbia my friends Edwin Black, Alan Cairns, Milton Moore and Paul Tennant shared their views and experiences with me and without their stimulation my studies on federalism would not have proceeded. In a more sporadic way, I have been very much helped over the years by my contacts with Ronald Cheffins of the University of Victoria and Ronald Burns of Queen's University. At the University of Toronto, Stefan Dupré has encouraged me, and by his own work strengthened my conviction that the tradition of political economy has continuing relevance. The academic editor of this series, Paul Fox, has helped me along at every stage and his vast patience and critical insight have made this book much better in style and in substance than it would otherwise have been. With all this help I have mentioned I, am to blame for all infelicities of expression and incoherencies of analysis.

I have incurred other debts too. I am grateful for a Canada Council Study Leave Fellowship in 1968-69 and I apologize to the Council for the delay in the publication of this book. During the past two years Dean E. A. Robinson of Erindale College has been generous enough to help me along from his very limited research budget. Mrs. Elinor Foden in typing the manuscript has gone much beyond the normal call of duty by her expert proofreading and her vigilant eye for awkwardness and ambiguity.

When I am writing, my wife and daughters are exposed to a great deal of quite unnecessary churlishness. I acknowledge their forgiveness.

— D. V. S.

NOTES

[1] *The Vertical Mosaic*, The University of Toronto Press, 1965, p. 384.

[2] *American Federalism: A View from the States*, Crowell, New York, 1966, pp. 4-5.

[3] *The Power of the Purse in a Revised Constitution*, Private Planning Association of Canada, Montreal, 1970, pp. 1-2.

[4] *Urban Political Systems: A Functional Analysis of Metro Toronto*, New York, Columbia University Press, 1967.

[5] Canada Publishing Company, Ottawa, 1971.

[6] With an introduction by John J. Deutsch, McGill-Queen's University Press, Montreal and London, 1971.

1

The Canadian Constitution and the Federal System

Among students of law and politics the term "constitution" is used in two different ways. In the first sense we refer to a legal code which within a geographically delineated area overrides all other enactments or acts of government and is usually amendable by a procedure less flexible than that related to other legislation. The second way we use the term constitution involves subject-matter, the laws and settled usages within a state which determine the respective powers and privileges of the various institutions of government and the essential aspects of the relations between citizens and the political community. In many circumstances the procedural and subject-matter definitions of what is constitutional will coincide where the legal document prescribing the basic political relations of a community is both paramount over other political acts and subject to amendment by procedures less flexible than those by which other laws can be changed. On the other hand, jurisdictions with codified constitutions in this sense sometimes include provisions about substantive public policy, as when the United States Constitution was amended in 1919 to prohibit the manufacture or sale of alcoholic beverages. Contrariwise, the United Kingdom does not have a codified constitution at all, and from time to time the most fundamental of political relations are determined by the Crown in Parliament through the same procedures by which enactments relating to the most trivial of public matters come into being. In general, the usual distinction between written and unwritten constitutions is not very helpful, and the more useful classification is between codified (procedural) and

1

uncodified (subject-matter) constitutions and between codified and un-codified elements of the same constitutional system.

There *is* a codified part of the Canadian constitution, including at a minimum the British North America Act of 1867 and its subsequent amendments and those British and Canadian statutes and Orders-in-Council providing for the entry of the various provinces and territories into Confederation after 1867. Although, as we shall see later in this Chapter, the Fulton-Favreau formula was not enacted, this proposed procedure for constitutional amendment agreed upon by the federal and provincial governments in the fall of 1964 included this definition:

> 11. Without limiting the meaning of the expression "Constitution of Canada", in this Part that expression includes the following enactments and any order, rule or regulation thereunder, namely,
>   (a) the British North America Acts, 1867 to 1964;
>   (b) the Manitoba Act, 1870;
>   (c) the Parliament of Canada Act, 1875;
>   (d) the Canadian Speaker (Appointment of Deputy) Act, 1895, Session 2;
>   (e) the Alberta Act;
>   (f) the Saskatchewan Act;
>   (g) the Statute of Westminster, 1931, in so far as it is part of the law of Canada; and
>   (h) this Act.[1]

There are a number of enactments of the Parliament of Canada which in a strict legal sense are solely at the discretion of that legislature but which are constitutional in their subject-matter. It is, however, unlikely that any group of students of such affairs could be brought to agreement on a list of Canadian constitutional statutes.[2] Certainly there should be included the War Measures Act, the Canadian Bill of Rights and the Supreme Court Act. But should such a categorization include, for example, the Canada Elections Act and the Canadian Citizenship Act? And moving away from enactments of Parliament, what about the minute of the Privy Council of October 25, 1935, which details the powers of the Prime Minister of Canada? Informed observers would differ.

Beyond its codified elements and certain statutes and Orders-in-Council of constitutional significance, the Canadian constitution can reasonably be regarded as including certain settled conventions of governmental structure and practice. The preamble of the British North America Act of 1867 stated that the colonies had expressed a desire to be federally united under the Crown "with a Constitution similar in Principle to that of the United Kingdom." We can suppose that by this phrase the framers of the Act were referring to the conventions of responsible parliamentary government, the independence of the judiciary and, outside Quebec, the common law system. Some of these understandings were enacted in the British North

America Act itself, e.g., the provision of Section 54 that a bill for taxation or for the expenditure of public funds must be brought before the House of Commons by the Governor General — in effect, by a Minister of the Crown — and by the provisions of Sections 44-47 related to the Speaker of the Commons. However, some of the most crucial aspects of British parliamentary government were not mentioned explicitly in the Act. To take outstanding examples, there is no reference to the office or powers of the cabinet as such[3] or of the Prime Minister or to the convention that to remain in office a ministry must retain the continuing support of a majority in the House of Commons.

THE FEDERAL DIVISION OF LEGISLATIVE POWERS

The most characteristic aspect of a federal constitution is its division of law-making powers between the central and regional governments. Contemporary federal systems have variegated institutional characteristics. Most, like Canada, have a unified judical system; the United States has parallel structures of federal and state courts. In several federations like the United States and the Federal Republic of Germany the regional governments as such have important responsibilities related to the functioning of the central authority; in Canada it is otherwise. The older federations have had separate and autonomous central and regional bureaucracies; in some of the newer ones there has been reliance on a unified civil service. Despite these and other institutional differences, the distinguishing characteristic of a federation is the constitutional distribution of legislative powers between national and state or provincial governments. There are many kinds of such distributions. In Canada, and most of the newer federations, the national legislature is given the residual powers, i.e. those not explicitly conferred on the provinces or states, while in the United States powers not explicitly vested in the national are reserved to the states and the people — although contradictory trends of judical interpretation in the two countries have gone a very long way toward reversing the intentions of those who framed these constitutional provisions. Some federations have a large number of concurrent legislative powers which can be exercised by either or both levels of government, but in Canada explicit provisions for concurrency are limited. In some federations, such as Canada and Australia, the distribution of legislative powers is exhaustive or nearly exhaustive in the sense that if one level cannot enact a particular kind of legislation the other has power to do so, while in the United States there are important constitutional restrictions against what any government can do. Some federations like the United States provide that all the constituents states/provinces have precisely the same law-making powers while in others, like the Republic of India, there is a differentiation among regional governments. Despite these variations, all federal constitutions provide for a distribution of legislative powers which cannot be altered or amended at the unilateral discretion of either level.

Those who framed the British America Act did not find it difficult to agree on a distribution of law-making powers between Parliament and the provincial legislatures. There have been several explanations of the relative ease with which the matter was resolved. In a study published in 1939, Donald Creighton suggested that so far as economic affairs were concerned the Fathers of Confederation made an implicit distinction between activities associated with land and activities associated with commerce, and on the basis of this distinction allocated powers to the provinces and the Dominion respectively.[4] The Report of the Quebec Royal Commission on Constitutional Problems published in 1956 argued that in general the subjects given to the provinces were those in respect to which the traditions and interests of the English and French-speaking communities were significantly different while Dominion matters were believed to have no such cultural incidence.[5] Peter Waite has said that by "the federal principle" the Fathers of Confederation did not mean the distribution of legislative powers at all but rather the structure of Parliament and in particular the relation between the Senate and the House of Commons.[6]

The formula for the distribution of legislative authority in the British North America Act assigned the residual powers to the Dominion. Section 92 enumerated fifteen classes of subjects about which the provinces exclusively might make laws with a sixteenth category "Generally all Matters of a merely local or private Nature in the province." Section 93 provided for exclusive provincial jurisdiction over education with safe-guards for the rights of denominational schools as these rights existed by law at the time of union or were subsequently so established. Section 95 enacted that both Parliament and the provinces might make laws in respect to agriculture and immigration with the proviso that those of the Dominion would prevail in the event of a conflict. These were, then, the legislative powers of the provinces. The opening words of Section 91 enacted "It shall be lawful for the Queen, by and with the Advice and Consent of the Senate and House of Commons to make Laws for the Peace, Order, and Good Government of Canada, in relation to all Matters not coming within the Classes of Subjects by this Act assigned exclusively to the Legislatures of the Provinces." If the Act had not gone on to elaborate this general grant of lawmaking power, the subsequent judicial interpretation of the Canadian constitution would have been very different from what it turned out to be. In passing on the validity of an enactment of Parliament the courts would have had no alternative to ascertaining whether or not it encroached on provincial legislation as specified in Sections 92 and 93 and any provincial enactment would have had to be justified as coming within one of these Sections or Section 95. However, Section 91 went on to enact "and for greater Certainty, but not so as to restrict the Generality of the foregoing Terms of this Section, it is hereby declared that . . . the exclusive

Legislative Authority of the Parliament of Canada extends to all Matters coming within the Classes of Subjects next herein enumerated . . ." There were then listed 29 classes of subjects. There has never been a satisfactory explanation of why the framers of the Act resorted to such an enumeration. As we shall see, judicial interpretation from the late-nineteenth century onward came to find the peacetime legislative powers of Parliament not in the authority to enact laws for the "Peace, Order, and Good Government of Canada" but rather in the enumerated headings of Section 91.

In terms of substance, most of the powers of the provinces can be subsumed under one or both of these classes of subjects: (1) those matters where the traditions of the English- and French-speaking communities of the former province of Canada differed significantly; (2) those matters which in British North America of the 1860s were usually the responsibility of local governments. Thus were included jurisdiction over education, what we would now call health and welfare matters, the control of provincial Crown lands, municipal instituions, the administration of justice in the province as well as concurrent powers with the Dominion over agriculture and immigration. The provinces were also given exclusive powers to legislate in respect to "Property and Civil Rights in the Province." From the Quebec Act of 1774 onward Quebec had been given the right to carry on the system of private law derived from France, and so the provinces were given jurisdiction over property and civil rights so that the civil and common law traditions might continue in Quebec and the provinces with English-speaking majorities respectively.[7]

The powers conferred on the Dominion were deemed necessary to secure military defence, the eventual inclusion of all remaining British territories in North America within Canada and the establishment of an integrated national economy. Under the enumerated headings of Section 91 were included powers over trade and commerce; the various aspects of interprovincial transportation and communication; banking, currency, interest, and legal tender; patents and copyrights. As we have seen, Section 95 conferred concurrent powers on the Dominion and the provinces in respect to agriculture and immigration with the proviso that federal laws should prevail in the event of a clash. Several Sections of the Act provided for the federal authorities taking action to include remaining British possessions in North America in the Dominion e.g. Newfoundland, and the western territories still under the control of the Hudson's Bay Company. Parliament was given the exclusive power to give legislative implementation to British treaties in Canada. The national authorities were to have exclusive powers over defence. Along with these nation-building and nation-maintaining powers, the exclusive authority to legislate in respect to the criminal law and to procedures in criminal matters was conferred on the Dominion and the central government was given crucial responsibilities in respect to a unified judicial system.

In conferring what were then the most costly functions of government on the Dominion the framers of the Confederation settlement provided that Parliament might raise moneys by "any Mode or System of Taxation" while the provinces were limited to direct taxes. The effect was to give the Dominion exclusive access to customs and excise duties, the sources of most public revenues at the time, while the provinces would be confined to taxes on real property, proceeds from the sale of Crown lands and the exploitation of natural resources and to incidental fees and revenues. The provinces were also to receive annual subsidies from the Dominion according to a schedule provided for in the British North America Act.

The B.N.A. Act provided for a single judical system in Canada rather than, as in the United States, a dual system of courts dealing with national and state matters respectively. Although the Act seemed to contemplate that for the most part the Dominion and the provinces would carry on their respective legislative and administrative responsibilities in relative independence of each other, the judicial system was clearly expected to operate through cooperation between the two levels. The provinces were given exclusive jurisdiction over "The Administration of Justice in the province, including the Constitution, Maintenance, and Organization of Provincial Courts, both of Civil and Criminal Jurisdiction, and including Procedure in Civil Matters in these Courts." However, the Governor General — in effect the federal cabinet — was to appoint the judges of the superior, district and county courts in each province, these judges were to be paid by the Dominion and were to serve during good behaviour, subject to removal by the Governor General on an address from the Senate and House of Commons. Parliament was given exclusive authority to legislate in respect to the criminal law and to procedures in criminal matters. It was further provided in Section 101 "The Parliament of Canada may . . . provide for the Constitution, Maintenance, and Organization of a General Court of Appeal for Canada, and for the Establishment of any additional Courts for the better Administration of the Laws of Canada."

Beyond the provisions for the dominance of the Dominion in the ways which have already been outlined, the British North America Act went even further in its attempts to secure federal supremacy by making provision for circumstances under which the central authorities might restrict the provinces in the exercise of the latters' legislative powers:

— under Sections 55 and 90 the provinces were put in a position of colonial subordination to the Dominion executive (as was the central government in respect to the United Kingdom). The Lieutenant Governor of a province, a Dominion officer, had the power to reserve provincial legislation and when this was done the bill did not become law unless the federal cabinet so decided. Whether reserved or not, any provincial law might be disallowed by the federal cabinet within a year of enactment.

— under Section 92 10(c) the Parliament of Canada was given the power to bring "Works" otherwise within provincial jurisdiction under federal control.

— under Section 93 the federal cabinet and Parliament were made the guarantors of the educational rights of denominational minorities against provincial encroachments. If such rights were overridden, the federal cabinet might take action but if this were ineffective Parliament was given the power to enact remedial legislation to secure execution of the cabinet's orders.

The distribution of legislative powers made by the British North America Act of 1867 has been explicitly changed by constitutional amendment on only three occasions. In each case the effect was to provide for federal responsibility in the field of income-maintenance programmes:

— in 1940 Parliament was given the exclusive legislative jurisdiction over unemployment insurance.

— in 1951 Parliament was given concurrent jurisdiction with the provinces in respect to old age pensions, with the proviso that "no law made by the Parliament of Canada in relation to old age pensions shall effect the operation of any law present or future of a Provincial Legislature in relation to old age pensions."

— in 1964 Parliament was given the power to enact legislation in respect to supplementary benefits to old age pensions, including survivors' and disability benefits, with the same provision as that of the 1951 amendment in respect to the paramountcy of provincial laws.

THE AMENDMENT OF THE BRITISH NORTH AMERICA ACT[8]

The amendment of a codified constitution is the most fundamental of political processes. Formal amendment is only one of the procedures of constitutional change, but as William S. Livingston points out, "It differs from the others in that it is superior to them and may be employed to transcend or repudiate any change that may be brought about by other means."[9] The failure of Canadians to agree on an amending procedure is the most obvious failure of their constitutional experience.

The British North America Act of 1867 did not specify an explicit procedure for its own amendment and the matter is mentioned only once in the Confederation Debates. It was undoubtedly taken for granted that the United Kingdom Parliament would be the amending authority but probably also, in the light of Canadian experience under the Act of Union,[10] that no amendment would be enacted without the request or consent of the Dominion. The procedure by which Canadian initiative would take place was not specified, perhaps because the Fathers of Confederation believed it unlikely they could come to agreement on such a procedure.

From Confederation until the period after the First World War the British North America Act was amended on several occasions by the Imperial Parliament at the request of Canada. However, no settled conventions developed to regulate the procedures within the Dominion for making such a request. Serious and protracted debates about a domestic amending procedure began only in the 1920s when Canada along with the other Dominions was on the verge of attaining full legal recognition of its self-governing status. However, when this development culminated in the enactment by the United Kingdom Parliament of the Statute of Westminster in 1931, it was provided at the request of the Canadian government that "Nothing in this Act shall be deemed to apply to the repeal, amendment or alteration of the British North America Acts, 1867 to 1930, or to any order, rule or regulation made thereunder." The federal and provincial governments had been unable to agree on an amending procedure.

A Dominion-Provincial Conference was called in 1935 and a sub-committee appointed to deal with a procedure for constitutional amendment. The Dominion and all the provinces except New Brunswick agreed that Canada should have the power to amend the constitution if a method satisfactory to all parties could be worked out. The desperate circumstances of the Great Depression soon halted even a desultory attempt to reach agreement. When the Royal Commission on Dominion-Provincial Relations was appointed in 1936 its terms of reference were limited to financial matters and did not include recommendations for an amending procedure.

In 1949 at the request of the Parliament of Canada the United Kingdom Parliament amended the British North America Act to provide the following:

> 1. The amendment from time to time of the Constitution of Canada, except as regards matters coming within the classes of subjects by this Act assigned exclusively to the Legislatures of the provinces, or as regards rights or privileges by this or any other Constitutional Act granted or secured to the Legislature or the Government of a province, or to any class of persons with respect to schools or as regards the use of the English or the French language or as regards the requirements that there shall be a session of the Parliament of Canada at least once each year, and that no House of Commons shall continue for more than five years from the day of the return of the Writs for choosing the House: provided, however, that a House of Commons may in time of real or apprehended war, invasion or insurrection be continued by the Parliament of Canada if such continuation is not opposed by the votes of more than one-third of the members of such House.

The British North America Act (No. 2) of 1949 was enacted when the federal government dominated the provinces more than at any peacetime period of Canadian history. In so bringing about this amendment without provincial consultation or consent the federal authorities undoubtedly wished to facilitate, or force, subsequent agreement with the provinces on an amending procedure. A Constitutional Conference took place in 1950.[11] There was unanimous agreement that the constitution should be divided into six categories with a different amending procedure for each.

Subsequently in the same year, discussions were held to divide the constitution into these categories but no agreement could be reached and discussions lapsed.

The 1949 amendment was the assertion by the federal government of two principles:

First, it became part of the constitution that the Parliament of Canada might unilaterally determine its own structure, composition and functioning — apart from those restrictions provided for the 1949 amendment related to the two official languages, to annual sessions and to the five-year life of each House of Commons. Quebec had unsuccessfully challenged this principle in protesting a 1943 amendment providing for the postponement of a reapportionment of seats in the House of Commons until after the war and an amendment of 1946 changing the basis of representation in the House. The federal authorities defended the 1949 change on the basis that Parliament's power over its own form and operations was a corollary of Section 92 (1) of the British North America Act which gave the provinces exclusive legislative authority to amend their own constitutions "except as regards the Office of Lieutenant Governor."

Second, it had been established that the federal Parliament might without provincial consultation or consent determine the procedure by which the constitution was to be amended. Constitutional amendment is the most fundamental of political processes, and, of amendments, those which determine how future amendments are made are most crucial. The 1949 amendment was on the whole an embodiment of existing practice, and by exempting the most critical aspects of the constitution from Parliament's amending power it was still left open for future resolution to determine the procedures by which Ottawa and the provinces would be associated in amendments relating to these matters. However, in effecting the 1949 amendment the federal government alone had drawn the distinctions between those matters subject to amendment by the Parliament of Canada and those by the Parliament of the United Kingdom, with the latter category by convention — but by convention only — involving the unanimous consent of the provinces.

From 1960 onward there was a new round of federal-provincial discussions on an amending formula. These discussions culminated in October, 1964, in the agreement of all eleven governments on what was called the Fulton-Favreau Formula in recognition of the successive federal Ministers of Justice who had chaired the proceedings.[12] The proposed amending procedure was very complex and had the following basic elements:

1. There was a "sign-off" provision by which no future statute of the United Kingdom would apply to Canada.

2. The most crucial elements of the constitution were to be amendable only with the consent of Parliament and all the provincial legislatures — provincial legislative powers, the use of the English and French languages,

denominational rights in education and the provisions of Section 51 A of the B.N.A. Act determining that a province would always have at least as many members of the House of Commons as Senators.

3. Certain basic aspects of the structure and functioning of the Government of Canada required the concurrence of at least two-thirds of the provinces having together at least half the Canadian population. This category included provisions related to the Crown and its Canadian representative, the five-year limit on the duration of each House of Commons, the number of members from each province in the Senate and representation of the provinces proportionate to their respective populations in the House of Commons. Except for these exceptions, Parliament had the exclusive authority to amend the constitution in respect to "the executive Government of Canada, and the Senate and House of Commons."

4. The rigidities of the proposed amending formula as these related to the distribution of legislative powers was somewhat tempered by provision for the delegation of powers between the two levels by mutual consent. Any of the powers of Parliament might be delegated to the provinces providing Parliament and at least four provincial legislatures enacted similar laws in respect to these powers. Provincial powers over prison and reform institutions, local works and undertakings, property and civil rights and "Matters of a merely local or private Nature" might be delegated to Parliament so long as at least four provinces had so consented or all the provinces had been consulted and Parliament had declared that the matter was of concern to fewer than four.

It thus seemed by the mid-1960s that Canada was on the verge of adopting a wholly domestic procedure for constitutional amendment. However, in January, 1966, Premier Lesage of Quebec informed Prime Minister Pearson that "the government of Quebec has decided to delay indefinitely the proposal for constitutional amendment."[13] He gave as the reasons for this action conflicting interpretations within the province about the meaning and effect of the proposed procedure and the view that its adoption would make impossible the abolition of the Quebec Legislative Council or the curtailment of its powers without the consent of that body. The more important reason for the Quebec action was undoubtedly the political storm the Fulton-Favreau Formula had raised in the province, including the challenge of the opposition Union Nationale to fight an election on the issue. Quebec governments in the past had always insisted on a rigid amending procedure and Premier Lesage and his colleagues had made as their major defence of the proposed procedure that Ottawa and the provinces had never previously been willing to accept unanimous provincial consent for amendments involving the distribution of legislative powers. However, by the mid-1960s the prevailing currents of thought and policy in Quebec had come to reject constitutional conservatism and to assert that the province's interests required radical constitutional changes. From this latter perspective, the rigidities of the proposed amending procedure became for Quebec what the Leader of the Opposition in the province called "une camisole de force", a straight-jacket, in the sense that even the smallest of the provinces could frustrate Quebec's aspirations for change.

Up until late 1970 or early 1971 the Federal-Provincial Constitutional Conferences begun in 1968 did not address themselves to a formula for constitutional amendment. The position of the federal government appears to have been that because agreement had proved impossible on this procedural question in the past it would be more expedient to press forward on reviewing the substantive content of the Canadian constitution. However, under pressure—apparently—from several of the provinces discussion was turned to an amending procedure at the Constitutional Conference of February, 1971, at Victoria, B.C. and the communique issued at the end of this meeting put forward a formula which the heads of government agreed was a "feasible approach." This formula in substantially the same form was embodied in the so-called "Charter" issuing from the Conference of June, 1971, and subsequently repudiated by Quebec.

Under the procedure of the Victoria Charter the most important parts of the Canadian constitution were to be amendable by resolution of the Senate and House of Commons and of at least a majority of the provinces which included:

(1) each province with a population at least 25 per cent of the population of Canada,
(2) at least two of the Atlantic provinces,
(3) at least two of the western provinces having together at least half the population of all the western provinces.

It was provided that the Parliament of Canada might unilaterally amend the constitution "in relation to the executive government of Canada and the Senate and House of Commons" and the provinces might as they chose amend their own constitutions. However, these provisions for unilateral action were qualified by a list of exceptions in respect to which amendments could be made only by the combined action of Parliament and the provincial legislatures as outlined above:

(1) the offices of the Queen, Governor-General and Lieutenant-Governor,
(2) yearly sessions of Parliament and the provincial Legislatures,
(3) the five-year maximum life of Parliament and the provincial legislatures, subject to provisions contained elsewhere in the constitution for extending the life of those bodies under emergency circumstances,
(4) the powers of the Senate and the number of members to which provinces are entitled in the Senate,
(5) the right of each province to at least as many members of the House of Commons as Senators,
(6) the representation of provinces in the House of Commons proportionate to their population as elsewhere detailed in the constitution,
(7) constitutional privileges of the English and French languages.

The procedure issuing from Victoria thus diverged from both existing practice and the Fulton-Favreau Formula by not requiring unanimous provincial consent for the most important of amendments. Unlike the 1964 proposal, however, the proposed amending procedure did not provide for the intergovernmental delegation of legislative powers. As we shall see in the next Chapter, the proposed change was part of a constitutional package rejected by Quebec. Thus for the time being Canadians are back to the 1949 amending procedure, with no immediate prospects of change.

CANADA'S OTHER CONSTITUTION: EMERGENCY POWERS[14]

The complex division of legislative powers between two levels of government which characterizes federalism is obviously inappropriate in times of domestic and international crisis. Contemporary federations make constitutional provisions for such emergencies in very different ways.[15] The Constitution of the United States contains very few and relatively specific provisions respecting emergencies and the late Clinton Rossiter has written of the American constitutional tradition in this respect. "The traditional theory of the Constitution is clearly hostile to the establishment of crisis institutions and procedures. It is constitutional dogma that this document foresees any and every emergency, and that no departure from its solemn injunctions could possibly be necessary."[16] At the other end of the spectrum the Constitution of India adopted in 1949 gave the federal executive sweeping powers to override the normal legislative powers of the states in cases of emergency caused by war, internal disturbances, the perceived inability of a state government to carry on its affairs in accordance with the Constitution and financial instability. These powers have been used by the national authorities on several occasions.

To return to the Canadian situation, the War Measures Act was enacted in August, 1914, and has since remained as a federal statute subject to being brought into effect by proclamation of the Governor-in-Council when, in his judgment, there exists "war, invasion, or insurrection, real or apprehended." The Act gives the federal cabinet discretion not only to declare the coming into being of such an emergency but also its passing. When the Act is proclaimed in force the cabinet is given almost unlimited powers to cope with the situation, to give effect to its will through orders and regulations and to prescribe penalties for violations of such orders and regulations, with the limitation that no such penalty shall exceed a fine of five thousand dollars or imprisonment for five years or both fine and imprisonment. When the Canadian Bill of Rights was enacted in 1960 there were provisions to associate Parliament with the cabinet in respect to War Measures Act powers. Under the 1960 legislation the cabinet is required to lay a proclamation declaring an emergency before Parliament "forthwith" or "if Parliament is then not sitting, within the first fifteen days next thereafter that Parliament is sitting." Further, when a proclamation is laid before Parliament any ten members of either House can force a debate that the proclamation be revoked and if both Houses so decide actions of the cabinet taken under the Act cease to have future effect. Thus under emergency conditions as determined by the federal cabinet Canada becomes what Rossiter has called a "constitutional dictatorship," with the federal cabinet assuming many of the most important functions of Parliament and overriding the normal legislative jurisdiction of the provinces.

As interpreted by the courts, the constitutional justification of emergency powers lies in the general authority of Parliament to legislate for the "Peace, Order and Good Government of Canada."[17] The national authorities may override provincial powers not only when international hostilities are in progress but also for a time after in dealing with the economic and other dislocations occasioned by the war. Further, "The length of time that an emergency may exist and hence relevant Dominion legislation may be upheld on emergency grounds is uncertain; but the question is essentially a political one and the courts are therefore very loath to question the decision of the Dominion Parliament on the length of the emergency period."[18] Canada was governed under emergency legislation during the First World War and afterward and also from 1939 to 1954 under the War Measures Act and subsequently under various federal emergency enactments of more limited scope.

Although the War Measures Act mentions insurrection, until the Quebec crisis of 1970 Canadians had almost universally regarded the Act within the framework of the country's involvement in international conflict. However, in the early morning hours of October 16 of that year the Act was proclaimed in force and the Public Order Regulations issued under its authority. The Regulations declared to be illegal Le Front de Libération du Québec, any successor organization or any group advocating force or crime as a means of accomplishing governmental change in Canada. There was specified a list of indictable offences for individuals who belonged to unlawful political associations, advocated force or crime to bring about political change or who gave assistance to such unlawful activities. Peace officers, including members of the Armed Forces, were given sweeping powers of search and arrest without warrants and at the discretion of the Attorney-General of a province a person might be detained up to twenty-one days before being charged with a specific offence under the Regulations. Prime Minister Trudeau gave this justification of the action of the federal cabinet:

> The first fact was that there had been kidnappings of two very important people in Canada and that they were being held for ransom under the threat of death. The second was that the government of the province of Quebec and the authorities of the city of Montreal asked the federal government to permit the use of exceptional measures because, in their own words, a state of apprehended insurrection existed. The third reason was our assess-

ment of all the surrounding facts ... the state of confusion that existed in the province of Quebec in regard to these matters:[19]

The Regulations were replaced by the Public Order Temporary Measures Act on December 3, 1970. The latter enactment shortened the period of detention without charge and required stronger proof of adherence to an unlawful political organization. Despite opposition from the government of Quebec, this Act lapsed on April 30, 1971, and Canada returned to a regime where illegal political activity was defined entirely by the normal processes of law. The War Measures Act remains, however, as a Canadian statute subject to proclamation by the Governor-in-Council.

The 1970 crisis was unique in Canadian constitutional theory and practice. Previously, emergency legislation in Canada had come into existence at the initiative of the federal government alone and had had the effect of overriding the normal legislative jurisdiction of the provinces. However, in 1970 the proclamation of the War Measures Act appears to have resulted from a common perception of the crisis by the federal, Quebec and Montreal governments, and the Public Order Regulations enhanced the powers of the law enforcement authorities under the immediate control of the Attorney-General of Quebec. During the debates of the House of Commons Prime Minister Trudeau and his colleagues asserted again and again the exclusive responsibility of the Quebec government for the administration of justice in the province and refused to intervene in these matters. However, in its refusal to renew the Public Order Temprary Measures Act when it expired in 1971 the federal authorities in a sense re-asserted their power to determine what legislative powers were necessary for the effective control of subversion in Quebec.

HUMAN RIGHTS AND CANADIAN FEDERALISM.

The protection of human rights in Canada is related directly to federalism because jurisdiction over what are variously regarded as rights is divided by the British North America Act between Parliament and the provincial legislatures. Judicial decision has left several crucial aspects of this division unclear. Further, in the past generation there has been an influential body of thought and policy in Canada which argues that human rights can be effectively protected only by their further constituional entrenchment.

The British North America Act of 1867 gave explicit protection to human rights only in respect to circumstances where a linguistic or religious group was in a minority position:

> 1. Section 93 restricted the rights of provinces to encroach on the privileges of separate Roman Catholic and Protestant schools existing "by Law" at the time of union or subsequently so established.

2. Section 133 provided that:

Either the English or the French Language may be used by any Person in the Debates of the Houses of the Parliament of Canada and of the Houses of the Legislature of Quebec; and both those Languages shall be used in the respective Records and Journals of those Houses; and either of those Languages may be used by any Person or in any Pleading or Process in or issuing from any Court of Canada established under this Act, and in or from all or any of the Courts of Quebec.

The Acts of the Parliament of Canada and of the Legislature of Quebec shall be printed and published in both those languages.

3. Various Sections protected the representation of the English-speaking minority in Quebec in Parliament and the Legislature of that province.[20]

Beyond these explicit recognitions of minority rights, the British North America Act was based on the principle of legislative supremacy qualified by a constitutional division of legislative powers. The protection of human rights was to rest on the traditional safeguards of the civil and common law systems as these safeguards were from time to time modified by enactments of Parliament and the provincial legislatures. Although there was a restricted entrenchment of human rights as such, there were significant constitutional prescriptions concerning the legislative bodies which would enact laws in respect to human rights and other matters.[21]

Judicial review of the Canadian constitution in respect to human rights has been dominated by what two writers of a recent text on constitutional law have called "the division of powers approach".[22] In this approach, what are variously regarded as human rights do not possess any independent constitutional value and when any federal or provincial enactment allegedly overriding such rights is subjected to judicial review the only relevant question to be decided by the courts is whether Parliament or the provincial legislature has trespassed on the powers of the other level. If it is determined that it did not, the legislation is valid even if it overrides the most fundamental of human rights.

The constitutional division of legistative powers over human rights is a complex and contentious matter whose elements are given here only in summary form.[23] Some of the most important of rights relating to arrest, detention and trial are squarely within Parliament's exclusive jurisdiction over the criminal law and criminal procedure, although in fact some of these rights may be qualified by practices of the provinces and their constituent municipalities in the processes of law enforcement and the administration of justice. Beyond the requirements of Section 133, Parliament and the provinces appear to have unlimited discretion in respect to linguistic rights as these relate to activities within the respective legislative powers of each level.[24] Similarly, the national and provincial authorities are free as they wish to protect egalitarian rights of non-discrimination on the basis of sex, religion, race, national origin or other individual characteristics.[25] The most contentious area relates to what Bora Laskin, now Mr. Justice Laskin of the Supreme Court of Canada, calls "political civil liberty," whose substance is "freedom of association, freedom of assembly, freedom of utterance, freedom of the press (or of the use of other media for dissemination of news and opinion) and freedom of conscience and religion."[26] Laskin argues that these freedoms "are embraced by federal power to make laws for the peace, order, and good government of Canada which includes power to legislate in relation to the criminal law."[27] The contrary argument is that in part at least these liberties are within provincial jurisdiction over "property and civil rights."[28] Both the historical circumstances of Confederation and subsequent judicial interpretation of the British North America Act support the Laskin opinion. In 1867 the conferring of jurisdiction on the provinces over property and civil rights was meant to preserve the system of private law based on civil law principles in Quebec, and although Section 92 (13) was subsequently interpreted by the courts to give the provinces extensive powers over economic matters, it cannot reasonably be used to justify provincial jurisdiction over political freedoms.[29]

From time to time some Canadian judges have attempted to break out of the seeming rigidities of the division of powers approach and to erect barriers to governments encroaching on human rights other than those of the jurisdiction of Parliament or the provinces as the case may be. The most important attempt in this direction has found in the preamble to the British North America Act an implied bill of rights. In *Reference re Alberta Statutes*[30] in 1938 an Alberta statute encroaching on freedom of the press was invalidated by the Supreme Court of Canada. In their opinions Duff C. J. and Cannon J. advanced the wholly unprecedented constitutional principle that because the preamble to the British North America Act stated that the colonies wished to be united with "a Constitution similar in Principle to that of the United Kingdom," provincial restrictions on rights essential to the workings of parliamentary government were invalid. This argument was used in several subsequent Supreme Court decisions striking down provincial legislation and in his *obiter* in the *Switzman*[31] case in 1954 Abbott, J. suggested that the preamble imposed similar restrictions on Parliament. It is significant, however, that in most of the opinions in which judges referred to the preamble of the 1867 Act as a restriction on provincial legislative power they also used more orthodox division-of-powers arguments, often that a province had encroached on Parliament's exclusive jurisdiction to legislate in respect to the criminal law.

Since the end of the Second World War Parliament and all the provinces have enacted legislation for the protection of human rights.[32] The most important of these statutes is the Canadian Bill of Rights of 1960.[33] Throughout his adult life Prime Minister Diefenbaker had been committed to the more effective protection of human rights and would clearly have preferred the entrenchment of such rights by a constitutional amendment binding on all governments in Canada. However, it appears to have been the judgment of the federal government that unanimous provincial consent for such an amendment could not be secured and the 1960 Bill of Rights applies only to matters otherwise within federal jurisdiction and can be altered or repealed by the same procedures as relate to other enactments of Parliament. The Bill of Rights affirms the existence of the traditional rights of religion, speech, assembly and the press; legal rights relating to arrest, trial and detention; and the right not to be discriminated against "by reason of race, national origin, colour, religion or sex." There were two contradictory directions in which the courts, and in particular the Supreme Court of Canada, could move in interpreting the meaning and effect of the Bill of Rights. The first was to regard it as only a guide to the interpretation of federal statutes which would not invalidate any enactment of Parliament unambiguously contrary to its terms. For almost a decade this interpretation appeared to be the authoritative one accepted by the Supreme Court.[34] However, in 1969 the Court by a 6-3 majority invalidated Section 94 (b) of the federal Indian Act which contained a harsher penalty for an Indian being intoxicated in a public place than for other citizens of the Northwest Territories where the particular offence occurred.[35] It was thus established that the Bill of Rights is a constitutional statute by whose provisions other federal legislation is to be measured and, if found wanting, invalidated.

For a generation there has been a strong current of influence pressing for the constitutional entrenchment of human rights in Canada. In the decade immediately after the Second World War this argument was often advanced in terms of Canada's alleged inability to fulfil its international obligations as a member of the United Nations without such entrenchment. This position now is less common. At the first Federal-Provincial Constitutional Conference of February, 1968, the federal government presented a comprehensive proposal for a constitutionally-entrenched Charter of what it classified as political, legal, egalitarian and linguistic rights.[36] In Ottawa's view, such a measure would not only give more effective safeguards but would also remove at one stroke the existing ambiguities of the division of legislative powers related to human rights. Subsequent discussions with the provinces soon made it apparent that no agreement was possible on entrenchment as extensive as that desired by Ottawa and the Charter issuing from the Constitutional Conference of June, 1971, provided for much more limited safeguards as we shall see in the next chapter.

Whether or not there is a further entrenchment of rights in the Canadian constitution, the question will remain in contention as to the extent to which courts should substitute their judgment for that of legislatures in the protection of human rights. In American terms, the issue is between judicial activism and judicial self-restraint. The recent textbook of Lyon and Atkey on Canadian constitutional law presents the case for activism in its most extreme form. These writers are impatient with the division-of-powers

approach to constitutional review in respect to human rights. Their
prescription is this: "If a fundamental rights issue is clearly perceived, a
court should attempt to meet the issue head-on, and should be loathe to
allow *any* level of government to deny this right through claims that it is
merely acting within its proper sphere of legislative jurisdiction."[37] Lyon
and Atkey are not very precise as to how courts would rationalize decisions
reached on this basis, although it may be conjectured that a heavy reliance
would be placed on the implied restrictions on federal and provincial
legislative power in the preamble to the British North America Act. The
Report of the Ontario Royal Commission of Inquiry into Civil Rights
published in 1969 contains the most sophisticated argument that has ever
been made in Canada on behalf of legislative supremacy in the determination of human rights.[38] Part of the McRuer Commission's argument is that
in terms of democratic theory legislatures have a better claim than courts to
make the final and authoritative decisions about rights. Further, the courts
of law suffer from certain institutional disabilities and the Report thus
states what it believes the appropriate role of the judiciary to be:

> In the judicial process, typical judicial law-making in response to the
> need for social change is interstitial. Cases are dealt with as they
> arise, proceeding gradually from precedent to precedent. In the
> modern world this is a valuable and necessary supplement to the
> primary legislative process; but the judicial system being interstitial
> so far as innovation is concerned, assumes that the main rules have
> been provided by the customs of the people (in older times) or by
> ordinary statutes (in modern times). Without these there would be
> no interstices — no gaps to be filled by sensible judicial adjustment
> and innovation.[39]

It needs to be emphasized that the dispute between proponents of judicial
activism and judicial self-restraint remains whether or not there is some
future entrenchment of rights in the Canadian constitution. The 1960 Bill
of Rights preserves the principle of legislative supremacy in that Parliament
retains the power to enact laws explicitly overriding such rights as are
specified, and it is also provided that when the War Measures Act is in
effect nothing done under its authority shall be deemed an "abrogation,
abridgement or infringement of any right or freedom recognized by the
Canadian Bill of Rights." However, in causing the Bill to be enacted it was
the intention of Prime Minister Diefenbaker and his government that the
courts would invalidate federal legislation which in their judgment
invalidated its prescriptions, and the *Drybones* judgment established the
Bill of Rights as a constitutional statute. On the other hand, *Drybones*
posed a clear circumstance where racial discrimination was sanctioned by
law. Most cases involving civil rights are more ambiguous and will
undoubtedly give the Supreme Court opportunities to defer to Parliament if
its members have an inclination to do so. The constitutional entrenchment

of human rights would of course be a directive to the judiciary to measure federal and provincial enactments by its standards. However, as American experience shows, the inevitably general provisions of a constitutional Bill of Rights give the final appellate court a very broad discretion in acting aggressively or otherwise in overriding the decisions of elected legislatures.

JUDICIAL REVIEW OF THE CANADIAN CONSTITUTION

The British North America Act of 1867 did not provide explicitly for judicial review, i.e. the procedure by which judicial bodies determine the validity of legislative enactments or executive acts in terms of their compatibility or otherwise with the terms of a codified constitution. The domestic constitutional system of the United Kingdom did not include such a procedure, the Crown in Parliament was sovereign and there could be no legal challenge to its will. From the early days of the British Empire, however, it had been customary to allow appeals to the Crown against enactments of colonial legislatures and the procedures for such appeals had been formalized with the establishment by Imperial statute of the Judicial Committee of the Privy Council in 1833.[40] As Peter Russell has pointed out, the power of the courts to pass on the validity of Canadian legislation in the early years of Confederation "might have been as much a corollary of imperialism as of federalism."[41] The British North America Act was an Imperial statute and according to the Colonial Laws Validity Act of 1865 enactments of colonial legislatures were invalid if they conflicted with those of the United Kingdom. However, as so happened, judicial review of the British North America Act did not evolve as an instrument for securing Imperial influence in Canadian affairs but rather as a practical device for delineating the respective legislative powers of Parliament and the provinces.

Until the abolition of appeals to this body by an act of the Canadian Parliament in 1949 the Judicial Committee of the Privy Council was the final appellate authority in interpreting the Canadian constitution. The Judicial Committee was composed of members of the House of Lords usually named to the Committee because of their distinguished judicial background.

There is a vast literature of analysis and criticism of the work of the Judicial Committee in reviewing the British North America Act[42] and its general directions in interpreting the Act are here summarized in very brief form. From the mid-1890s onward the dominant trends of judicial interpretation by the Committee worked in the following directions:

— the general power of Parliament to legislate for the "Peace, Order, and Good Government of Canada" was interpreted restrictively. Thus in most circumstances federal enactments had to be justified as coming within one of the enumerated powers of Section 91.

— the power of Parliament to legislate in respect to "Trade and Commerce" was interpreted restrictively. The United States Supreme Court has found in the power of Congress to regulate interstate commerce a very wide scope for national control over economic matters but the dominant Canadian tradition of interpreting the trade and commerce power has been otherwise.

— the exclusive power of the provinces to legislate in respect to "Property and Civil Rights" was interpreted broadly. In respect to economic matters this became the *de facto* residual power of the constitution.

In *Re Regulation and Control of Aeronautics* in 1932 Lord Sankey speaking for the Judicial Committee thus summarized "four propositions"[43] about the division of legislative powers which had been developed through previous decisions of that body:

(1) The legislation of the Parliament of the Dominion, so long as it strictly relates to subjects of legislation expressly enumerated in Section 91, is of paramount authority, even though it trenches upon matters assigned to the provincial legislatures by Section 92.

(2) The general power of legislation conferred upon the Parliament of the Dominion by Section 91 of the Act in supplement of the power to legislate upon the subjects expressly enumerated must be strictly confined to such matters as are unquestionably of national interest and importance, and must not trench on any of the subjects enumerated in Section 92, as within the scope of provincial legislation, unless these matters have attained such dimensions as to effect the body politic of the Dominion.

(3) It is within the competence of the Dominion Parliament to provide for matters which, though otherwise within the competence of the Provincial Legislature, are necessarily incidental to effective legislation by the Parliament of the Dominion upon a subject of legislation expressly enumerated in Section 91.

(4) There can be a domain in which Provincial and Dominion legislation may overlap, in which neither legislation will be ultra vires if the field is clear, but if the field is not clear and the two legislations meet, the Dominion legislation must prevail.

Three decisions by the Judicial Committee in 1937 denied the federal government the powers which many thoughtful Canadians believed necessary to deal with the social and economic circumstances of the Great Depression.

— three enactments of Parliament in 1935 dealing with minimum wages, the limitation of working hours and a weekly day of rest in industrial undertakings were declared invalid. This legislation was declared to be within provincial jurisdiction over property and civil rights.[44] In justifying this legislation the federal authorities had asserted that it was in fulfilment of international obligations accepted by Canada as a member of the

International Labour Organization. The Judicial Committee denied this claim, and asserted the important principle that Parliament did not acquire any legislative power it would not otherwise have had by virtue of Canada as such incurring an international obligation.

— the Judicial Committee declared *ultra vires* federal legislation providing for the regulation of the marketing of natural products through a national Board.[45] The Committee found the legislation to be an encroachment on property and civil rights because it dealt in part with intra-provincial trade in natural products.

— the Judicial Committee struck down a national scheme of unemployment insurance.[46] Again the major grounds were that federal legislation encroached on provincial jurisdiction over property and civil rights.

There was what one might call a counter-tradition of interpretation by the Judicial Committee which found in Parliament's power to legislate for the "Peace, Order, and Good Government of Canada" an independent source of legislative authority.[47] Although from the mid-1890s onward this was not the prevailing tradition, from time to time it did allow Dominion legislation to be upheld on the grounds that some matter could be dealt with only by the national government. By reliance on the general power Parliament and the federal cabinet were permitted to override the legislative jurisdiction of the provinces in the two World Wars and to deal with the economic and other dislocations occasioned by international conflict after hostilities had ended. In other circumstances the Judicial Committee was able to find justification in the general power for federal legislation regulating the sale of alcoholic beverages and broadcasting and for the incorporation of companies with Dominion objects.

Until the past few years at least it has been the conventional wisdom in English Canada to be critical of the work of the Judicial Committee in interpreting the Canadian constitution. There have been two currents of criticism. The first asserts that according to the rules of statutory interpretation accepted in the Anglo-Canadian tradition the Judicial Committee misinterpreted the clear meaning of the British North America Act. The most exhaustive argument along these lines was made in a Report of the Parliamentary Counsel of the Senate, William F. O'Connor, published in 1939.[48] On the basis of a thorough review of Canadian constitutional experience up to and including the events surrounding Confederation, O'Connor concluded that the framers of the British North America Act had clearly embodied a scheme for the distribution of legislative powers in its terms. However, from 1896 onward this scheme had been repealed by "judicial legislation." O'Connor proposed that this situation be righted by a constitutional amendment which would in effect direct the judicial authorities to interpret the B.N.A. Act by the normal legal rules. The second line of criticism has come from the judicial activists.[49] According to this kind of argument, the normal rules of statutory interpretation are not in themselves adequate guides to courts in reviewing a constitution. Judicial review is inevitably a policy-making role and in performing it judges should explicitly take into account their own considered views of the basic nature of the polity and its needs and the social and other contexts of the matters before them. Within this formulation, the tradition of "black letter" statutory interpretation followed by the Judicial Committee was inadequate in resolving some of the basic problems of Canadian life. The criticisms based on technical standards of statutory interpretation and on the perspectives of the judicial activists were in a logical sense contradictory, although some detractors of the Privy Council supported both at once. The two streams of criticism were in agreement, however, in their general conclusion that the powers of the Dominion had been unduly restricted and those of the provinces unduly expanded by the Judicial Committee.[50]

The Judicial Committee has of course had its supporters. Using a highly technical approach, a recent book by G. P. Browne has attempted a refutation of the O'Connor argument that the Judicial Committee deviated from the normal rules of statutory interpretation in review of the British North America Act.[51] Among French-speaking scholars it has been argued that the result of the Judicial Committee's work was to recognize in a prudent and basically statesmanlike way the pervasive cultural and other particularisms of Canadian life. In a 1951 article Louis-Phillipe Pigeon, now Mr. Justice Pigeon of the Supreme Court of Canada, defended the way the B.N.A. Act has been interpreted in these terms:

> A great volume of criticism has been heaped upon the Privy Council and the Supreme Court on the ground that their decisions rest on a narrow and technical construction of the B.N.A. Act. This contention is ill-founded. The decisions on the whole proceed from a much higher view. As appears from passages I have quoted, they recognize the implicit fluidity of any constitution by allowing for emergencies and by resting distinctions on matters of degree. At the same time they firmly uphold the fundamental principle of provincial autonomy: they staunchly refuse to let our federal constitution be changed gradually, by one device or another, to a legislative union. In doing so they are preserving the essential condition of the Canadian confederation.[52]

Pierre Elliott Trudeau put the same view pithily in 1964. "It has long been a custom in English Canada to denounce the Privy Council for its provincial bias; but it should perhaps be considered that if the law lords had not moved in this direction, Quebec separatism might not be a threat today: it might be an accomplished fact."[53] A distinguished English-Canadian scholar of the constitution, G. F. G. Stanley, assented to the Pigeon-Trudeau viewpoint in 1969:

The decisions handed down by their Lordships of the Judicial Committee set the pattern of our constitution for over seventy years. Uninfluenced by local sympathies or party affiliations they set out conscientiously to maintain the true federal character of Canada and to resist the encroachments of the Federal Parliament upon the powers of the Provincial Legislatures and *vice versa*. The Judicial Committee, by its careful and unprejudiced approach to Canadian problems, lessened the political dangers of excessive centralization and preserved that federalism which is the distinctive feature of our country.[54]

Both critics and supporters of the Judicial Committee appear to have exaggerated its importance in determining the shape of Canadian federalism. By the end of the nineteenth century several important developments other than judicial review had worked toward enhancing the strength and independence of the provinces — the parliamentary enactment of 1873 ending joint membership in Parliament and the provincial legislatures, the emergence of strong provincial leaders and parties able and willing to challenge the dominance of the Dominion, the adverse economic circumstances of 1873 onward which denied the federal government some of the legitimacy it might otherwise have had, the failure of the Dominion authorities to give effective aid to the educational minorities in the provinces when the privileges of these minorities were challenged by provincial action, the election in 1873 and again in 1896 of federal Liberal governments more sympathetic to provincial sensibilities than the Conservatives they displaced. Thus it can plausibly be argued that the Judicial Committee's decisions in 1896 and soon after did little more than give retroactive recognition to the underlying particularisms of Canadian life which the framers of the Confederation settlement had too sanguinely believed would yield to the integrative thrust of Dominion power.

The context of Privy Council decisions of the 1930s restricting federal jurisdiction is perhaps more complex. Although the domestic measures whose validity was denied have sometimes been called the "Bennett New Deal," these and other national measures of the decade taken together did not constitute a basic change in the relations of business, agriculture, labour and government as was true of the Roosevelt programme in the United States. Critics of the Judicial Committee's decisions in the 1930s and subsequently have sometimes argued as if all right-thinking Canadians recognized the need for a significant extension of Dominion powers to meet the exigencies of the Great Depression. The Canadian electorate, however, seems to have been divided on the relative powers of the provinces and the federal authorities. The Bennett government which had brought forward the reforms sustained one of the most decisive defeats in Canadian political history in the general election of 1935 dropping in the 1930 election from 137 to 40 seats in the House of Commons and from 48.8 per cent to 29.6

per cent of the popular vote. The incoming Liberal administration was significantly more hesitant in asserting federal power. Also, the 1930s brought to office strong and able provincial leaders devoted to provincial autonomy — Duplessis in Quebec, Hepburn in Ontario, Macdonald in Nova Scotia, Aberhart in Alberta, Patullo in British Columbia — and in 1940 the Premiers of Ontario, Alberta and British Columbia were able to block serious federal-provincial discussion of the Rowell-Sirois Report. In general, it is somewhat of an exaggeration to say that the Judicial Committee followed the election returns, as was once claimed of the Supreme Court of the United States. However, in those periods where the Privy Council enhanced provincial powers there was a rough congruence between its decisions and the prevailing political currents in Canada.

Until 1949 the Supreme Court of Canada was very much subordinate to the Privy Council in judicial review of the constitution. A large number of cases from provincial courts went directly on appeal to the latter body and bypassed the Supreme Court; in 1938 such appeals had outnumbered those from the Supreme Court by 329 to 198.[55] The Supreme Court also believed itself rigidly bound by the precedents of the Judicial Committee as Bora Laskin wrote, "As Privy Council decisions multiplied, the Supreme Court became engrossed in merely expanding the authoritative pronouncements of its superior. The task of the Supreme Court was not to interpret the constitution but rather to interpret what the Privy Council said the constitution meant."[56]

Since it became the final appellate court in Canada the Supreme Court has shown some disposition to give a more extended scope to federal power than was true in the dominant tradition of constitutional interpretation bequeathed by the Privy Council.[57] In a few cases the Court has resorted to the minor tradition which finds in "Peace, Order, and Good Government" an independent source of Parliament's peacetime legislative power. Also in a few cases the Court has been willing to give a somewhat more generous interpretation than did the Judicial Committee of Parliament's power to legislate in respect to Trade and Commerce. There have, however, been relatively few decisions under these two headings mentioned above. The Supreme Court in no case has turned its back explicitly on precedents established by the Judicial Committee. The Court has on occasion, however, shown some tendency to attenuate the positivistic tradition of constitutional interpretation which dominated the Privy Council. W. R. Lederman has lucidly summarized the two different ways in which courts may approach judicial review. ". . . there are principally two types of interpretation — literal or grammatical interpretation emphasizing the words found in statutes and constitutional documents — and, sociological interpretation which insists that constitutional words and statutory words must be carefully linked by judicially noticed knowledge and by evidence to the ongoing life of society."[58] Judicial review of the Canadian constitution has been predominantly in the first tradition, but in a tentative and hesitant way the Supreme Court of Canada since 1949 has come to accept some of the perspectives of the second.

In the post-1945 period judicial review has played a less important part in shaping the Canadian federal system than was the case in the earlier history of Confederation. There have been several factors at work. J. A. Corry suggested in 1958 that the business elites in Canada had come to think in national terms and to find fewer incentives than before to press legal challenges to federal power.[59] F. R. Scott in 1961 pointed out the influence of new kinds of fiscal policies on the way that powers were distributed between Ottawa and the provinces:

> From the time of its economic proposals in 1945, the federal government became committed to a policy of high and stable levels of employment and income. Keynes became kind of a post-natal Father of Confederation . . . The emergence of fiscal and monetary policy as economic regulators has become so important a factor today as almost to make us forget the question of legislative jurisdiction. It seems to have by-passed Sections 91 and 92 of the B.N.A. Act. The lawyers are moving out and the economists are moving in. Since Ottawa has the most money, and exclusive control of banking and currency, the fiscal approach restores federal influence though no new judgements are forthcoming from the courts to enlarge federal jurisdiction."[60]

Since Corry and Scott wrote, the nationalizing trends in Canadian federalism have been attenuated but the Court has not assumed a crucial role in delineating the respective powers of Parliament and the provinces. With one possible exception, no judicial decision has in any direct way affected the changing relations between the English and French communities which developed from 1960 onward. In a 1971 decision, as yet unreported, a judge of the Supreme Court of Ontario turned back a challenge by J. T. Thorson, former President of the Exchequer Court of Canada, to the constitutionality of the federal Bilingual Districts Advisory Board established under the Official Languages Act on the grounds that Mr. Thorson had not demonstrated a sufficiently direct interest in the legislation to have judicial standing. The effect of this decision is to sustain the federal position that it has jurisdiction to enhance the protection of the two official languages within the scope of matters conferred on Parliament by Sections 91, 93 and 95 as against the argument that such action might validly be taken only after an amendment to Section 133. However, judicial review has had little impact on the relations between Canada's two historic communities in contrast to the United States where over a generation the courts have played a decisive role in the relations of blacks and whites.

From Quebec itself there has come a series of direct challenges to the legitimacy of the Supreme Court of Canada as the final appellate tribunal in constitutional matters. The dominant argument here is that because the

Court operates entirely under federal law and because its members are appointed by the federal cabinet a neutral and objective interpretation of the constitution is impossible. After an exhaustive review of this kind of criticism Peter Russell concluded. ". . . this viewpoint . . . has been sustained, not by any tangible evidence that members of the Supreme Court are biased in favour of the level of government which appointed them, but by an objection in principle to the constitutional arbitration by a tribunal which is organically part of the federal level of government."[61] Other Quebec arguments, usually advanced less urgently, point to the lack of bilingual capacity of the Court and its staff and the alleged dilution of the civil law when cases involving that legal system are decided by a Court composed of a majority of judges from the common law tradition.

Beyond the Quebec challenge to the legitimacy of the Supreme Court as umpire of the federal system, there has grown up a disposition among the federal and provincial governments that it is more appropriate to try to resolve their conflicts by negotiation than to submit these to the courts for authoritative resolution. In 1967 the Supreme Court of Canada delivered an advisory opinion which in effect conferred jurisdiction over off-shore mineral resources on the national government. The federal authorities had sought such an opinion only after several years of negotiation with the provinces had failed to lead to agreement. Several of the provinces have refused to accept the legitimacy of the Court's opinion. For its part, the federal authorities refused the request of the western provinces in 1968 that the proposed Official Languages legislation be submitted to the Supreme Court for an opinion as to its constitutionality. On two other occasions angry provincial governments have threatened to appeal to the courts in pressing their claims. After one of the most turbulent Federal-Provincial Conferences in recent history Premier Lesage of Quebec asserted in April, 1964, that the whole edifice of the federal spending power would be submitted by Quebec to judicial challenge. In the wake of Prime Minister Trudeau's calling Premier Bennett of British Columbia a "bigot" at an Ontario Liberal meeting in February, 1972, the Attorney-General of the province announced his intention to challenge the legal validity of federal equalization payments.

In general then, it is unlikely that judicial review will come to play a decisive role in delineating the respective roles of Parliament and the provinces. For whatever reasons, private business corporations are less willing than in the past to mount judicial challenges to the authority of one level of government or the other. So far as federal-provincial relations are concerned, the most important conflicts relate to fiscal issues which are not easy of resolution by the courts, although it is possible that in the next few years the judiciary will be called upon to define the limits, if any, to the federal spending power. The failure of the judiciary to delineate the respective jurisdictions of Parliament and the provinces in several crucial areas may in itself be an inhibition to either private litigants or governments seeking judicial clarification of these matters because of the vast uncertainties as to what the courts would do in being confronted with circumstances on which they have not previously decided.

Within those matters brought to them for decision, the courts have perhaps unrealized opportunities for facilitating the adjustment of the constitutional division of legislative powers to evolving circumstances. B. L. Strayer in his recent book makes several positive suggestions in this direction.[62] The courts may broaden the grounds of judicial standing in constitutional cases so that it is easier for individuals and groups to establish that they have a sufficiently direct interest in a matter to be litigants. The Supreme Court might without breaking directly with the rule of precedent become more creative in distinguishing among precedents as evolving circumstances so require. The courts should in their constitutional decisions "take more cognizance of the world of facts" and broaden the grounds of admissible evidence to include an examination of the social and economic contexts of the matters before them. Such directions could be taken without any dramatic breaks with the past in an evolving recognition by the courts that inflexible adherence to the ordinary rules of statutory interpretation are not completely adequate to judicial review of the constitution.

THE FLEXIBLE CONSTITUTION[63]

In a developed federal system the relation between the constitution as judically interpreted and the operation of the federal system is extraordinarily complex. As we have seen, the Canadian constitution during the past generation has proved somewhat resistant to change through amendment and evolving patterns of judical review. However, the constitution has demonstrated flexibility in other directions. It has not unduly frustrated federal-provincial collaboration. It has sustained several areas of *de facto* concurrency where either or both levels can find jurisdiction to act when they desire to do so. Through various devices the national government in the years after the Second World War was able to overcome the apparent constitutional impasse of the 1930s and to dominate the federal system. From the late 1950s onward provincialist trends set in and Canada has evolved as one of the most decentralized federations now in existence. The influences toward national supremacy and subsequently toward the reassertion of provincial powers were overwhelmingly a result of the joint and unilateral action of the federal and provincial governments. Although this statement is subject to minor qualifications, it can be said that the constitution as judically interpreted contributed to this development only in a negative way by not erecting insurmountable barriers to what governments wanted to do either unilaterally or by mutual action.

It is, however, prudent not to underemphasize the influence of the constitution as interpreted by the courts in determining the shape of Candian federalism. The Confederation settlement as embodied in the B.N.A. Act of 1867 delineated some of the most important features of the continuing federation and the years in which judicial review was more crucial than more recently in delineating the respective powers of the two levels of government have contributed important influences to our present circumstances. I wrote in 1961, "The federal aspects of the Canadian constitution, using the latter term in its broadest sense, have come to be less what the courts say they are than what the federal and provincial Cabinets and bureaucracies in a continuous series of formal and informal relations have determined them to be."[64] This statement is somewhat of an exaggeration and W. R. Lederman has wisely pointed out:

> . . . the text of the federal constitution as authoritatively interpreted in the courts remains very important. It tells us who can act in any event. In other words, constitutionally it must always be possible in a federal country to ask and answer the question — What happens if the federal and provincial governments do not agree about a particular measure of cooperative action? Then which government and legislative body has power to do what? And even though federal-provincial agreement on some matter may come at the end of difficult negotiations, the question and answer just referred to will have influenced the result because the answer is a primary element in defining the bargaining power of the federal government on the one hand and the provincial governments on the other.[65]

Lederman points out that in the periodic renegotiation of the federal-provincial taxation agreements Ottawa has usually been able to get its way partly because under the constitution "the federal taxing power is a much more potent instrument than the taxing Power of a province" and that in the Canada-Quebec bargaining about contributory retirement pensions in the mid-1960s Quebec's ability to make its will prevail was based on the provisions of Section 94A of the B.N.A. Act which provides for the paramountcy of provincial powers in respect to old age pensions.

A federal distribution of legislative power as interpreted by the courts may either facilitate or frustrate cooperation between two levels of government. The 1937 decision of the Judical Committee in striking down the federal National Products Marketing Act of 1934 provides a dramatic illustration of the obstruction of intergovernmental collaboration by judical review.[66] The public regulation of the marketing of natural products in Canada has thrown up a difficult constitutional problem because to be effective the grading must take place at a point in the productive process where it is in practice impossible to tell what part will be channeled into extra-provincial trade and thus come under federal jurisdiction and what will be sold and consumed in the provinces where it was produced.[67] The 1934 enactment setting up a national board to deal with all transactions in natural products was the result of a joint attempt by Ottawa and the provinces to overcome this constitutional hurdle. In invalidating this legislation Lord Atkin in delivering the judgment of the Judicial Committee said:

> The Board were given to understand that some of the Provinces attach much importance to the existence of marketing schemes such as might be set up under this legislation: and their attention was called to the existence of Provincial legislation setting up Provincial schemes for various Provincial products. It was said that as the Provinces and the Dominion between them possess a totality of complete legislative authority, it must be possible to combine Dominion and Provincial legislation so that each within its own sphere could in co-operation with the other achieve the complete power of regulation which is desired. Their Lordships appreciate the importance of the desired aim. Unless and until a change is made in the respective legislative functions of Dominion and Province it may well be that satisfactory results for both can only be obtained by co-operation. But the legislation will have to be carefully framed, and will not be achieved by either party leaving its own sphere and encroaching upon that of the other. In the present case their Lordships are unable to support the Dominion legislation as it stands. They will therefore humbly advise His Majesty that this appeal should be dismissed.[68]

Despite Lord Atkin's references to the possibilities of federal-provincial cooperation in the marketing of natural products, it might well have proved impossible with even the most ingenious of legislative drafting to provide for a joint scheme which met the Privy Council's test.

In the past generation the flexibility of the federal system has been enormously enhanced by the exercise of the power of the national government to lend and spend in respect to matters within the legislative jurisdiction of the provinces.[69] Although it is possible — although perhaps not likely — that the courts will in the future impose limitations on the federal spending power, the present constitutional position is that this power is subject only to the following restrictions, none of which is of great practical importance. (1) So far as a matter within provincial jurisdiction is concerned, the failure of individuals or groups to conform to the conditions of eligibility for federal largesse cannot be made an offence in federal law. (2) Parliament may not finance a programme within provincial jurisdiction partly or wholly from the proceeds of a levy made for that specific purpose. (3) The national authorities may not under the guise of the spending power set up what is in essence a regulatory scheme encroaching on provinical jurisdiction.[70] The federal spending power has been used for purposes as diverse as providing a national system of family allowances, collaborating with the provinces in building the Trans-Canada Highway, giving financial assistance to universities and cultural groups and supporting comprehensive provincial plans of hospital and medical insurance.

A second procedure making for flexibility is the inter-delegation of powers between the federal government and the provinces. In 1950 the Supreme Court of Canada denied the constitutionality of a proposed Nova Scotia enactment providing that the province might delegate its legislative powers concerning labour relations under Section 92 to the Parliament of Canada.[71] However, in 1952 the Court decided that it was valid for one level to delegate its powers to administrative bodies created under the legislative authority of the other.[72] As the exercise of the federal spending power provides a measure of constitutional flexibility where large public expenditures are involved, so delegation mitigates the rigidities of the division of legislative powers in respect to public regulation. This device has been employed in the regulation of the marketing of natural products and interprovincial motor transport.

Flexibility in a federal system may be furthered not only by the facilitation of intergovernmental collaboration but also by procedures which permit the level of government which develops more urgency than the other about particular aspects of public policy to take action in such matters. The most explicit of procedures here is for the constitution explicitly to vest certain concurrent powers in both levels with provisions determining which is to prevail in the event of a clash. Under the Canadian constitution such concurrency is limited to agriculture, immigration, and old age pensions; and both Parliament and the provinces may levy direct taxes. However, there are now several other areas of jurisdiction which are *de facto* concurrent in the sense that either or both levels may find jurisdiction to act when this is deemed expedient.[73] The exercise of the spending power can be and has been used not only to facilitate federal-provincial collaboration, but also to provide for unilateral federal action in respect to matters within provincial jurisdiction as in the case of family allowances and financial assistance for cultural and scientific development. In public regulation either or both levels can find jurisdiction in respect to environmental pollution, credit-granting institutions, insurance, driving offences, the sale of securities and various aspects of consumer protection. The exercise of the criminal law power may yet prove to be the most effective device by which the national authorities can involve themselves in regulatory activities otherwise partly or exclusively within provincial jurisdictions. Under this justification Parliament has already enacted legislation prohibiting the adulteration of food products, measures in restraint of competition certain labour practices and particular actions which pollute the natural environment. Although the courts have not yet fixed the boundaries of the criminal law power, it is even possible that this power could be used to given constitutional validity to a federal scheme of either comprehensive or selective controls over prices and wages in peacetime.

There are prices to be paid for constitutional flexibility. It attenuates the accountability of governments to their respective legislatures and electorates and gives politicians plausible constitutional justifications for their failure to act when public action is clearly required. Provinces or regions which are, or believe themselves to be, in a permanent minority position in national affairs can be expected to be anxious when in relation to many important matters their actual position is determined not so much by the constitution as judically interpreted but by their own political bargaining power — and in relative terms the procedures of flexibility give Ottawa more scope for encroaching on provincial responsibilities than the reverse. Before he entered elective politics, Pierre Elliott Trudeau wrote the most trenchant criticism of flexibility in the Canadian federal system that has ever been made.[74] He said in 1961 that "whenever an important segment of the Canadian population needs something badly enough, it is eventually given to them by one level of government or the other, regardless of the constitution."[75] The main drawback of this circumstance according to Trudeau was that "it tends to develop paternalistic instincts in more enterprising governments, at the expense of democratic maturation in others."[76] Thus if one level finds that it cannot discharge its responsibilities the better remedy is to seek an explicit transfer of jurisdiction through constitutional amendment. Although he and Trudeau were fundamentally opposed in their prescriptions for Canadian federalism, the late Daniel Johnson while Leader of the Opposition in Quebec also opposed the flexible nature of the Canadian federal system when he wrote in 1965:

> Au lieu d'une véritable constitution, nous avons un régime mouvant, qui est constamment en mutation et qui est le produit des accords formels ou tacites entre Ottawa et la majorité des provinces.[77]

The Canadian constitution has proved a very flexible instrument in the sense that Canadians have been able to effect very great changes within its framework in the absence of any abrupt breaks with the past. Whether it continues to meet contemporary needs is a matter of dispute. Efforts toward constitutional revision and review are the subject of the next chapter.

AN EXAMPLE: CONSTITUTIONAL FLEXIBILITY AND EDUCATION

Constitutional flexibility, as the term was used in this chapter, manifests itself in its most fully developed form in respect to educational activities in Canada. Section 93 of the British North American Act of 1867 gives the provinces exclusive legislative jurisdiction over education, subject to safeguards for the rights of denominational minorities. However, apart from these denominational rights there has been almost no authoritative definition by the courts about what education means, and in particular what activities of a broadly educational kind the federal government may validly undertake. For the most part the provinces with English-speaking majorities have not been much exercised about such involvement and have in most cases been willing to tolerate and even to welcome Ottawa's educational involvements although in recent years Ontario has held strong views about its control over educational television. However, it is understandable that dominant currents of thought and policy in Quebec have been otherwise inclined.

In a speech made in 1966, when he was Minister without Portfolio in the Pearson government, the Honourable John Turner put forward a restrictive definition of the meaning of education under Section 93, "In the federal view, education means the imparting of knowledge through a standard curriculum during the period of childhood, adolescence and youth."[78] This definition, in the Minister's view, "does not preclude" federal action in respect to occupational training or retraining, cultural activities, research and aid to individuals (for educational purposes) as against aid to institutions.

The Royal Commission of Inquiry on Constitutional Problems which reported to the Quebec government in 1956 gave a formulation of provincial responsibilities for education directly opposed to that of Mr. Turner.[79] The Commission said "Education, whose object is to improve Man, may be defined as a processus (*sic*) of cultural access."[80] The Report made a very complex analysis of culture with an emphasis on the preservation of the "national culture" of French-Canada as "the totality of the rational and spiritual values forming the collective patrimony of a determined human group: modes of life, morals, customs, traditions, language, laws etc."[81] This definition of course precluded direct federal involvement in educational activities, and the Commission was critical of all such activity even when it was justified by reference to federal powers over defence, agriculture, immigration and Indians.[82] According to this analysis, Ottawa had a legitimate concern with education, but this concern should be manifested by policies which gave the provinces adequate fiscal resources to meet educational needs rather than direct federal intervention.[83]

In justifying its manifold activities of an educational nature the federal government has resorted to several distinctions.

1. *Between education and culture.* The federal Royal Commission on the Arts, Letters and Sciences made this assertion in its Report published in 1951, "All civilized societies strive for a common good, including not only material but intellectual and moral elements. If the Federal Goverment is to renounce its rights to associate itself with other social groups, public and private, in the general education of Canadian citizens, it denies its intellectual and moral purpose, the complete conception of the common good is lost, and Canada, as such becomes a materialistic society."[84] If this close association between education and culture were accepted literally there would be no limits to Ottawa's involvement in the "general education

of Canadian citizens." Federal policy has never gone this far, but has been influenced by the Commission's formulation of the national government as a general repository of cultural values.

2. *Between general education and occupational training or retraining.* In its policy as enunciated in the fall of 1966 the federal government undertook to pay all the costs of occupational training and retraining.[85] A distinction was made between such training related directly to the labour market and general education, with Ottawa's responsibilities in the former matter arising because of its generalized role in respect to levels of employment and its specific jurisdiction over unemployment insurance.

3. *Between assistance in the education of specific groups of Canadians and other kinds of educational involvement.* The federal government has asserted its right to direct involvement in the education of specific groups either through provision of these services or through payments directly to these individuals or to institutions providing educational services. Such groups include Indians and Eskimos, immigrants, federal employees, members of the Armed Forces and their dependent children and veterans of military service.

4. *Between universities and other kinds of educational institutions.* In the past two decades successive federal governments have accepted the general viewpoint of the Royal Commission on the Arts, Letters and Sciences that universities as distinct from elementary and high schools were national institutions and thus in some sense partially Ottawa's responsibility.

5. *Between the advancement of knowledge and the transmission of knowledge.* At least since the establishment of the National Research Council in 1916 successive federal governments have maintained their right to support research — a term almost as elastic in its meaning as education — whether in connection with specific federal responsibilities or otherwise.[86]

6. *Between "making a gift and making a law."* In F. R. Scott's terms, the federal power to expend funds on matters within provincial legislative jurisdiction, including of course education, rests on the argument that "making a gift is not the same as making a law".[87] Thus is respect to education Ottawa can and does insist that parents and guardians of children eligible for family allowances observe the school-attendance laws of the respective provinces as a condition of receiving these "gifts," but the federal government cannot make non-attendance a legal offence. The federal spending power as so interpreted leaves the national government free to support education and other activities within provincial jurisdiction by making loans or gifts to individuals, private groups, local governments and provinces and to impose such conditions as it chooses to make potential beneficiaries eligible for federal financial assistance.

7. *Between education for official language majorities and minorities.* From 1969 onward there has been a programme of federal grants-in-aid of the official language minorities in the provinces.

The distinctions which have been outlined above have justified a very considerable amount of federal intervention in matters which are, broadly speaking, educational. Apart perhaps from the spending power, these distinctions rest on pragmatic considerations of policy and on general assumptions about the nature of the Canadian polity rather than constitutional law. In a similar way, the contrary Quebec formulation which restricts the federal role in education as a requirement of the cultural survival of French-Canada is related only in a tangential way to the consitution as interpreted by the courts.

In the past decade there have been disputes between the federal and provincial governments about education in respect to two kinds of matters where judicial review of the constitution provides partial but not complete guides to a delineation of the respective powers of the two levels.

1. *Educational broadcasting.*[88] Is educational broadcasting primarily broadcasting or primarily education? In 1932 the Judical Committee decided that Parliament had exclusive jurisdication over radio communications, including both the transmission and reception of broadcasting.[89] Under this power the federal authorities have allocated broadcasting licences, controlled the content of broadcasting and operated national radio and television networks. It was not until the 1960s when the potentialities of television as an instrument of formal instruction emerged that the respective responsibilities of the federal and provincial governments in broadcasting became a crucial, and as yet unresolved, issue.

2. *International conferences on education.* As we have seen, the Judicial Committee in 1937 decided that Parliament did not acquire any legislative powers it would not otherwise have had by virtue of such powers being necessary to the fulfilment of an international obligation incurred by Canada. During the 1960s there was a protracted and bitter dispute between the federal and Quebec authorities centring on the appropriateness or otherwise of the province participating independently of Ottawa in international conferences on education.[90] In summary form, the Quebec position was that it was in law and practice inappropriate to separate the power to conclude international agreements from the power to give legislative implementation to such agreements, and thus the province should be able to participate without federal interference in international conferences on education and other matters where the subject-matter was within provincial legislative jurisdiction.[91] The federal viewpoint was that responsibility for foreign affairs could not be so divided, that Quebec's position if acceded to would project the province into the community of sovereign states and that — where the subject-matter of international relations was within provincial jurisdiction — cooperation between Ottawa and the provinces was essential.[92]

The situation relating to education points up both the advantages and difficulties of constitutional flexibility. The level of government which has shown more urgency than the other about a particular public problem has been able to find the jurisdiction to take action. For example, in the early

1960s the provinces showed little disposition to establish the kinds of vocational training facilities essential to an industrialized country, but Ottawa was able to induce this development by generous if somewhat indiscriminate grants-in-aid. Similarly, the provinces have been for the most part unwilling without federal encouragement to make the necessary contributions to the development of the more specialized kinds of scientific research and the fine arts. Flexibility brings its difficulties. So far as many kinds of educational activities are concerned, Ottawa maintains that its support is in a sense *ex gratia* and thus may and has in some cases cut back on its involvement leaving those who are directly affected to seek assistance from provinical or other sources. Flexibility, as we have seen, leads to claims and counter-claims which have no basis, or almost no basis, in constitutional law and to conflicts for which there is no procedure for authoritative resolution. Most importantly perhaps, flexibility dilutes the accountability of governments to their respective legislatures and electorates.

NOTES

[1]The Honourable Guy Favreau, *The Amendment of the Constitution of Canada*, Queen's Printer, Ottawa, 1965, p. 13. Reproduced by permission of Information Canada.

[2]See the collection by Maurice Ollivier, *The British North America Acts and Selected Statutes, 1867-1962*, Queen's Printer, Ottawa, 1962. This collection contains a very large number of items which are of a constitutional nature but unfortunately the compiler gives no statement of the tests he used to include or exclude documents.

[3]There is reference in Sections 11 and 13 to the Queen's Privy Council for Canada. However, this body consists at any one time of all living persons who have ever taken the Canadian Privy Council oath, generally all incumbent and former members of federal cabinets and other honorific Privy Councillors, and thus is not the cabinet.

[4]*British North America at Confederation*, A Study Prepared for the Royal Commission on Dominion-Provincial Relations, Queen's Printer, Ottawa, Section IX "The Division of Economic Powers at Confederation."

[5]Queen's Printer, Quebec, Volume I, First Part, Chapter III "The Political Work of the Fathers of Confederation and the Spirit of the Federative Pact."

[6]*The Life and Times of Confederation, 1864-1867*, University of Toronto Press, 1962, Chapter VIII, "Confederation and the Federal Principle."

[7]Section 94 contemplated an early assimilation of the private law of the common law provinces into a single code under Dominion jurisdiction. This Section never became operative.

[8]For detailed treatments of this subject see Paul Gérin-Lajoie, *Constitutional Amendment in Canada*, University of Toronto Press, 1950; William S. Livingston, *Federalism and Constitutional Change*, Oxford University Press, 1965; and Guy Favreau, *The Amendment of the Constitution of Canada*, Queen's Printer, Ottawa, 1965.

[9]Livingston, p. 13.

[10]See generally Sir J. G. Bourinot, *A Manual of the Constitutional History of Canada*, Copp Clark, Toronto, 1901, pp. 24-37.

[11]*Proceedings of the Constitutional Conference of Federal and Provincial Governments*, (Second Session), September 25-28, 1950, King's Printer, Ottawa, 1950.

[12]Favreau, *The Amendment of the Constitution of Canada.*

[13]The correspondence between Premier Lesage and Prime Minister Pearson is contained in *House of Commons Debates*, January 28, 1966, pp. 421-423 and March 24, 1966, p. 3162. This correspondence is reprinted in Paul Fox, Editor, *Politics: Canada*, Second Edition, McGraw-Hill of Canada, Toronto, 1966, pp. 146-149.

[14]For an excellent analysis of the relation between constitutionalism and emergency conditions see Clinton Rossiter, *Constitutional Dictatorship: Crisis Government in the Modern Democracies*, Second Edition, New York, 1963.

[15]The newer federations in the Commonwealth have provided more explicitly for emergency powers than do the constitutions of the older federations. See R. L. Watts, *New Federations: Experiments in the Commonwealth*, Oxford University Press, 1966, pp. 315-319.

[16]Rossiter, p. 212.

[17]The leading case here is *Fort Frances Pulp and Paper Co. v. Manitoba Free Press*, (1923), A.C. 695.

[18]R. MacGregor Dawson, *The Government of Canada*, Fifth Edition, Revised by Norman Ward, University of Toronto Press, 1970, p. 92.

[19]*House of Commons Debates*, Oct. 23, 1970, p. 510. Reproduced by permission of Information Canada.

[20]Section 22 and Section 23(6) (Senate of Canada), Section 40 (House of Commons of Canada), Section 72 (Legislative Council of Quebec), Section 80 (Legislative Assembly of Quebec).

[21]Section 20 (annual sessions of Parliament); Section 39 (no joint membership in Senate and House of Commons); Sections 44-47 (Office of the Speaker of House of Commons); Section 51 (basis of representation in House of Commons); Sections 53-54 (money bills).

[22]J. Noel Lyon and Ronald G. Atkey, *Canadian Constitutional Law in a Modern Perspective*, University of Toronto Press, 1970, p. 375.

[23]For a comprehensive account of the division of powers over human rights at that time see Bora Laskin, "An Inquiry into the Diefenbaker Bill of Rights," XXXVII *Canadian Bar Review* (March 1959), pp. 77-134.

[24]This proposition has been challenged and Section 133 has been asserted to imply that Parliament cannot *extend* the recognition given to English and French without a constitutional amendment to that effect. The Alberta government put forward this argument in respect to the federal measure which was enacted as the Official Languages Act of 1969 and pressed Ottawa to submit the bill to the Supreme Court of Canada for an advisory opinion. This the federal authorities refused to do.

[25]However, it is possible that Parliament might validly under the criminal law power make discrimination on such grounds offences.

[26]Laskin, "An Inquiry into the Diefenbaker Bill of Rights," p. 80.

[27]p. 116.

[28]The clearest statement of this position is in the opinions of Justices Cartwright and Fauteux in *Saumur v. City of Quebec and A.-G. Que.*, (1953), 2 S.C.R., 299.

[29]See the exhaustive discussion of the meaning of property and civil rights in *Report Pursuant to Resolution of the Senate to the Honourable the Speaker by the Parliamentary Council Relating to the Enactment of the British North America Act, 1867, and any lack of consonance between its terms and judicial construction of them and cognate matters*, King's Printer, Ottawa, 1939, pp. 109-145. (Hereafter cited as *O'Connor Report*). See also D. A. Schmeiser, *Civil Liberties in Canada*, Oxford University Press, 1964, pp. 74-78.

[30](1938) S.C.R. 100.

[31]*Switzman v. Elbling and A.-G. Quebec* (1957) 7 D.L.R. (2nd), 337.

[32]See the summary in the Honourable Pierre Elliott Trudeau, *A Canadian Charter of Human Rights*, Queen's Printer, Ottawa, 1968, pp. 171-174.

[33]For a detailed discussion of this legislation and its early judicial interpretation see Walter S. Tarnopolsky, *The Canadian Bill of Rights*, Carswell, Toronto, 1966. The March, 1959, issue of the *Canadian Bar Review*, was given over to a discussion of the Bill of Rights prior to its enactment.

[34]See particularly *Robertson and Rosetanni v. the Queen* (1963) S.C.R. 651.

[35] *The Queen v. Joseph Drybones*, (1970) 71 W.W.R. 161.

[36] *Trudeau, A Canadian Charter of Human Rights.* For a criticism of the proposed Charter see Donald V. Smiley, "The Case against the Canadian Charter of Human Rights", *Canadian Journal of Political Science*, Vol. II, No. 3, September, 1969, pp. 277-291. The issue of entrenchment was discussed at the first Constitutional Conference of February, 1968, *Proceedings*, Queen's Printer, Ottawa, 1968, pp. 265-332.

[37] *Lyon and Atkey*, Emphasis in original, p. 377. For a critique of this view of the proper role of the courts in protecting human rights see my article on the Lyon-Atkey book in a forthcoming issue of the *Canadian Bar Review*.

[38] Queen's Printer, Toronto, Report No. 2, Volume 4, Chapters 106-108.

[39] pp. 1581-1582. See my article dealing with this aspect of the Report, "The McRuer Report: Parliamentary Majoritarian Democracy and Human Rights", V *Journal of Canadian Studies*, (May, 1970) pp. 3-10. For a similar view to that of the Report see R. I. Cheffins, *The Constitutional Process in Canada*, McGraw-Hill Series on Canadian Politics, Toronto, 1969, pp. 161-169.

[40] See Lord Sankey's short account of the history of the Judicial Committee of the Privy Council in *British Coal Corporation v. The King* (1935) A.C. 500 at pp. 510-512. This is reprinted in *The Courts and the Canadian Constitution*, W. R. Lederman, Editor, Carleton Library No. 16, McClelland and Stewart, Toronto, 1964, pp. 63-65.

[41] "Introduction" in *Leading Constitutional Decisions*, Peter H. Russell, Editor, Carleton Library No. 23, McClelland and Stewart, Toronto, 1965, p. XI.

[42] See particularly the *O'Connor Report* (Note 29); G. P. Browne, *The Judicial Committee and the British North America Act*, Toronto, 1967; and, more generally, Edward McWhinney, *Judicial Review in the English-Speaking World*, 4th Edition, Toronto, University of Toronto Press, 1969. See also Alan C. Cairns' brilliant article "The Judicial Committee and Its Critics," IV. *Canadian Journal of Political Science* (September 1971), pp. 301-345.

[43] (1932) A.C., 54 at pp. 71-72. By permission of Information Canada.

[44] *A.-G. Can. v. A.-G. Ont.* (1937) A.C. 326.

[45] *A.-G. B.C. v. A.-G. Can.* (1937) A.C. 377.

[46] *A.-G. Can. v. A.-G. Ont.* (1937) A.C. 355.

[47] For a comprehensive review of the Judicial Committee's treatment of the general power see Bora Laskin, " 'Peace, Order and Good Government' Re-examined" in *Lederman, The Courts and the Canadian Constitution*, pp. 66-104.

[48] *O'Connor Report.*

[49] For one of a number of articles on this general line see Vincent C. MacDonald. "The Privy Council and the Canadian Constitution", 29 *Canadian Bar Review*, 1948, pp. 1021ff.

[50] See Cairns' article cited in n. 42.

[51] *The Judicial Committee and the British North America Act*, Toronto, 1967.

[52] "The Meaning of Provincial Autonomy" by Louis-Phillipe Pigeon, Vol 29 *Canadian Bar Review* (1951). By permission of the author and the *Canadian Bar Review*.

[53] "Federalism, Nationalism, and Reason" in Pierre Elliott Trudeau, *Federalism and the French Canadians*, Macmillan of Canada, Toronto, 1968, p. 198.

[54] *A Short History of the Canadian Constitution*, The Ryerson Press, Toronto, 1969, p. 142.

[55] Peter H. Russell, *The Supreme Court of Canada as a Bilingual and Bicultural Institution*, Documents of the Royal Commission on Bilingualism and Biculturalism, Queen's Printer, Ottawa, 1969, p. 26.

[56] Bora Laskin, "The Supreme Court of Canada: A Final Court of and for Canadians," *Lederman, The Courts and the Canadian Constitution*, p. 143, Laskin's 1951 article at pp. 125-151 is an excellent analysis of the previous status and future prospects of the Court written near to the time when it became the final appellate tribunal for Canadian cases.

[57] For general reviews see Peter H. Russell, "The Supreme Court's Interpretation of the Canadian Constitution since 1949" in Paul Fox, Editor, *Politics: Canada*, Third Edition, McGraw-Hill Series on Canadian Politics, Toronto, 1970, pp. 439-452; Martha Flet-

cher, "Judicial Review and the Division of Powers in Canada" in *Canadian Federalism: Myth or Reality*, J. Peter Meekison, Editor, Methuen of Canada, 1968, pp. 140-158; and the Honourable Vincent C. Macdonald, *Legislative Power and the Supreme Court in the Fifties*, Butterworth, Toronto, 1961.

⁵⁸"Thoughts on Reform of the Supreme Court of Canada", *The Confederation Challenge*, Ontario Advisory Committee on Confederation, Background Papers and Reports, Vol. II, Queen's Printer, Toronto, 1970, p. 295.

⁵⁹"Constitutional Trends and Federalism", reprinted in *Meekison, Canadian Federalism: Myth or Reality*, pp. 58-60.

⁶⁰"Our Changing Constitution" in *Lederman, The Courts and the Canadian Constitution*, p. 27. By permission of F. R. Scott.

⁶¹*Russell, The Supreme Court as a Bilingual and Bicultural Institution*, p. 37. For an extended argument along these lines in comparative perspective see Jacques Brossard, *La Cour Suprême et La Constitution*, Les Presses de l'Université de Montréal, 1968.

⁶²*Judicial Review of Legislation in Canada*, University of Toronto Press, 1968, particularly Chapter 8, "The Future of Judicial Review."

⁶³In this section I have been very much influenced by two articles — W. R. Lederman "Some Forms and Limitations of Cooperative Federalism," XLV *Canadian Bar Review*, September, 1967, pp. 409-436 and Barry Strayer, "The Flexibility of the BNA Act" in *Agenda: 1970*, Edited by Trevor Lloyd and Jack McLeod, University of Toronto Press, 1968, pp. 197-216.

⁶⁴"The Rowell-Sirois Report, Provincial Autonomy and Post-War Canadian Federalism," in *Meekison, Canadian Federalism*, p. 70.

⁶⁵"Some Forms and Limitations of Cooperative Federalism," XLV *Canadian Bar Review* (September, 1967), p. 410. By permission of W. R. Lederman and the *Canadian Bar Review*.

⁶⁶*A.-G. B.C. v. A.-G. Can.* (1937) A.C. 377.

⁶⁷See J. A. Corry, *Difficulties of Divided Jurisdiction*, A Study prepared for the Royal Commission on Dominion-Provincial Relations, King's Printer, Ottawa, 1939, Chapter II "Marketing of Agricultural Products."

⁶⁸At p. 389. Reproduced by permission of Information Canada.

⁶⁹J. A. Corry, "Constitutional Trends and Federalism" in *Meekison, Canadian Federalism: Myth or Reality*, pp. 62-63 and *Lederman*, "Some Forms and Limitations of Cooperative Federalism," pp. 428-433.

⁷⁰On this constitutional issue see Gerald V. La Forest, *The Allocation of Taxing Power under the Canadian Constitution*, Canadian Tax Foundation, Canadian Tax Paper No. 46, Toronto, 1967, pp. 36-41 and Donald V. Smiley, *Conditional Grants and Canadian Federalism*, Canadian Tax Foundation, Canadian Tax Paper No. 32, 1963, Chapter II.

⁷¹*A.-G. N.S. v. A.-G. Can.* (1950) 4 D.L.R. 369.

⁷²*P.E.I. Potato Marketing Board v. H. B. Willis Inc. and A.-G. Can.* (1952) 4 D.L.R. 146. Lederman examines and criticizes delegation as a device of federal-provincial cooperation "Some Forms and Limitations of Cooperative Federalism," pp. 418-428.

⁷³*Strayer, The Flexibility of the BNA Act.*

⁷⁴"Federal Grants to Universities" in *Federalism and the French Canadians*, pp. 79-102. His argument went much beyond university grants in its implications.

⁷⁵*Federalism and the French Canadians*, p. 138.

⁷⁶p. 138.

⁷⁷*Égalité ou Indépendance*, Editions Renaissance, Montréal, p. 73. Emphases in original.

⁷⁸*Politics of Purpose: Politique d'Objectifs*, McClelland and Stewart, Toronto/Montreal, 1968, p. 62.

⁷⁹Particularly Volume II, Part Four, Chapter VII "Practices and Theories in the Field of Education."

[80]Vol. II, p. 19.

[81]Vol. II, p. 15.

[82]pp. 234-237.

[83]p. 249.

[84]*Report*, King's Printer, Ottawa, p. 8.

[85]For the federal proposal see *Federal-Provincial Conference, Ottawa, Oct. 26-28, 1966*, Queen's Printer, 1968, pp. 48-55.

[86]See *The Role of the Federal Government in Support of Research in Canadian Universities*, John B. Macdonald *et al.*, Queen's Printer, Ottawa, 1969. See also the dissenting Report to this document of L. P. Dugal, pp. 357-361 emphasizing the constitutional problems and the special needs of French-language institutions.

[87]"The Constitutional Background of the Taxation Agreements", 2 *McGill Law Journal*, 1955, p. 6.

[88]For the fullest account of the issues here see Ronald G. Atkey, "The Provinical Interest in Broadcasting under the Canadian Constitution" in *The Confederation Challenge*, Ontario Advisory Committee on Confederation, Background Papers and Reports, Volume 2, pp. 189-255.

[89]In *Re Regulation and Control of Radio Communication*, (1932), A.C. 304.

[90]For a description and analysis of these conflicts see Edward McWhinney, "Canadian Federalism: Foreign Affairs and Treaty Power" in *The Confederation Challenge*, Vol. 2, pp. 115-152.

[91]Paul Gérin-Lajoie, the Minister of Education in the Lesage government and a distinguished constitutionalist, made the most coherent defences of the province's powers in foreign affairs that are available. See his Address to the Montreal Consular Corps, April 12, 1965 (mimeo), his interview with *Le Devoir* 1er Mai, 1965 and his article in the *Montreal Star*, March 19, 1968.

[92]See the two statements of the federal government, the Honourable Paul Martin, *Federalism and International Relations*, Queen's Printer, Ottawa, 1968, and the Honourable Mitchell Sharp, *Federalism and International Conferences on Education*, Queen's Printer, Ottawa, 1968.

2

Constitutional Reform and Review

In the past decade the federal and provincial governments together have made two series of attempts to revise the Canadian constitution. Both attempts have foundered on the refusal of the incumbent political leadership of Quebec to agree to solutions acceptable to Ottawa and the governments of the other provinces. The circumstances surrounding the repudiation of the Fulton-Favreau formula for constitutional amendment have been outlined in the preceding chapter. An attempt at more comprehensive reform was begun with the Confederation for Tomorrow Conference of the provinces sponsored by the government of Ontario in November, 1967, and continued through a series of Federal-Provincial Conferences from February, 1968, to June, 1971. The second process of constitutional review is the subject of this chapter.

The Confederation for Tomorrow Conference was an Ontario initiative directed toward commencing — or resuming — a dialogue on the future shape of Canadian federalism and in particular on the place of Quebec in Confederation. From the Ontario perspective the situation, as it had developed when planning for the Conference began early in 1967, must indeed have appeared critical and unsatisfactory. The Quebec general election of June, 1966, had brought to power a government committed to urgent and early reform of the constitution on bi-national lines. The emerging attitudes in Ottawa toward the provinces, and in particular toward Quebec, had become increasingly less conciliatory and the growing influence of Pierre Elliott Trudeau and the Liberal "new guard" from Quebec over federal policies combined both a personal distrust of the Union Nationale leaders and an inflexibility toward Quebec's continuing demands for an increased scope of autonomy. From the Ontario point of view, the mutual isolation of Ottawa and Quebec posed grave challenges both to national unity and to the role in national reconciliation that the province, and in particular Premier John Robarts, had assumed. A polarization between the federal and Quebec governments would in the long run give Ontario only the unpalatable options of siding with one of these contenders or of standing aside and leaving some of the most critical issues of the Canadian federation to be resolved without significant Ontario influence on the outcome. Further, there seems to have been some anxiety in the Ontario government that during the past few years many important but piecemeal changes had been effected in federal-provincial relations without adequate consideration of the cumulative impact on the federal system.[1]

The 1967 Conference consisted of a frank and general discussion of the views of the provincial leaders on Confederation with of course a focus on the place and demands of Quebec. No formal resolutions were put forward and the crucial matter of federal-provincial financial relations was excluded from the agenda. At the end of the meeting a committee of four Premiers — those of Alberta, Ontario, Quebec and Nova Scotia — was established to analyze the results of the Conference and to "explore the subjects and form of future discussion." The final communique isolated these broad subjects for subsequent consideration — "constitutional change; regional disparities; language practices and rights."

The reaction of the federal government to the Ontario initiative was cool if not hostile and Ottawa declined an invitation to participate in the November meeting. Prime Minister Trudeau in his press conference of July 27, 1971, reconstructed the federal view of late 1967.[2] It was that revising the constitution was not an urgent priority. The comprehensive reform of the Canadian constitution was much more complex than many supposed. The existing constitution was a flexible instrument and under it there had been in the years before a shift of relative power to the provinces. However, once the provinces had in fact embarked on a process of constitutional review Ottawa would be irresponsible to stand aside. Thus late in 1967 the federal government announced that the terms of the reference of a federal-provincial conference already called for early in 1968 to discuss the more effective protection of individual rights, including linguistic rights, would be broadened to include a comprehensive review of the Canadian constitution.

At the first Constitutional Conference of February, 1968, the federal government presented its plan for reviewing the constitution.[3] The process as suggested would proceed in three stages. First there would be discussion of the more effective protection of human rights through their constitutional entrenchment. Then there would be consideration of "the central institutions of Canadian federalism" — specifically, Parliament, the Supreme Court of Canada, the federal public service and the national capital — in order to make these more representative of the "federal character of the country." At the end of the process the federal and provincial governments would turn their attention to the division of powers between the two levels. The rationale for this sequence seems to have been that if individual rights and cultural and provincial particularisms were more effectively protected by constitutional entrenchment and by restructuring certain institutions of the federal government there would be less pressure than otherwise for safeguarding these rights by an extension of provincial powers.[4] It was also decided by Ottawa that constitutional review should be comprehensive rather than piecemeal, in effect that the governments would not commit themselves to particular changes as the review proceeded but rather would await the eventual negotiation of a new constitutional package.[5]

The federal plan was based on the assumption that rationality in the review procedure required the governments first to discuss and, it was hoped, agree on general principles about the nature of the Canadian community and then to embody these principles in concrete constitutional changes. Such general statements would be enacted as a preamble to the new constitution and the federal emphasis on the entrenchment of human rights seems to have been based partly on the conviction that such individual rights rather than the older and more collectively oriented purpose of "Peace, Order, and Good Government" had become the primary objective of the Canadian political community. For reasons that were never explained, the federal government felt with some urgency that the new constitution would be — as the existing one had never been — a symbolic focus of Canadian political allegiance.[6] The federal approach reflected very directly the views of Pierre Elliott Trudeau who throughout his adult life had been deeply concerned with constitutional matters.

Most of the first Constitutional Conference of February, 1968 was devoted to a consideration of what most if not all of the participating governments agreed were the two most pressing substantive problems of the Canadian federation — regional economic disparities and language rights.[7] On the second matter there was a prevailing disposition among all the governments that there should be an extension of the recognition of the French language, and the leaders of all the governments except that of Quebec gave an account of what his administration was doing and proposed to do in this respect. At the end of the Conference a "consensus on language rights" was accepted in terms of a recognition that " . . . French-speaking Canadians outside of Quebec should have the same rights as English-speaking Canadians in Quebec".[8] There were, however, deep disagreements among the governments in respect to linguistic matters. The so-called "consensus" had been reached after the Premiers of Alberta and British Columbia had left the meeting and throughout the previous discussions Alberta, with some support from Saskatchewan and British Columbia, had argued against the "constitutional and legalistic approach to linguistic matters" and in particular against the constitutional entrenchment of linguistic rights. The federal government and those of several of the other provinces were favourably disposed or at least open-minded to such entrenchment as had recently been recommended by a Report of the Royal Commission on Bilingualism and Biculturalism.[9] The Quebec position was that the division of powers rather than linguistic rights was the matter of urgency, and that a more extensive recognition of such rights should be imposed neither by the Conference nor the federal government.

From the beginning, the provinces showed various degrees of commitment to the process of constitutional review. In one of his first policy statements after the 1968 general election Prime Minister Trudeau was critical of some provinces, which he did not name, for their reluctance about the review process.[10] It is broadly accurate to say that apart perhaps from an amending procedure, a matter absent from the 1968 federal plan for constitutional revision, neither Ottawa nor the governments of any of the provinces with English-speaking majorities felt any urgency about substantive change in the constitution except as such changes might provide for some form of "great new act of accommodation" between the English and French communities as foreseen by Prime Minister Pearson in his opening address to the Conference of February 1968.[11] The governments of the western provinces were generally conservative about constitutional matters, although from time to time the Premier of British Columbia indulged his highly developed talents for obstruction by introducing into discussions daring proposals quite incapable of being taken seriously by the other governments.[12] As a price for their continuing participation in the review process, all the provinces from time to time insisted on raising issues which were only in a tangential way if at all constitutional, particularly matters of financial relations with Ottawa. At the Conference of February, 1970, for example, there was no discussion of constitutional review at all but rather consideration of substantive problems facing the two levels — inflation, western agriculture, environmental pollution and the administration of shared-cost programmes.

Between the first of the Conferences in 1968 and the proceedings leading up to those of February and June, 1971, the process of review was rather diffuse. The sequence for discussion suggested by Ottawa in the first meeting was soon put aside, and the governments encouraged to put forward "propositions" related to constitutional reform. The status of such recommendations was thus defined in a federal document of February, 1969: "The propositions submitted by the Government of Canada, like those of other governments, are for discussion purposes only and are in no sense final. Nor are they intended as proposed drafts of constitutional articles. Propositions may be withdrawn, altered or replaced as discussions continue."[13] At this Conference Ottawa presented a series of detailed proposals related to individual rights and the restructuring of several of the institutions of the federal government. Quebec throughout pressed its plans for a radical reform of the constitution on bi-national lines.[14] The other provinces responded to the call for propositions with widely varying degrees of seriousness and urgency. Under these circumstances it was impossible for discussion to be focused, and from about the middle of 1969 onward the emphasis appears to have shifted for a time to a consideration of several federal position papers related to the division of taxing[15] and spending powers[16] and the respective responsibilities of the two levels of government for income security and social services.[17]

By the fall of 1970 it seemed that the process of constitutional review had almost broken down. The Federal-Provincial Conference of September of that year, like the one held in the preceding February, dealt entirely with intergovernmental problems other than those directly related to the constitution, although in a formal sense both were constitutional conferences. In a position paper published in June, 1970, the Premier of Alberta analyzed the lack of progress that had been made and concluded". . . the process of constitutional review has not in any meaningful way reduced the inherent conflicts in the federal system, nor has it facilitated changes in the federal bargain."[18] The Alberta position was basically critical of the "holistic" approach to constitutional review and suggested that more progress could be made if problems narrower in scope could be considered. Other governments than that of Alberta were undoubtedly dissatisfied with the way in which reform of the constitution was proceeding, and so far as public expectations of change had been aroused, the process was losing its credibility.

Sometime late in 1970 there was a renewed effort to focus constitutional review and bring it to some kind of conclusion. The hopeful new element in the situation was the election of the Bourassa Liberals in the Quebec general election of April, 1970, on a straightforwardly federalist platform. Unlike its predecessor the new government was not disposed to advance the Quebec position through nationalist rhetoric or abstract and doctrinaire statements of principle. Perhaps here there appeared the elements of a possible constitutional accommodation in which Quebec would trade its support for a new amending formula, the first priority in constitutional change for most if not all of the other governments, in exchange for extended provincial powers over social policy. The Constitutional Conference of February, 1971, gave its attention to "the questions of an amending formula and an early patriation of the Canadian Constitution" and published a proposed amending procedure which the "First Ministers agreed . . . was a feasible approach." Consideration was also given to the constitutional entrenchment of human rights, Quebec's demands in the field of social policy and other matters which in a refined form finally appeared in the Victoria Charter.

Between the February Conference and the one held in Victoria the succeeding June there were intensive constitutional discussions between Ottawa and the individual provinces. The federal government appears to have been determined to achieve *some* conclusion from the review process, and in particular to focus discussion on constitutional matters exclusively without the previous diversions to other aspects of federal-provincial relations.[19]

The most difficult substantive problem to be dealt with in the constitutional discussions was in respect to social security. The basic elements of the Quebec proposal were these:[20]

1. Subject to the important qualifications outlined below, the Parliament of Canada would have the power to legislate in respect to the major areas of income-maintenance where it is now active — family allowances, manpower training allowances, guaranteed old-age income supplement, youth and social allowances, unemployment insurance, old age pensions and supplementary benefits to survivors and disabled persons regardless of age.

2. In respect to family and manpower training allowances and to the old-age income supplement, any province might enact to the effect that federal law would prevail within the province only to the extent the province so decided. When such action was taken, the non-participating province would receive from the federal government the fiscal equivalent of what otherwise would have been disbursed in the province had the federal law applied. The same provision would apply to new federal income-security schemes.

3. In respect to youth and social allowances, unemployment insurance and old age pensions and survivors' benefits no federal law would affect the operation of any present or future provincial enactment. These fields would be concurrent with provincial paramountcy.

The Quebec government argued for its proposal largely in terms of rationalization and efficiency in designing and implementing income-maintenance policies and of the benefits of integrating all aspects of social policy under one level of government.

The net effect of the Quebec proposal would have been to place existing and future federal powers in the income-security field at the discretion of the provinces and this contradicted squarely Ottawa's position that the central government could not responsibly give up its role in equalizing incomes among individuals throughout Canada. Prime Minister Trudeau thus summarized the federal position in his opening statement to the Victoria Conference:

> Quebec's proposal that provincial legislatures should have the power to limit the authority of Parliament to make income security payments such as old age pensions and family allowances within their province is one of the important issues before this conference. By the present system of income security, Parliament transfers billions of dollars a year to the old, the poor, the unemployed and families with children, from taxpayers and contributors who have the ability to pay. This federal redistribution is particularly important to poor people in those parts of Canada where opportunities and incomes are less than average — and that includes seven of

our ten provinces. If, as the government of Quebec proposes, provincial laws could nullify federal income security laws in a province, and divert the federal revenue through the provincial treasury to be spent as the provincial government decided, then provincial governments would have a strong inducement to have such laws. But in those circumstances Parliament would be less likely to impose taxes on Canadians generally to make payments to provincial governments than it would to make payments directly to the needy old people and families with children. Taxpayers themselves would be less prepared to pay taxes to the federal government for programmes controlled by provincial governments other than their own, than to support programmes of the federal parliament which they themselves elect. Consequently, the constitutional change proposed by Quebec would, over the years, lead to an erosion of federal income security programmes and their replacement by purely provinical plans. In the latter case, the old and the poor in the wealthier provinces might do as well as if the federal government were making the payments, but in the other provinces including Quebec, the tax base would not support as good income security payments as Parliament could provide.[21]

The so-called "Victoria Charter" emerging from the June Conference in 1971 had the following elements:

1. There was a formula for the patriation and amendment of the Canadian constitution. This formula was outlined in the previous chapter.

2. There was to be constitutional entrenchment of certain human rights in three categories:

(a) No federal or provincial law was to abrogate "freedom of thought, conscience and religion; freedom of opinion and expression and freedom of peaceful assembly and association". However there was this qualification:

Art. 3. Nothing in this Part shall be construed as preventing such limitations on the exercise of the fundamental freedoms as are reasonably justifiable in a democratic society in the interests of public safety, order, health or morals, of national security, or of the rights and freedoms of others, whether imposed by the Parliament of Canada or the Legislature of a Province, within the limits of their respective legislative powers, or by the construction or application of any law.

(b) Universal suffrage and free elections were declared to be fundamental principles of the constitution. There should be no discrimination against citizens voting or holding elective office because of "national origin, colour, religion or sex." Parliament and each provincial legislature had a maximum life of five years, except under emergency conditions as determined by the federal cabinet when such period might be extended if not opposed by more than one-third of the members of such bodies. There were to be annual legislative sessions.

(c) In terms of linguistic rights, both English and French might be used in the Parliament of Canada and all the provincial legislatures except those of Saskatchewan, Alberta and British Columbia. Statutes, records and journals of Parliament were to be published in both languages. The statutes of each province were to be published in English and French. Both languages could be used in the courts established by Parliament and in the courts of Quebec, New Brunswick and Newfoundland. An individual had the right to use either language in communicating with the head offices of any agency of the government of Canada or the governments of Ontario, Quebec, New Brunswick, Prince Edward Island and Newfoundland. If any province subsequently extended the rights of the two languages beyond those contained in the constitution such privileges could be revoked only by an amendment to the constitution of Canada.

3. Certain changes were to be made in the Supreme Court of Canada. Of the nine judges, three were to be chosen from the Bar of Quebec. The Governor in Council was to continue to appoint judges but there was a complex procedure for consulting with the provinces in making such appointments. When cases involving the Quebec civil law were before the Court there were safeguards that these would be heard by judges a majority of whom were trained in the civilian tradition of Quebec.

4. Parliament might make laws in respect to old age pensions and supplementary benefits and to family, youth and occupational allowances but such legislation was not to "affect the operation of any law present or future of a Provincial Legislature in relation to any such matter." Enactments could be made only after the provinces had been consulted.

5. There was to be a conference of Prime Ministers and Premiers each year unless a majority of the heads of government decided otherwise.

6. The existing provisions providing for the reservation and disallowance of provincial legislation were to be repealed.

It is significant that the Victoria Charter did not include several matters which had been the subject of previous discussion between Ottawa and the Provinces and others which might have been expected to come to resolution in a review of the constitution which purported to be comprehensive. In terms of the entrenchment of rights, the Charter omitted entirely traditional rights connected with arrest and trial and linguistic rights in education, and in a sense the Charter was a retreat from the protection of existing rights as it would have abolished the constitutional protection of denominational minorities in the existing constitution. Apart from the Supreme Court of Canada, there were no changes in the structure and functioning of the institutions of the central government. With the exception of limited fields of social security there was no change or clarification in respect to the division of legislative powers and the relation between the two levels of government in regard to such matters as taxing and spending, external relations, etc. There was here a very small constitutional package.

Before the first Ministers left Victoria it was agreed that within eleven days each would notify the Secretary of the Constitutional Conference whether or not his government was willing to recommend the adoption of the Charter to the respective legislature. This procedure has been the subject of conflicting interpretations. To some observers, it has been viewed as an ultimatum to Quebec, an indication to the province that the Charter was all that the other governments were willing to give. The federal Minister of Justice has denied the validity of this interpretation. According to Mr. Turner, the eleven-day waiting period was requested by the provinces.[22] Reports of the Victoria meeting indicate that of all the heads of government Premier Bourassa was alone in being unable or unwilling to commit his administration to a particular solution at the Conference, and among the other leaders there was apparently a good deal of annoyance at this apparent vacillation.

On June 23, five days before the eleven-day limit expired, Premier Bourassa announced that his government would not accept the Charter in the form that had issued from Victoria.[23] The operative part of the public announcement stated:

> This decision arises from the necessity to agree to as great an extent as possible on clear and precise constitutional texts, thus avoiding to transfer to the judiciary (*sic*) authority a responsibility which belongs first and foremost to the political authority, that is to those elected by the people. The texts dealing with income security have an uncertainty that meshes badly with the objectives inherent in any idea of constitutional revision. If this uncertainty were eliminated, our conclusion could be different.

The Premier's statement reiterated the general commitment of the Quebec goverment and people to the federal option and suggested by implication that constitutional review should continue despite Quebec's rejection of the Charter.

What was behind Premier Bourassa's statement, "If this uncertainty were eliminated, our conclusion could be different"? Was only textual ambiguity in the way of Prime Minister Pearson's 1968 hope of a "great new act of accommodation" among Canadians? It is undeniable that the meaning and effect of the terms of the Charter relating to social security were not very clear. The proposal that in the defined areas of income-security no federal law "shall effect the operation of any law present or future of a province" comes from the existing provisions of Section 94A of the B.N.A. Act and the courts have never had the occasion to clarify what this provision means. If, under the terms of the Victoria Charter, a province enacted a scheme of family allowances would this action cause the federal family allowance plan to be terminated within the province? In such circumstances would the provincial government or citizens eligible for benefits establish a valid legal claim for financial compensation by the federal authorities? The constitutional vesting of concurrent powers in both Parliament and the provinces with one or the other having priority in the event of a clash has a reasonably precise application so far as regulatory activities are concerned. For example, although this seems not to have happened, any clash between Ottawa and a province about those eligible for entry to Canada as immigrants would be resolved in favour of the federal authorities. The situation is much less clear in regard to the service-providing activities of government.

It is reasonable to suppose that Quebec's objections to the Charter were based on more fundamental grounds than its textual ambiguity, and it is significant to remember that Premier Lesage advanced the same reason of ambiguity for his repudiation of the Fulton-Favreau formula in 1966. Various nationalist groups in Quebec mobilized opposition to the Charter very quickly after the end of the Victoria meeting and the Premier was undoubtedly responding to this pressure. Within Quebec there are continuing objections to any amending formula which would put Quebec's future constitutional position at the discretion of the other provinces.[24] One can only conjecture whether the present or any future Quebec government will be able or willing to support such an amending procedure, regardless of other concessions it is able to gain for such support. In general, the proposals relating to income security as these emerged from the Victoria meeting were quite obviously the reflection of deep and unresolved differences among the participating governments rather than inexpert legal draftsmanship.

The failure to secure agreement on the Victoria Charter appears to have brought the process of comprehensive constitutional review to an end for the time being. The federal position is that the initiative now rests with Quebec if constitutional reform is to be resumed and on this basis there may be a continuing discussion involving either Quebec and Ottawa alone or all eleven governments on Quebec proposals of a very specific kind. However, the failures of 1964 and 1971 have undoubtedly attenuated whatever hopes there were in governmental circles either that a major English-French accommodation might emerge through constitutional review or that agreement could be reached on a new and allegedly better constitution than the one we now have.

The decision to engage in a comprehensive review of the constitution was from the first a risk, although among the politicians who promoted the enterprise the costs were not very carefully calculated. Such a review almost inevitably caused specific and particular matters to be discussed within the framework of fundamental principle. Contrary to nearly everything in the country's political experience, federal politicians proceeded on the assumption that it would be possible for Canadians to agree on general principles about the nature of their political community and then to embody these principles in specific reforms. Contrary to common political prudence, the opportunities to negotiate on limited and specific matters were passed by in favour of the vision of agreement on some comprehensive constitutional package.

The breakdown of the process of constitutional review seriously attenuated the legitimacy of the existing constitution without replacing it by something allegedly better. The ambiance of review was a climate of opinion in which the Canadian constitution and the Canadian constitutional experience were denigrated.[25] Canadians have never found in their constitution a primary focus of political allegiance. On the other hand, in the period between Confederation and the 1960s citizens and groups often made claims against one another in terms of the constitution, or, more exactly, the broad political and economic settlement of Confederation. In some cases these claims were expressed in terms of the theory of Confederation as a compact among provinces or between English and French. At other times the peripheral provinces demanded compensation for the alleged disabilities they suffered from national economic policies. In yet other circumstances it was asserted that the Fathers of Confederation had established a centralized political union, that this original objective met the continuing needs of the Canadian community and must be sustained and to an extent restored by remedying the depredations of judicial misinterpretation of the constitution. All these ways of asserting claims implied an allegiance to Canada and asserted the continuing validity of its historical experience. This has now passed. Compact theories of Confederation have few supporters, and apparently almost none in Quebec. Many argue as did Prime Minister Pearson at the Constitutional Conference of February, 1968, that because the constitution is more than a century old it must to a greater or lesser degree be inadequate to contemporary needs,[26] ignoring of course that the operative constitution of today is not that of 1867 and that the original settlement is worthy of respect because it proved flexible enough to be adaptable to evolving circumstances without decisive breaks from the past.

The comprehensive approach to constitutional reform seems thus to have ended in failure. During the fall of 1971 bilateral discussions between Quebec and Ottawa were begun about specific aspects of social policy and in particular about the relation of the proposed Quebec family allowance system to the federal plan then in process of revision. It is possible, but in my view unlikely, that agreement on these specifics will lead to a revival of the Victoria Charter. The Bourassa government, unlike its immediate predecessors, has based its argument largely on grounds of administrative rationalization rather than in terms of cultural and nationalist considerations.[27] Thus there appears within the incumbent Quebec administration little urgency for comprehensive constitutional revision if the province can get its way on the specific matters it believes to be of importance, particularly in the field of social policy. The status of the Victoria Charter among the other governments is obscure. Some, if not all, have objections to certain of its aspects, objections which they were willing to put aside in

June, 1971, for the sake of a comprehensive settlement but which might be advanced if an attempt were made to reactivate the process of review. Most crucially, the federal government seems to have demonstrated its lack of desire to maintain any momentum for constitutional reform by its action in disbanding the Constitutional Secretariat early in 1972.[28]

Table of Constitutional Conferences

November, 1967	Confederation for Tomorrow Conference convened by the government of Ontario.
February, 1968	First Meeting of the Constitutional Conference. A Continuing Committee of Officials established and also a Constitutional Secretariat authorized. The following questions to be examined in the future process of review: official languages, fundamental rights, distribution of powers, reform of institutions linked with federalism including the Senate and Supreme Court of Canada, regional disparities, amending procedure and provisional arrangements and mechanisms of federal-provincial relations.
February, 1969	Second Meeting of the Constitutional Conference. Four ministerial committees established for the study of official languages, fundamental rights, the judiciary and the Senate. The Continuing Committee authorized to give immediate attention to the distribution of powers, particularly the taxing and spending powers and constitutional aspects of regional disparities.
June, 1969	First Working Session. Discussions of taxing and spending powers and regional disparities. Reports from Continuing Committee of Officials.
December, 1969	Third Meeting of the Constitutional Conference. Discussion of the distribution of powers in relation to income security and social services, the spending power and regional disparities.
September, 1970	Second Working Session. Priority to be given to study of amending procedures and mechanisms for intergovernmental relations. Discussion of constitutional aspects of regional disparities.
February, 1971	Third Working Session. Preliminary agreement on "elements which might be incorporated into the Constitution at time of early patriation." Agreement on proposed amending formula as a "feasible approach."
June, 1971	Fourth Constitutional Conference. Discussion of what subsequently emerged as the "Victoria Charter."

Source: From Process of Constitutional Review, Secretariat of the Constitutional Conference, Ottawa, 1971 (mimeo).

NOTES

[1] Ontario Provincial Parliament, *Debates*, 1967, pp. 3566-3568.

[2] *Transcript* (mimeo) from Prime Minister's Office.

[3] The Right Honourable Lester B. Pearson, *Federalism for the Future*, Queen's Printer, Ottawa, 1968.

[4] *Federalism for the Future*, pp. 34-36.

[5] For a justification of the comprehensive approach see the Right Honourable Pierre Elliott Trudeau, *The Constitution and the People of Canada*, Queen's Printer, Ottawa, 1969, p. 2.

[6] *The Constitution and the People of Canada*, pp. 4-22.

[7] *Proceedings*, Queen's Printer, Ottawa, 1968.

[8] *Proceedings*, p. 545.

[9] Book I, *The Official Languages*, Queen's Printer, Ottawa, 1967, *Recommendations*. pp. 147-149.

[10] To the Canadian Bar Association National Convention, Vancouver, September 1968 (mimeo).

[11] *Proceedings*, p. 5.

[12] Such as those for ousting Ottawa completely from the direct tax fields, creating five provinces in place of the existing ten and changing the federal role from emphasis on inter-provincial equalization to equalization among individuals wherever they lived in Canada.

[13] *The Constitution and the People of Canada*, p. 46.

[14] See a summary of the position taken by the Union Nationale contained in the compilation *The Government of Quebec and the Constitution*, L'Office d'Information et de Publicité du Québec, Québec, 1969.

[15] The Honourable E. J. Benson, *The Taxing Powers and the Constitution of Canada*, Queen's Printer, Ottawa, 1969.

[16] The Right Honourable Pierre Elliott Trudeau, *Federal-Provincial Grants and the Spending Power of Parliament*, Queen's Printer, Ottawa, 1969.

[17] The Right Honourable Pierre Elliott Trudeau, *Income Security and Social Services*, Queen's Printer, Ottawa, 1969.

[18] The Honourable Harry E. Strom, *The Process of Constitutional Review: A Position Paper*, Edmonton, p. 15.

[19] In particular, Ottawa resisted the requests of Ontario and perhaps other provinces that the Victoria Conference should discuss fiscal relations.

[20] *Outline of Quebec's Constitutional Proposals on Social Security*, Cabinet du Premier Ministre, June, 1971, (mimeo).

[21] Prime Minister's Office (mimeo), pp. 3-4.

[22] Canadian Broadcasting Interview "Encounter," July, 1971, *Transcript* (mimeo). Mr. Turner's point was that there were no new issues introduced at Victoria and that what was under debate there had been subjects of intensive discussions from February onward both between Ottawa and individual provinces and at a meeting of the Attorneys-General.

[23] Communique from Premier Bourassa's office, June 23, 1971 (mimeo).

[24] Prior to the Victoria Conference all three Opposition parties in the Quebec National Assembly had expressed their hostility to what came to be called the Trudeau-Turner formula for amendment. See Assemblée national, *Journal des Débats*, Commission permanente de la Constitution, 18 Mai 1971, pp. B1316-1335.

[25] Alan C. Cairns, "The Living Canadian Constitution," LXXVII *Queen's Quarterly* (Winter, 1970), pp. 1-16.

[26] *Federalism for the Future*, pp. 2-4. See also Cairns' account of the contemporary denigration of the Canadian constitution and the Canadian constitutional experience in *The Living Canadian Constitution*.

[27]See the perceptive article on the Bourassa strategy by Michel Roy, Le Devoir, 14 Juin 1971.

[28]After this Chapter was written Premier Lougheed in a speech in the Alberta Legislative Assembly asserted that his province would not participate in future constitutional discussions unless Ottawa spelled out provincial constitutional jurisdiction in advance and that Alberta was not committed to the Victoria decision. (*Toronto Star*, March 28, 1972). The next day Premier Bennett of British Columbia made a similar announcement, with the difference that the prior commitment would be required from Quebec rather than the federal authorities. (*The Globe and Mail*, March 29, 1972).

3

Executive Federalism

Canada like other federations has moved away from the so-called "classical federalism" in which each level of government performed the responsibilities assigned to it by the constitution in relative isolation of the other.[1] In the contemporary world, both the citizens and constituent governments of nations have become so interdependent that if some matter within the sphere of public decision is of concern only to particular state or provincial communities it is not crucial even to them. For example, if some jurisdictions maintain inadequate health or education services some of those who are victims of such deprivations move elsewhere in the country and create burdens for the public authorities where they go. A province which maintains lax regulations over the sale of securities defeats the objectives of other governments which wish such regulation to be more stringent. Policies toward economic stabilization can be effective only by appropriate actions by all three levels of government. Examples of such interdependence could be multiplied. Under contemporary conditions it is unhelpful to see a division of powers and responsibilities in terms of the central government being given those relating to the nation "as a whole" while conferring on the provinces those of concern only to these smaller communities.

As we saw in Chapter One, constitutional amendment and evolving patterns of judicial review have been somewhat unresponsive in re-delineating the respective powers of the two levels of government as circumstances change. In the next chapter, it will be argued that relations between the federal and provincial wings of the political parties are not very effective in giving authoritive resolution to conflicts between centrifugal and centripetal tendencies in Canada. Thus in managing the ongoing federal system a very heavy burden is placed on what may be called executive federalism, which may be defined as the relations between elected and appointed officials of the two levels of government.

THE INFLUENCES LEADING TO EXECUTIVE FEDERALISM

There are at least four interrelated factors at work to make the interaction between federal and provincial governments increasingly important:

1. The ever-broadening scope of public decision brings into being new circumstances where federal and provincial objectives must somehow be harmonized if public policy is to be effective. To take an important example, government responsibility for employment opportunities can be effectively discharged only through a plethora of measures relating to economic stablilization, regional economic development, vocational education and occupational retraining for adults, etc.

2. Nationalist and egalitarian sentiments propel the federal government into action toward establishing minimum standards throughout Canada in respect to such public services as are defined to be within an ever-broadening social minimum. These services are frequently within the constitutional jurisdiction of the provinces. Gunnar Myrdal has pointed out that the welfare state is a manifestation of nationalism,[2] and at successive Federal-Provinical Conferences Premier Smallwood used his gifts of vivid exposition to call attention to the unequal opportunities lying ahead of a baby born in a Newfoundland outport compared with those available in more favoured parts of Canada and demanded that these inequalities be mitigated.[3] As in other nations, citizenship in the Canadian community has come increasingly to be defined in terms of equal access to opportunities provided by or influenced by public action. The federal government has considerable scope for meeting these demands through levying its own taxes and providing directly certain services at country-wide levels. However, this scope is limited by the circumstances that many important services within the social minimum are under provincial jurisdiction and thus in regard to these Ottawa can move toward removing inequalities only through collaboration with the provinces.

3. Contemporary rates of taxation and the deliberate use of fiscal policy to ensure economic stability and growth mean both that there is increasingly intense competition for tax sources and that the expenditure policies of each level have direct and immediate consequences for the other. This subject will be discussed in Chapter 5.

4. The constitution as judicially interpreted provides for an increasing number of matters of public policy where both levels of government are active. In fact, it is no longer easy to name many important areas of public decision in respect to which only one level is involved. During the period between the end of the World War and the early 1960s, Ottawa came increasingly to take action in respect to matters within the constitutional

jurisdiction of the provinces, mainly through the exercise of the federal spending power. More recently, the federal authorities have been somewhat more discriminating in the use of this power and have preferred to give financial aid to the provinces unconditionally or with fewer and less restrictive conditions than before. In the past decade, however, there has come to be a significant degree of provincial involvement in matters previously believed to be exclusively or almost exclusively of federal concern — broadcasting, international economic relations, the determination of the federal tax structure, etc. In general then, the constitution as it actually operates provides for an increasing number of areas of shared jurisdiction.

In the face of the growing interdependence of the two levels of government, the development of federal-provincial institutions and procedures to manage such interdependence has consistently lagged behind what informed observers of Canadian federalism have believed necessary. Apart from the judicial system, the framers of the Confederation settlement seem not to have foreseen the necessity of consultation and collaboration between Ottawa and the provinces, and in the early years of the federation relations were of a formal, legal nature carried out through communication between the Lieutenant-Governors and the federal Secretary of State.[4] In more recent times, the desperate circumstances of the Great Depression and the dominance of the federal government during the Second World War and for the decade afterward inhibited the development of institutionalized means of federal-provincial collaboration. Although in respect to many matters of a rather specialized kind such collaboration developed after 1945, there was little machinery for dealing with questions of a more comprehensive nature until the 1960s.

It is significant that pressures for more formalized means of federal-provincial interaction have often come from provinces interested in challenging federal power. At the Dominion-Provincial Conference on Reconstruction in 1945-46 Premier Drew of Ontario put forward a plan for institutionalizing relations between the two levels in respect to economic matters but with no result.[5] The Lesage government, in office in Quebec from 1960 to 1966, pressed for more formalized machinery of intergovernmental relations as part of its overall campaign for safeguarding and extending provincial autonomy.[6] According to this version of "cooperative federalism," Ottawa was to show a fastidious respect for matters within the constitutional jurisdiction of the provinces. However, because most federal economic policies had immediate implications for the provincial governments, these latter required an institutionalized part in devising and implementing such policies. Further, through regularized means of interprovincial cooperation the provinces might regulate many matters where Ottawa was involved. In the same direction, Premier William Davis of Ontario at the Federal-Provincial Conference of November, 1971, made a proposal that the First Ministers constitute themselves as a "Joint

Economic Committee" whose purpose would be "to review and determine, on a continuing basis, national economic goals of a strategic order."[7] This Ontario proposal was part of the province's campaign against the allegedly centralizing tendencies then dominant in Ottawa.

The development in the past decade of increasingly institutionalized machinery for intergovernmental collaboration has been concomitant with the attenuation of the federal dominance which was established during the Great Depression and Second World War and perpetuated for more than a decade after the latter ended. Effective intergovernmental cooperation means that governments will give up their unqualified discretion over matters within their constitutional jurisdication. Such a surrender is unlikely where one level or the other is dominant. What came in the 1960s to be characterized with some inaccuracy as "cooperative federalism" was a response to the attenuation of the power of the central government under provincial pressures.

THE MACHINERY OF FEDERAL-PROVINCIAL RELATIONS

There have been several recent attempts to catalogue the institutions of federal-provincial relations. K. W. Taylor in 1957 listed 67 federal-provincial committees.[8] In 1965 the federal government distributed a list of 125 federal-provincial conferences and meetings in that year,[9] although using a somewhat different classification Edgar Gallant found 121 of such.[10] Gérard Veilleux discovered that 119 federal-provincial ministerial and official committees had held 159 meetings in 1967[11] while for the same year the Institute of Intergovernmental Relations of Queen's University enumerated 190 federal-provincial *and* interprovincial committees. However, these various counts do not proceed from a common basis of classification, and although such enumerations convey a broad impression of the incidence of intergovernmental collaboration they are not otherwise very useful for analysis.

In the period between the end of the Second World War and the establishment of the Continuing Committee on Fiscal and Economic Matters in 1955 institutionalized federal-provincial interaction was for the most part limited to two kinds of matters — the periodic renegotiation of the tax agreements and cooperation in respect to specific services and facilities, the latter often within the framework of shared-cost arrangements.[12] There was relatively little integration of these two kinds of matters and the sharing of taxes and revenues was determined by finance and treasury departments in relative isolation from collaboration between officials and agencies of the two levels with concerns limited to specific programmes. Neither, as we shall see in Chapter 5, was there institutionalized collaboration in fiscal policy as an instrument of economic stabilization.

The establishment of the Continuing Committee on Fiscal and Economic Matters in 1955 was a break-through in the institutionalization of federal-provincial fiscal relations.[13] The press communique issued by the Conference of Prime Ministers and Premiers on October 3 of that year stated:

> By general agreement the Conference established a committee of federal and provincial officials to meet from time to time to exchange information and examine technical problems in the field of federal-provincial fiscal and economic relations. Representation on this committee will be designated by the Prime Minister or Premier of each government respectively and the chairman will be designated by the Prime Minister of Canada. The Committee will not take collective action but each of its members will report to his own government on the subjects discussed.[14]

It should be noted that the Committee was authorized only to share information and discuss technical matters and was to have no collective responsibility for either recommendation or action. It was made up of senior appointed officials. The Committee performed useful work in connection with the tax agreements which came into effect in 1957 and acted as a Secretariat for several future Federal-Provincial Conferences. However, it was not until seven years later that more important progress was made in institutionalizing financial relations between the two levels.

The Federal-Provincial Conference of March 31-April 1, 1964 provided for the establishment of the Tax Structure Committee.[15] This new and more ambitious attempt to establish a machinery for fiscal cooperation came at one of the most turbulent of Conferences in recent times, at the end of which an angry Premier Lesage of Quebec issued his own dissenting communique and threatened to challenge in the courts Ottawa's alleged encroachments on provincial jurisdiction. The Tax Structure Committee was to consist of Ministers of Finance and Treasurers. It was given the collective responsibility to report on several important matters to the Federal-Provincial Conference of heads of government early in 1966 — probable trends of public expenditure in the 1967-72 period, general problems in shared-cost programmes in this period, the joint occupancy of tax fields, equalization grants to the provinces and "future inter-governmental liaison on fiscal and economic matters." The Continuing Committee on Fiscal and Economic Matters was in effect to be the staff agency of the Tax Structure Committee. It was also decided in 1964 that the Treasurers and Ministers of Finance should meet toward the end of each calendar year just prior to the time when each government's budget was being formulated to discuss the general economic and financial situation. This procedure was not regularized until nearly the end of the 1960s but is now in effect.

The beginning of constitutional review in 1968 brought into existence a Continuing Committee of Officials to supervise the process and a Federal-

Provincial Constitutional Secretariat to serve the Committee and the Constitutional Conferences of First Ministers. With the virtual termination of constitutional discussions in the wake of the Victoria Conference the Secretariat was disbanded in early 1972.

Along with the machinery relating to the most comprehensive concerns of the two levels, there is a vast and complex network of federal-provincial organizations dealing with more specific matters ranging in particularity from annual meetings of animal pathologists to those of ministers of health, welfare and labour. Often, but by no means always, these groupings are focussed on one or more programmes of federal conditional grants to the provinces.[16] As a general rule, the more limited the focus of such interactions the more likely there is to be agreement — agreement based on the norms of such experts as engineers, correctional officials, public health specialists, professional foresters, etc. In the past decade there has been a general trend toward subsuming federal-provincial relations at the middle and lower levels of the civil services where professional and technical considerations are most important to machinery where ministers and their deputies are participants. The concerns of these latter officials are more directly related to broader policy and to partisan politics.

The Federal-Provincial Conference of Prime Ministers and Premiers has come to be one of the most crucial institutions of Canadian federalism. Prior to the beginning of constitutional review in 1968 such Conferences dealt almost exclusively with fiscal and economic matters and, from time to time, with attempts to agree on a formula for constitutional amendment. However, this range of discussions has come to be more extensive and such meetings are held with increasing frequency, at least twice each year.

The Federal-Provincial Conference very much needs detailed study. It is inaccurate to suggest, as some have done, that it has become the third level of government in Canada. Such an assertion ignores the important difference between the actual and potential powers of this emergent institution. In terms of potentiality, the Conference could prevail over even the constitution because the constitution could and would be amended in any direction on which the federal and all the provincial governments could agree. In fact, the capacity to reach agreement is very much circumscribed by the divergent policy and partisan-political interests of its members. In the absence of further research the following generalizations can be made about this emergent institution:

1. The Conference has come to be a highly visible forum for the discussion of some of the most important issues facing Canada. The proceedings of the Confederation for Tomorrow Conference of November, 1967, were nationally televised as were those of the Constitutional Conferences of February, 1968, and February and December, 1969. Some if not all of the participants dislike this degree of openness and certainly none of the decisive processes of intergovernmental negotiation is going to be conducted before the television cameras. However, the increasing

frequency of Conferences and their extensive reportage by the media ensure the prominence of this institution in the consciousness of Canadians concerned with public affairs, and in recent years the exposure of the provincial Premiers in this setting has made them to widely-varying degrees national figures. Parliament and the provincial legislatures spend relatively little of their time debating federal-provincial relations, and the publicity given to Conferences contributes to public awareness of these issues.

2. Although most of the discussions of the Conferences have centred on fiscal matters and on constitutional reform and review, there has been a tendency to include other matters of joint concern as well as to establish sub-committees, sometimes at the ministerial and sometimes at the official levels, reporting directly to the Conference. In the past five years there have been discussions about environmental pollution, Indian affairs, western agriculture, foreign investment, winter unemployment, the reform of the federal tax structure, the participation of municipalities in federal-provincial relations and other aspects of intergovernmental structures. With the termination in mid-1971 of attempts at comprehensive constitutional reform, it is likely that the Conference will continue to meet at least annually and to deal with an ever-broadening range of problems confronting the participating governments.

3. During recent years there has been an improvement in the staff work of the Conferences. At the intergovernmental level this has been aided by the work of the Continuing Committee on Fiscal and Economic Matters, the Tax Structure Committee and the Secretariat of the Constitutional Conference as well as by the large number of committees at the ministerial and official levels with more specialized concerns. Just as importantly, within the federal government and those of some of the provinces there have been established specialized executive agencies dealing with federal-provincial relations as such. There is thus a small but important group of officials to whom these relations are an exclusive or almost exclusive concern. The extent to which heads of government rely on this specialized concern varies widely among governments. At the federal level, there is an Assistant Deputy Minister of Finance whose major responsibility is in federal-provincial relations and a Federal-Provincial Secretariat in the Privy Council Office. Alberta, Manitoba and Quebec have Departments of intergovernmental relations and in the Department of Treasury and Economics Ontario has an impressive array of bureaucratic talent involved in those relations on a full-time basis. At the other end of the spectrum, Premier Bennett of British Columbia — like the former Premier of Newfoundland — carries on his province's external relations in a highly personalized style with little specialized assistance.

4. Federal-provincial relations at the level of general policy have not evolved formalized and agreed-upon procedures and are carried on in a somewhat personalized way. Who has the authority to cause a Conference to be called? How is its agenda determined? Are Conferences to be open or

closed? Should their final communiques contain references to disagreements among the participating governments? Is it appropriate for governments to introduce new proposals into Conferences without prior consultations with other participants? Is it legitimate to expect governments to commit themselves at Conferences or may they appropriately reserve their judgments? Such matters have never been resolved. The highly personalized fabric of federal-provincial relations is being subjected to severe strains because of the rapid turnover of personnel. At the level of heads of government, only two of the eleven participants in the first Constitutional Conference of February, 1968, remained in office four years later — Premiers Campbell of Prince Edward Island and Bennett of British Columbia. There has been a similar turnover of appointed officials. R. B. Bryce, the former federal Deputy Minister of Finance and perhaps the most experienced and respected official in federal-provincial relations of his generation, has assumed other duties and Edgar Gallant, successively head of the Federal-Provincial Secretariat and the Secretariat of the Constitutional Conference, has been seconded to the Committee of Maritime Premiers. In Quebec three of the government's most experienced advisers in the past decade have resigned — Claude Morin, Louis Bernard and Jacques Parizeau, all three now belong to the Parti Québécois. Such turnovers subject federal-provincial relations to added stress when there are few formalized procedures by which these relations are carried on.

5. The Conferences require the Prime Minister of Canada to assume roles which may be in conflict. In this context he is at one time chairman, the head of a government with interests to safeguard and the leader of a national political party. Lester B. Pearson has recently asserted that in Federal-Provincial Conferences the Prime Minister of Canada "should often act more in an diplomatic capacity than in a political negotiating capacity."[18] In accord with this strategy Mr. Pearson while in office made it a practice at Conferences to let one or other of his Ministers put forward and defend the federal government's inevitably contentious viewpoints while he himself preferred to carry on negotiations in a more informal setting. The major aim of the Prime Minister was thus to preside over the formal meetings of Conferences in such a way as to facilitate harmony and constructive negotiation. Prime Minister Trudeau's style inclines him towards confrontation and toward discussion through sharpening points of disagreement. He has also more firmly-held convictions about the shape of Canadian federalism than did his predecessor and has thus emphasized his role as the defender of federal interests.

During the past decade federal-provincial relations have become of increasing importance to all governments and have been generalized in the sense that particularized policies have come to be dealt with within a framework of more comprehensive concerns than was so in the recent past. To a very large degree this can be explained by the severe strains Quebec was imposing on Confederation and by the attenuation of Ottawa's dominance which made necessary intergovernmental negotiation about matters which were formerly decided by the federal government alone. Under such circumstances no responsible administration could continue to regard federal-provincial relations as the almost exclusive business of middle-level officials in treasury or programme departments which engaged only the intermittent attention of elected and appointed officials with broader concerns. There also grew up by the middle and late 1960s a generalized dissatisfaction in some influential government circles with *ad hoc* and expedient solutions. Certainly too, the process of constitutional review almost by its inherent nature induced governments to rationalize their interests and conduct federal-provincial relations in terms of more abstract principle than had been the pattern before. Edgar Gallant pointed out that whereas in international relations the establishment of diplomatic machinery with generalized concerns preceded for the most part the growth of specialized functional agencies, the development in Canadian federalism had been in the other direction.[19]

INTERPROVINCIAL AND TRI-LEVEL RELATIONS

Since 1960 there has been an increased institutionalization not only of relations between the federal and provincial governments but of relations among the provinces.[20] Further, although few formal procedures have as yet developed, it appears likely in the years immediately ahead that progress will be made in associating the three levels of governments with one another, particularly in the field of urban development.

At the Dominion-Provincial Conference of July 25-27, 1960, the newly-elected Premier Lesage of Quebec indicated his intention to invite the heads of the provincial governments to a meeting to discuss common problems[21] and from that year onward the Premiers have had an annual Conference in August. In his more extended analysis of cooperative federalism presented to the Federal-Provincial Conference of November, 1963, the Quebec leader put forward the view that federal involvement in provincial matters could and should be lessened if all the provinces or groups of provinces developed institutionalized procedures for formulating economic policies.[22]

The annual Premiers' Conferences, held by invitation of the various provinces, are informal meetings. Unlike the Federal-Provincial Conferences the heads of government are each accompanied by not more than two or three advisers. It is usual for the federal government to send observers, usually officials of the Department of Finance and/or the Federal-Provincial Affairs Secretariat of the Privy Council Office. The Conferences apparently consist of a sharing of views on matters of mutual concern and it is unusual for them to seek agreement on specific policies; there appears little disposition to arrive at a specifically provincial view or to gang-up on Ottawa. There seems no strong support at the present for a permanent interprovincial secretariat, as suggested by Premier Lesage a decade ago, performing functions similar to those of the Council of State Governors in the United States. In the past five years or so there appears to have been a declining interest among several of the premiers in these August conferences.

In the past decade there has been some development in regional associations of the Maritime and Prairie provinces. For many years the Premiers of Prince Edward Island, New Brunswick and Nova Scotia have met annually to discuss matters of common concern. In 1971 a joint committee of the three Maritime legislatures was established and recommended that attempts be made to devise uniform legislation, including a common bill of rights; Edgar Gallant, formerly head of the Federal-Provincial Relations Secretariat in the Privy Council Office and later Director of the Constitutional Secretariat, was seconded from federal service to this committee for two years. An interesting development took place at the Federal-Provincial Conference of November, 1971, at which Premier Regan of Nova Scotia on behalf of the Council of Maritime Premiers presented a proposal that the base of federal equalization payments be broadened "to include local or municipal levies, starting at least with those required to finance . . . primary and secondary education services".[23] Since the mid-1960s the Premiers of the three Prairie provinces have been constituted as the Prairie Economic Council. The Prairie Premiers have from time to time been able to agree on joint representations to the federal government in respect to the Report of the Royal Commission on Taxation, the need for regional representation on federal agricultural marketing boards, and railway freight-rates. During the past decade there has been considerable discussion and study of the organic union of the provinces in the Maritime and Prairie regions. This appears unlikely in, say, the next decade but it is reasonable to anticipate greatly increased cooperation among the provincial governments in these regions.

There is a growing complex of interprovincial relations in respect to specific functions of government.[24] The Council of Resource Ministers is a unique intergovernmental body in Canada in that it is constituted with its own letters patent and its own research staff; it consists of provincial and federal ministers and directs itself to promoting research and advising governments on policies for the development of natural resources. There is also an interprovincial Mines Ministers Conference which meets annually. In June, 1967, the provincial Ministers of Education constituted themselves as a permanent body with its own secretariat and concerned with research in education matters and the development of joint approaches to the federal government.

During recent years there has been sporadic discussion of the desirability of somehow associating the local governments with Ottawa and the provinces in the discussion of social and economic policy and constitutional reform. The traditional federal position has been based on the assumption that both in law and in fact the local governments are creatures of the provinces. So far as Federal-Provincial Conferences are concerned, the provinces are free as they wish to include municipal representatives in their delegations and from time to time some have done so. In its shared-cost and other arrangements where the local governments are involved Ottawa has been relatively fastidious in working through the provinces and there are few instances of direct national-local relations which are common in the United States. The provinces are of course jealous of their position as intermediaries between the federal government and the local authorities in the increasing number of national programmes involving the latter in such fields as the education of official language minorities, housing, urban transportation and development, public assistance, etc.

What have come to be called "tri-level" relations are most likely to develop in the field of urban affairs. In 1971 Prime Minister Trudeau designated the Honourable Robert Andras as Minister of State for Urban Affairs. At the Federal-Provincial Conference of November, 1971, the Prime Minister explained the rationale for the new Ministry:

> . . . the Ministry is not a Department. It does not have a programme responsibility in the normal sense and it does not have a large store of funds directly at its disposal. But it does have, within the federal government's areas of responsibility, a specific mandate for policy development that is wide and unrestricted in relation to all matters affecting urban development. Its role is to assist in the search for precise definitions of what are or what will be the real problems in our urban areas and to propose solutions for the consideration of all concerned . . . a function of the Ministry of State will be to consult with your governments, and through you your municipalities, in achieving an integrated approach to solving the problems that none of our three levels of governments can solve alone.[25]

Further, according to Mr. Trudeau, the new Ministry was to be seen largely as a coordinating agency within the federal government itself of the manifold national activities affecting urbanization already underway. At the Conference the Premiers were firm in their determination that tri-level consultations should not undermine the provinces' supremacy in respect to their constituent municipalities or result in direct federal-local relations. The Communiqué issued at the end of the Conference stated, "It was agreed that there must be close co-operation between the federal and provincial governments toward the effective co-ordination of their relevant urban policies and programs: the involvement, if any, of municipal governments in the co-ordination mechanisms was discussed, and it was agreed that the determination of such involvement must rest with each provincial government."[26]

EXECUTIVE FEDERALISM: EVALUATION AND PROSPECTS

Contemporary circumstances have imposed a heavy burden on a relatively small number of elected and senior appointed officials of the federal and provincial governments in adjusting the Canadian federal system to the changing demands made upon it. In evaluating executive federalism only very modest criteria of performance are realistic. In general terms we might ask how well the existing complex of relations has done in mitigating the disabilities inherent in a situation of autonomous though interdependent levels of government. By these modest standards, the achievements are considerable:

1. There have been developed both formal and informal channels by which the federal and provincial governments can and do communicate information, perceptions and intentions to each other. This circumstance need not and often does not lead to agreement and in some cases may sharpen disagreement; it is one of the superstitions of the contemporary age that human conflict is overwhelmingly the result of faulty communications rather than genuinely contradictory aspirations and interests. In reality, all communications can do — and this is sometimes decisive in the resolution or mitigation of conflict — is to ensure that individuals and groups who are both autonomous and interdependent proceed from accurate perceptions of each other. Executive federalism has had a large measure of success in this direction.

2. Through executive federalism the role of the federal government in mitigating regional economic disparities has gained a measure of legitimacy among the people and governments of the more prosperous parts of Canada. For example, it is somewhat remarkable that the "have" provinces accepted, albeit grudgingly, the very extensive measures of interprovincial revenue equalization embodied in the tax agreements in effect from 1957. However, from 1945 onward the more prosperous provinces have remained ambivalent about the desirability of interprovincial equalization and from time to time explicit opposition to such equalization is expressed. As in the 1930s Premier Hepburn of Ontario spoke of his province as the "milch-cow of Confederation", so Premier Bennett now asserts that so far as Ottawa is concerned British Columbia is "a goblet to be drained," and in February, 1972, his Attorney-General threatened a judicial appeal on the constitutionality of equalization payments. It may be that this recognition of the claims of the less prosperous regions which has developed gradually over the past generation is being attenuated. This is confirmed by the increasingly more aggressive stances of British Columbia, Alberta and Ontario in fiscal matters in the face of a federal administration committed more fully than any of its predecessors to narrowing regional disparities without any profound disposition to educate the people and the governments in the more prosperous parts of Canada on the rationale of these policies. Despite what appears to be a setback, the legitimacy of Ottawa's

role in this direction has been established as part of the operative Canadian constitution.

3. As we shall see in Chapter 5, Canada has achieved important elements of an integrated tax structure in the crucial fields of personal and corporate income taxes. This tax-sharing combined with revenue equalization is particularly striking in comparison with the United States where such has not been attained.

4. Executive federalism has been able to remove most barriers to the free movement of Canadians from one part of the country to another, as these obstructions result from provincial and local residence requirements for access to public services. Particularly through federal grants-in-aid of hospital and medical insurance plans and of public assistance, residents are able to move throughout Canada without any break in their eligibility to secure these benefits. Similarly, the Canada Pension Plan and the Quebec Pension Plan have been harmonized to facilitate free movement.

As in international politics, the autonomous but interdependent governments of Canada and its provinces from time to time bypass the cumbersome processes of consultation. During recent years the pressures toward consultation have more often than not been directed toward a one-way process — from Ottawa to the provinces — and provincial administrations characteristically exercise their discretion unilaterally in determining their policies toward, for example, higher education, the development of natural resources or the conditions under which their constituent local governments may borrow in capital markets, although in these and other circumstances important federal interests are engaged. On the other hand, prior consultation with the provinces was scanty or non-existent in several of Ottawa's recent decisions such as those involving the conditions of federal support for provincial medical insurance plans, the 1966 scheme for assistance to post-secondary education and the 1968 Social Development Tax.

There are influences at work to attenuate the levels of federal-provincial integration developed in the past generation and to move Canada part of the way back toward classical federalism. These influences will be discussed more fully in Chapter 5 but may be noted briefly here:

1. Ottawa's current fiscal policies run in the direction of forcing the provinces to meet rising expenditures from their own tax sources rather than decreases in federal income taxes. Under the abatement system in effect from 1957 onward the provinces were from time to time able to influence Ottawa to lower its rates of income taxes so that the provincial governments could increase theirs without raising the total burden on the taxpayer. This abatement system was ended in 1972.

2. Current developments in conditional grants almost inevitably decrease the levels of federal-provincial collaboration in respect to highly particularized matters. During recent years several grant-in-aid arrangements such as those related to forestry and specific activities in the field of public health

have been terminated, and the Canada Assistance Plan of 1966 incorporated several conditional grant programmes into a coordinated scheme by which Ottawa would meet half of all provincial social assistance costs regardless of the circumstances under which recipients were in need. Federal legislation related to medical insurance enacted in 1966 also differed from previous grant-in-aid schemes in that it provided that assistance would be given to provincial plans which met certain specified conditions without subsequent procedures of detailed overhead controls, and a new federal proposal made in late 1971 provided for what in effect would be a block grant for all health services, including medical and hospital insurance. Quebec has accepted the alternative of contracting-out of certain established conditional grant schemes and two other provinces, Ontario and Alberta, have more recently announced their intention to do the same if acceptable conditions can be negotiated with Ottawa. Since the Trudeau government came to power in 1968 there has been only one major new grant-in-aid scheme established — that for minority official-language facilities — and the general developments in conditional grants work in the general direction of reducing federal-provincial collaboration in respect to specific programmes.

3. The integration of federal and provincial taxation has been lessened by federal withdrawal from the field of estate taxes. It is also possible that Ontario and perhaps other provinces will, like Quebec, set up their own systems for collecting individual income taxes rather than levying these taxes on the federal base and having them collected by the national authorities.

Federal-provincial relations are the despair of those who place a high value on rationality in the devising and implementing of public policy. The key terms are "consultation" and "coordination." But consultation is a notably imprecise idea and may be regarded at one extreme as no more than jurisdictions giving each other advance notice about their intentions and at the other as a situation where governments have in fact surrendered their independent discretionary powers to joint agencies of decision-making. Between these poles, there are various circumstances where the interests of one level are granted influence over the actions of the other. Coordination is capable of more exact definition. Thus according to the economist Charles E. Lindblom, "A set of decisions is co-ordinated if adjustments have been made in it such that the adverse consequences of any one decision for other decisions in the set are to a degree and in some frequency avoided, reduced, counterbalanced, or outweighed."[27] Or in other terms, coordination would consist of all levels of government engaging in a joint process of ranking the priorities of public expenditures so that the last dollar spent on each public service or facility, however categorized, would contribute equally to agreed-upon objectives. Those who are dismayed by the complex and seemingly haphazard processes of decision-making in Canadian federalism often posit, implicitly or otherwise, the alternative of a centralized structure of decision where objectives are specified and ranked in a deliberate way. There are compelling reasons for believing that such a process in the Canadian context at least would not lead to such a degree of rationality and efficiency in decision-making as is sometimes supposed, particularly by professional economists.

There is universal agreement that federal-provincial cooperation should be extended. There is also a notable unwillingness of governments to surrender their powers of independent discretion. In referring to conversations with ministers and senior appointed officials on federal-provincial liaison the Report on Intergovernmental Liaison on Fiscal and Economic Matters stated:

> Most of those with whom we talked agree with co-operative federalism as an idea. Some were prepared to accept it in the abstract as the logical working government form in Canada, but really with little idea of what this might mean in the long run. But in all too many cases we found an unwillingness, or at least an inability, to relate the principle to the practice and it is perhaps less interesting but nevertheless true that it is in the practice in particular cases that effective cooperation in government will succeed or fail. Part of the trouble may be in the fundamental state of uncertainty as to what kind of country we really want.[28]

The last sentence of this quotation indicates that the failure of federal and provincial governments to come to agreement on particular matters arises from genuine and intractable differences about fundamentals, differences based on the conflicting partisan objectives of governments and their different kinds of public responsibility. It is unrealistic to expect that those differences can be eliminated through even the most sophisticated machinery of intergovernmental liaison.

Paradoxically perhaps, the increasing rationality and administrative maturity of both the federal and provincial governments may contribute to increasingly intense conflicts between the two levels. There are several reasons for this somewhat pessimistic view.

1. G. Bruce Doern has recently written of the impact of Planning, Programming and Budgeting procedures on federal-provincial relations:

> There is already a sense of competitiveness between the federal government and the Ontario government regarding the best way to introduce PPB. It does not tax the imagination to see that we have reached a new era of analytical and bureaucratic competitiveness between the federal and provincial bureaucracies, especially between the big provincial bureaucracies of Ontario, Quebec and British Columbia.[29]

After the publication by the federal Minister of Finance of his White Paper on Tax Reform in 1969 there was a vigorous debate with the Ontario authorities. The substantive issue at dispute was whether Ottawa was concealing tax increases under the guise of tax reform. This debate about the validity of the federal projections of the tax yields consequent to its proposals can reasonably be regarded as a trial of bureaucratic competence between experts of the two governments.

2. The renewed conflicts in respect to conditional grants from 1960 onward can be explained partly in terms of the sharpening of federal and provincial objectives. The earlier grant-in-aid programmes were begun in periods of buoyant federal revenues and of limited concern for the precise measurement of federal objectives. On the provincial side, "fifty cent dollars" were more attractive than otherwise in the absence of precise programme and budgetary goals. With relative financial stringency in Ottawa and with emphasis on rational priority-setting there has come a growing restiveness among federal officials about "open-ended" arrangements in which federal expenditures are determined by provinces, local governments and institutions of post-secondary education. In the provinces administrative rationalization has made grants-in-aid less attractive than before because of their impact on programme standards and expenditure-priorities.

3. The increasing concern of the provinces with fiscal policy as an instrument of economic stabilization may well sharpen federal-provincial conflict. As we shall see in Chapter 5, this has certainly been so in the case of Ontario which has gone much further than any other province in designing and implementing its own independent fiscal policy in terms of the generalized requirements of full employment, price, stability and economic growth.

4. The provinces have come increasingly to view taxation and expenditure by governments as instruments for deliberate policies of income redistribution and to challenge federal policies in terms of these redistributive goals. Not only Ottawa but most of the provinces sponsored comprehensive fiscal investigations in the 1960s and the work of these groups contributed greatly to provincial sophistication in fiscal matters. Thus Ontario waged a determined battle against federal proposals for reforming the individual income tax base in 1969 on the grounds that these proposals did not effectively embody certain conditions regarded by the province as equitable. The current Quebec pressure for exclusive authority over the administration of family allowances is justified partly in terms of the argument that Ottawa's proposal for the reform of family allowances does not go for enough in meeting the needs of low-income families. In respect to equity in taxation and public expenditures as in other matters, the increasing maturity and sophistication of the provincial governments lead to more coherent policies, and these policies to clashes with the federal administration.

As we have seen, the Ontario government has recently proposed a Joint Economic Council of heads of government to "review and determine, on a continuing basis, national economic goals of a strategic order." According to the argument made by Premier Davis in November, 1971, "the present structure of federal-provincial ministerial meetings and technical committees simply does not work effectively to this end."[30] The problems of "immediate concern" for the Committee would be the role of the provinces in economic stabilization, the coordination of winter works programmes and the devising of a permanent framework for dealing with winter unemployment. The Communique issued at the end of the November 1971 Conference indicates that Ontario had not been able to secure the agreements of the other governments to its proposal. In a press conference following the Conference Prime Minister Trudeau criticized the Ontario plan from the traditional view that it was the responsibility of each level to set its objectives.

The Ontario proposal goes further than most other recommendations for the further institutionalization of intergovernmental relations by its suggestion that the projected Joint Economic Committee should determine national economic objectives. In a lucid commentary on this scheme R. M. Burns objects on several counts.[31] The national government could not responsibly surrender its duties toward the economic welfare of Canada to such a committee. The pressures for joint decision-making come from the provinces and for the most part are directed toward matters within federal responsibility. The role of committees and of consultation is to adjust and reconcile not to govern. In general, one might say that there is not the slightest evidence that the provinces which are most insistent about new machinery for federal-provincial collaboration have any inclination to give up important elements of what they regard as exclusive provincial powers to joint decision-making agencies.

It is unrealistic to contemplate a Committee like that recommended by Ontario operating as a kind of super-cabinet in respect to the most basic of Canadian economic policies.[32] The conflicts between Ottawa and the provinces involve for the most part the most basic of political choices and interests and these conflicts will not yield to highly sophisticated economic analysis or even more elaborate procedures of federal-provincial collaboration than have as yet been developed. The cabinet working within the framework of the British parliamentary tradition has several institutional characteristics which facilitate the resolution of political conflict among its members. It is presided over by a leader to whom its other members owe their offices and who can relieve them of these offices. It works within conditions of secrecy. It has a tradition of collective responsibility which dictates that its members abide by its decisions. It is chosen from members of a single party and the partisan interests of its members are in most circumstances either the same or at least not basically incompatible. In devising and implementing policy it relies on a common bureaucracy. The Conference of Prime Ministers and Premiers has none of these institutional characteristics facilitating agreement.

There are thus no recognized procedures for giving authoritative resolution to federal-provincial conflicts.[33] Neither have the federal and provincial governments developed firm conventions about the rules as to which their relations are to be regulated. Some of these uncertainties and ambiguities in connection with the Conference of Prime Ministers and Premiers have already been mentioned. But there are others. How can effective consultation in fiscal matters be reconciled with the traditions of budget secrecy? How can consultation work in situations where a federal or provincial opposition party succeeds to power on the basis of certain election promises directly affecting the other level? What reasonable expectations can governments have about other jurisdictions respecting the secrecy of consultations? What is the appropriate time in the legislative process at which intergovernmental consultations should take place? — prior to the notice of legislation? after first reading? at the committee stage? Is it appropriate for provinces to appear as witnesses before committees of Parliament? In broad terms, what, if any, are the limits of partisanship in federal-provincial relations? There are thus few agreed-upon guidelines in the relations between the provinces and Ottawa and of course this deficiency exacerbates conflict.

J. A. Corry once remarked that a tidy mind was a disability in dealing with Canadian federalism, and it is presumed that Principal Corry was referring to both observers and practitioners. On this basis there may be dangers in attempts at what one might call over-rationalization of federal-provincial relations. The piecemeal consideration of very specific matters has the disadvantages that resolution characteristically takes place outside the framework of coherent policy or principle and that the cumulative impact of these incremental adjustments is something that no one wanted or intended. On the other hand, when highly particularized problems are subsumed under more comprehensive concerns the most fundamental of political interests and perceptions of the federal system are engaged and on these agreement is often impossible. Flexibility, pragmatism and opportunism thus appear essential elements in the effective working of executive federalism in Canada.

NOTES

[1] For example although R. L. Watts was a student of K. C. Wheare and his writings are generally within that tradition, in his study of the newer federations he gives much more emphasis to intergovernmental relations, to what he calls "interdependent federalism"; *New Federations: Experiments in the Commonwealth*. Oxford University Press, 1966. Similarly in their studies of American federalism Daniel Elazar and the late Morton Grodzins focus on the complex of intergovernmental relations. See especially Grodzins, *The American System: A New View of Government in the United States*, Rand McNally, Skokie, Ill., 1966 and Elazar, *The American Partnership*, University Press, Chicago, 1962. For readings on Canadian intergovernmental relations see J.

Peter Meekison, Editor, *Canadian Federalism: Myth or Reality*, 2nd Edition, Methuen of Canada, Toronto, 1971, Part 4.

[2]*Beyond the Welfare State*, Yale University Press, New Haven, 1960, Chapter 10, "Economic Nationalism in the Western World".

[3]The entry of Newfoundland into Confederation in 1949 and Premier Smallwood's defence of the needs of its citizens has given a new slant to economic nationalism. Prior to the Second World War the Maritime and Prairie provinces characteristically put their cases in terms of compensation for the allegedly adverse effects of national economic policies. In the nature of the circumstances Newfoundland could not and did not argue in this way and thus helped to develop a system of claims based on the rights of citizens as Canadians.

[4]Gérard Veilleux, *Les relations intergouvernmentales au Canada, 1867-1967*, les presses de l'université du Québec, Montréal, 1971, Chapitre Premier.

[5]*Dominion-Provincial Conference (1945) Dominion and Provincial Submissions and Plenary Conference Discussions*, King's Printer, Ottawa, 1946, pp. 15-19. Premier Drew also stated, "It is our intention to designate a minister who will be responsible for Dominion-Provincial relations and who will spend much of his time in Ottawa in connection with this work" (p. 16). This intention was never implemented.

[6]*Federal-Provincial Conference 1963*, Queen's Printer, Ottawa, 1964, pp. 38-41 and pp. 44-46.

[7]*Questions on Federal-Provincial Economic Co-Operation*, Statement by the Honourable William G. Davis to the Meeting of First Ministers, Ottawa, November 15-16, 1971 (mimeo), p. 3.

[8]"Coordination in Administration,"*Proceedings of the Ninth Annual Conference, 1957*, Toronto, Institute of Public Administration of Canada, 1957, p. 253.

[9]Edgar Gallant, "The Machinery of Federal-Provincial Relations" in *Canadian Federalism: Myth or Reality*, J. Peter Meekison, Editor, Methuen of Canada, 1968, p. 288.

[10]*op. cit.*, p. 295.

[11]*The Machinery for Intergovernmental Cooperation in Canada*, Unpublished M.P.A. research essay, Carleton University, 1968, p. 100. I am indebted to Mr. Veilleux for a copy of this essay. See also Appendix A to his *Les Relations Intergouvernmentales, op. cit.*

[12]*Report: Intergovernmental Liaison on Fiscal and Economic Matters*, Queen's Printer, Ottawa, 1969, Appendix D.

[13]A. R. Kear, "Cooperative Federalism: A Study of the Federal-Provincial Continuing Committee on Fiscal and Economic Matters" in Meekison, *Canadian Federalism*, First Edition 1968, *op. cit.*, pp. 305-317.

[14]Quoted in *Kear*, pp. 309-310.

[15]For the terms of reference as given to the Tax Structure Committee in October, 1964, see *Federal-Provincial Conference of Ministers of Finance and Provincial Treasurers*, Ottawa, November 4-5, 1968, Queen's Printer, Ottawa, 1969, Appendix G.

[16]Donald V. Smiley, *Conditional Grants and Canadian Federalism*, Canadian Tax Paper No. 32, Canadian Tax Foundation, Toronto, 1963, pp. 37-42.

[17]In an interview with Thomas Hockin in February 1970 former Prime Minister Pearson gave as the reasons for televising these Conferences that pressure for this had been built up — presumably largely from the mass media and some of the provinces — and that if the press and public were exposed to these Conferences they might in the future be more willing to let them be held *in camera* with only an occasional public conference. *Apex of Power: The Prime Minister and Political Leadership in Canada*, Thomas A. Hockin, Editor, Prentice-Hall of Canada, Scarborough, 1971, pp. 191-192.

[18]*op. cit.*, p. 190.

[19]*The Machinery of Federal-Provincial Relations*, p. 290.

[20]There have been no studies on interprovincial relations as they have developed since the mid-1960s. For earlier studies see Richard H. Leach, "Interprovincial Cooperation: Neglected Area of Canadian Federalism", *Canadian Public Administration* II (June, 1959), pp. 83-99 and J. H. Aitchison, "Interprovincial Co-operation in Canada" in J. H.

Aitchison, Editor, *The Political Process in Canada: Essays in Honour of R. MacGregor Dawson*, University of Toronto Press, Toronto, 1963, pp. 153-170.

[21]Queen's Printer, Ottawa, 1960, pp. 126-127.

[22]Queen's Printer, Ottawa, 1964, pp. 45-46.

[23]*Mimeo.*

[24]For a list of these groupings see *Report: Intergovernmental Liaison on Fiscal and Economic Matters, op. cit.,* Appendix D.

[25]*Outline for remarks by Prime Minister to the First Ministers Conference on the subject of tri-level consultation,* Press Release, Office of Prime Minister, Nov. 15-17. 1971, pp. 1-2.

[26]*Mimeo*, pp. 8-9.

[27]*The Intelligence of Democracy*, Free Press, New York and Collier-Macmillan Limited, London, 1965, p. 154.

[28]pp. 120-121. By permission of R. M. Burns, Director, Institute of Intergovernmental Relations, Queen's University.

[29]"The Budgetary Process and Policy Role of the Federal Bureaucracy" in *The Structures of Policy-Making in Canada*, Edited by G. Bruce Doern and Peter Aucoin, Macmillan of Canada, Toronto, 1971, pp. 104-105.

[30]*Questions of Federal-Provincial Economic Co-Operation, mimeo*, p. 3.

[31]Letter to the Editor, *The Globe and Mail*, Toronto, November 19, 1971.

[32]I am grateful to Paul Tennant for this comparison.

[33]Donald V. Smiley "Canadian Federalism and the Resolution of Federal-Provincial Conflict" in *Contemporary Issues in Canadian Politics*, Frederick Vaughan, Patrick Kyba and O. P. Dwivedi, Editors, Prentice-Hall of Canada, Scarborough, 1970, pp. 48-66.

4

The Politics of
Canadian Federalism

It is only within the past decade that students of federalism have turned their attention to the study of political parties. Successive editions of K. C. Wheare's influential *Federal Government* exclude parties.[1] Neither does W. S. Livingston's perceptive analysis of the sociology of federalism deal with political parties as such.[2] There is a growing literature on political integration which focuses on the economic, cultural and attitudinal aspects of the building and maintenance of political communities but gives parties little or no attention in its analyses of these processes.[3]

Several recent books on comparative federalism by R. L. Watts,[4] Carl Friedrich[5] and Ivo D. Duchacek[6] give some place to party systems, but it is only William H. Riker's *Federalism: Origin, Operation, Significance* published in 1964[7] which makes political parties the crucial determinant of what form federations take. Riker's political explanation of federalism is in marked contrast both to those students who proceed exclusively or almost exclusively in terms of formal legal and institutional forms and those who emphasize popular attitudes, degrees of integration and other circumstances outside the political system. There are, he claims, two explanatory foci through which federalism may best be investigated and understood. The first is the original political bargain concluded by the leaders of political jurisdictions who come together to form a federation. Certain of these leaders, if not all, will desire union to increase the diplomatic, military and economic power of themselves and their respective communities. Under modern conditions it is often more expedient to pursue such aggrandizement through negotiation rather than force, through imperial expansion.[8] However, other leaders and other political communities are less urgent about the formation of a union and a bargain between centralization and decentralization is struck through the establishment of a federation. But once the original bargain is concluded will it subsequently be sustained in a centralized or "peripheralized" form? Riker's second explanatory factor comes into operation — the degree of centralization in the party system. Thus,

> Whatever the general social conditions, if any, that sustain the federal bargain, there is one institutional condition that controls the nature of the bargain in all the instances here examined and in all others with which I am familiar. This is the structure of the party system, which may be regarded as the main variable intervening between the background social conditions and the specific nature of the federal bargain.[9]

Riker's political explanation of federalism can be summarized briefly: federations are centralized to the extent that national political parties can and do impose their wills on their respective provincial/state parties. This argument is suggestive in calling attention to the neglected role of the party system in federations. But Riker nowhere presents conclusive evidence for his assertion that parties do in fact "control" the nature of the federal bargain in the eight countries, including Canada, which he examines. In the absence of such evidence it seems plausible to argue that in some if not all of Riker's eight federations important decisions determining, in the short run at least, the degree of centralization or peripheralization are made by other institutions and processes than intraparty relations — by judicial review of the constitution, by what I called in the previous chapter "executive federalism," by legislative committees at the national level drawing members from more than one party. Riker's attribution of primacy to intraparty relations in determining the shape of federal systems remains assertion and is devoid of any analysis of the widely divergent roles that parties do play in different political systems.

This chapter is organized around an answer to three questions about political processes and the Canadian federation:

1. What are the capabilities of the patterns of relation between national parties and provincial parties of the same designation for resolving differences in favour of one or the other? This question in itself does not involve consideration of how crucial these differences are for controlling the nature of the federal bargain.

2. What are the capabilities of popular elections and plebiscites for resolving authoritatively differences between the federal government and the governments of provinces? The asking of this question assumes that *some* important aspects of federal-provincial conflict will *not* be amenable to resolution through intraparty relations.

3. What is the relation between the partisan-political dimensions of Canadian federalism (as examined in 1 and 2 above) and other institutions and processes of public decision in shaping the federal system? This

question leaves open for investigation, as Riker's analysis does not, whether and to what extent intraparty relations "control" the nature of the continuing federal bargain.

RELATION BETWEEN FEDERAL AND PROVINCIAL PARTIES

It may be useful in examining relations between federal and provincial parties to proceed from alternative models of federal party systems which will be called "integrated" and "confederal" respectively.

Integrated	Confederal
1. *Electoral dependence*. National and provincial parties of the same designation draw very largely on common voter allegiances to both. When there are shifts in voter support at one level these are characteristically accompanied by shifts in the same direction at the other in subsequent elections.	1. *Electoral dependence*. National and provincial parties have significantly different bodies of voter allegiance. Changes in electoral support for parties characteristically arise from circumstances prevailing at one level only and are not accompanied by changes in the same direction at the other level.
2. *Party organization*. The same party machinery is used to select and elect candidates of both national and provincial parties. There are authoritative processes within the parties to commit both levels to policy.	2. *Party organization*. The national and provincial parties are autonomous. This autonomy prevails in respect to nomination of party candidates, electoral competition and policy direction.
3. *Party careers*. Those who pursue party careers characteristically move between national and provincial office. The most important careers are those involving popular election.	3. *Party careers*. Party careerists characteristically fulfil their ambitions through serving at only one level. The most crucial of these careers involve office by popular election.
4. *Party finance*. Donors to political parties characteristically contribute to the party as such. Intraparty procedures distribute those funds between the two levels.	4. *Party finance*. Donors to parties characteristically contribute to one level or the other separately. The federal and provincial parties are financially independent of one another.
5. *Ideology*. Federal and provincial parties share a common ideology. This ideology distinguishes them from other parties in the political systems of both levels.	5. *Ideology*. Federal and provincial parties characteristically do not share distinctive ideologies. Parties at both levels adjust themselves to the ideological currents prevailing among their respective activists and electorates.
6. *Party symmetry*. The same political parties contest elections at both levels. The major federal parties are major parties at the provincial level.	6. *Party symmetry*. Federal and provincial elections often see different parties as the major contestants. Important parties are often wholly or largely oriented to political competition at one level rather than both.

These models can be applied to the Canadian party system, with particular but not exclusive emphasis on the two major parties:

FEDERAL-PROVINCIAL ELECTORAL DEPENDENCE

The electoral dependence of federal and provincial parties is an extraordinarily complex phenomenon which has only recently begun to be investigated. Sophisticated and inevitably costly survey research is needed to determine, for example, the extent to which Canadian voters perceive they live in one integrated political system or in two or more relatively discrete ones.[10] It is probable from the fragmentary evidence now available that the degree of dependence varies greatly as among parties, regions and smaller areas within particular provinces, and much detailed work needs to be done even in the preliminary step of isolating the relevant variables.

The institutional forms under which Canadian elections take place clearly work toward the mutual independence of federal and provincial parties. With only a very few constitutional limitations, Parliament and the provincial legislatures have unfettered discretion to determine constituency boundaries, who may vote in their respective elections and other circumstances shaping the electoral process. Elections at the two levels take place at different times and under different administrative auspices. It does indeed seem remarkable to a Canadian student of federalism that scholars of American politics give so little attention to the contrary circumstance in which a complex of intraparty dependencies must surely arise when voters make their choices at the same time and on the same ballot for candidates for elective office at two or more levels. Although the Republic of India has retained most of the British parliamentary forms, R. L. Watts has pointed out: ". . . with only a few exceptions, state elections have generally been called at the same time as Union elections, and . . . in these elections the candidates for state legislatures were finally selected by the All-India Board of the (Congress) Party."[11]

Some students of Canadian politics have propounded what has come to be called the balance theory of federal-provincial voting behaviour. Frank Underhill stated in 1955, "By some instinctive sub-conscious mental process the Canadian people have apparently decided that, since freedom depends upon a balance of power, they will balance the monopolistic power of the Liberal government in Ottawa by setting up the effective countervailing power not in Ottawa but the provincial capitals."[12] The late Robert MacGregor Dawson put it this way, "The records suggest . . . that provincial electorates show a decided tendency to fall away from the party which gains control of the Dominion Parliament. The provinces would appear to feel happier when they are able to assert their independence of the party in control of the Dominion Parliament: and this tendency steadily grows and spreads and is virtually never reversed until a party change in Ottawa gives impetus in the opposite direction."[13]

Recent investigation gives reason for qualifying if not rejecting the balance theory:

1. Howard Scarrow investigated patterns of "alternating party choice" in federal and provincial elections between 1930 and 1957[14] with such choice being defined as "an election victory for a party at one level of government surrounded by election victories for another party at the other level of government." He found that of a total of 104 elections there had been alternating choices in only 16 and concluded ". . . when a provincial electorate has registered a preference for one party over a number of years and then changes that preference, the change is reflected in both provincial and federal election results . . . In Canada . . . as in other federations, the normal presumption is that a voter will exhibit relatively consistent voting behaviour in both federal and provincial elections."[15]

2. In an article published in 1970 John Wilson and David Hoffman turned their attention to explaining the continuing weakness of the Liberal party in the provincial politics of Ontario while the Liberals dominated the province in federal elections. In investigating the prevalence of a belief in the balance theory among a sample of Ontario voters they found that 52 per cent of their respondents disagreed with the theory and only a third agreed. However,

> . . . those who voted for the Liberal party in both (1965 federal and 1967 provincial) elections were actually *more* inclined to agree that the same party should not control both levels of government at the same time than were the federal Liberals. Nearly two-fifths of those who supported the Liberal party in 1965 and again in 1967 claimed to be adherents of the balance theory, while only 27 per cent and 17 per cent respectively of those federal Liberals who switched to the provincial Conservatives and to the provincial NDP gave such a response to the question.[16]

Further, ". . . federal supporters of the Conservatives and the New Democrats who counted as consistent supporters of the balance theory — and who might have been expected to vote again for their party at the provincial level because of their opposition to the Liberals winning on Ontario as well — were actually more inclined than the sample as a whole to switch to the Liberal party in 1967."[17] Wilson and Hoffman conclude, ". . . the theory of balance has played little part in shaping the voting behaviour of Ontario citizens in recent years."[18]

3. Jean Havel examined the voting behaviour of a sample of Sudbury voters in the federal general election of April, 1963, and the Ontario general election of September, 1963. He concluded, "There does not appear to be in Sudbury . . . any desire to balance power in Ottawa with power in Ontario. The interviewers discovered no indication of feeling in that direction."[19]

There are several recent studies of federal-provincial voting behaviour in individual constituencies using survey research. The results of these studies are outlined briefly:

1. John C. Courtney and David E. Smith investigated the voting behaviour in Saskatoon at a provincial general election in 1964 and a federal by-election two months later.[20] This constituency was an interesting one because it had a previous record of electing provincial CCF-NDP and federal Conservative candidates and this record held in the 1964 election. Of the 1075 voters in the sample 875 (81.4 per cent) voted for the same party both provincially and federally while 200 (18.6 per cent) supported different parties. The allocation of support of these 200 voters was as follows:

Party supported in federal by-election

Party supported in provincial election	CCF-NDP	Lib.	PC	Total
CCF-NDP	——	26	94	120
Lib.	——	——	58	58
PC	2	20	——	22
Total	2	46	152	200[21]

Courtney and Smith examined some of the characteristics of those who split their vote. Women split their vote to a greater extent than men. Voting articulation increased with age, except that splitting was highest in the 65-and-over age group. The occupational groups which split most frequently were the professional, sales and clerical groups and least frequently the service, transportation and managerial groups. Vote splitting increased with length of residence in the constituency.

2. Jean Havel examined the voting behaviour of a sample of 537 voters in Sudbury in the federal election of April, 1963, and the Ontario general election of September, 1963. His results are as follows:

Comparison of Choice Between General Election and Provincial Election in 1963

	PARTIES			
	PC	Liberal	NDP	Soc. Cr.
General Election	100.0%	100.0%	100.0%	99.9%
Same in Provincial Election	79.5%	66.1%	61.7%	22.2%
Different in Provincial Election	10.6%	18.4%	12.3%	33.3%
No Answer	7.9%	6.3%	17.8%	22.2%
Did not vote in Prov. Election	2.0%	9.2%	8.2%	22.2%

$100\% = 151 + 304 + 73 + 9.$[22]

3. George Perlin and Patti Peppin undertook pilot surveys just before the Ontario provincial election of 1967 in the federal constituencies of Eglinton and Wellington South.[23] The first constituency had elected a Liberal in the federal general election of 1965 and a Conservative in the

provincial election of 1963 while Wellington South had chosen a Conservative in 1965 and a Liberal in 1963. The results of the survey were as follows:

Percentages of Party Vote in the First Election of Each Set Remaining Constant and Changing to Another Party in the Second Election

	Provincial-federal 1963-1965		Federal-provincial 1965-1967*		Provincial-provincial 1963-1967*	
	%	N	%	N	%	N
Percentage remaining constant						
PC	54.1	46	66.3	55	77.6	66
Liberal	60.2	56	44.9	48	66.7	62
NDP	75.0	12	50.0	14	81.3	13
Percentage changing to another party						
PC	42.3	36	25.3	21	13.0	11
Liberal	34.4	32	41.1	44	22.6	21
NDP	25.0	4	39.3	11	18.8	3

*The calculation of 1967 preferences is based upon vote intentions rather than actual votes.[24]

Interestingly, Perlin and Peppin found that the usual demographic classifications (sex, age, income, education, occupation and religion) had no statistically significant relation to vote-switching. There were also suggestive results about the differing perceptions of federal and provincial politics:

> Among the more interesting findings . . . is the significantly greater influence attached by changers to leadership affect in federal politics. Personality generally seems to have been rather more important than we might have assumed since the (local) candidate is maintained at the federal level by more than 60 per cent of the changers and at the provincial level by as many as 47 per cent. Another comparison of interest is the greater frequency with which general past record is mentioned at the provincial level. It might be inferred from this that provincial politics is perceived more frequently in terms of generalized images, while in federal politics leader, candidate, policy and party are more frequently treated as independent objects.[25]

4. Jean Laponce in his 1965 survey of the federal constituency of Vancouver-Burrard caught the provincial election of October 1963 between a series of federal elections in 1962, 1963 and 1965.[26] Between the federal and provincial elections of 1963, 49 per cent of the respondents "migrated"

between one party and another, while between the two federal elections of 1962 and 1963 only 29 per cent changed parties. Of these migrants in the provincial election 93 per cent transferred to Social Credit; the NDP lost 8 per cent of its 1963 federal supporters to Social Credit and the Liberals and Conservatives 55 per cent and 62 per cent respectively. In the ensuing 1965 federal election the NDP recovered all its migrants, the Liberal and Conservative recovery rates were 60 and 71 per cent respectively. The federal-provincial switchers did not have significantly different demographic characteristics than the rest of the voting population. Laponce gives ideology a significant effect and he asserts, "The more ideological an electorate, the greater is the degree of perception of the boundaries around it and the less likely is the electorate to change in behaviour when moved from one political system to the other."[27] Thus the NDP neither gains nor loses significantly from federal-provincial migrations, while the Liberals, and to an even greater extent the Conservatives, are vulnerable to defections of their federal supporters to Social Credit in provincial elections in British Columbia.

5. In the Wilson-Hoffman article to which reference has been made the authors set out to explain the relative weakness of the Liberal party in recent Ontario politics, a weakness particularly striking because of the Liberal dominance of the province in federal elections. As we have seen, the balance theory was rejected. Gross results for the province indicate a close correlation between Liberal weakness and strength in provincial and federal elections respectively and voter-abstention at the provincial level. However, there are important regional variations. Liberal declines from federal to provincial elections accompanied by a corresponding increase in abstentions is most marked in the larger cities and the urbanized areas of the province from the Toronto-Hamilton areas to the Niagara Peninsula. In a number of rural constituencies of traditional Liberal strength the party's vote holds relatively consistent in both federal and provincial elections. All Ontario parties lose some of their federal supporters because of abstentions in provincial elections but the Liberals more than others, in 1967 the provincial Liberals retained only 49 per cent of their 1965 federal supporters in Toronto and Hamilton. Throughout the province high-status federal Liberals were more prone than other voters to switch to the Conservatives in provincial elections, lower-status Liberals to abstain. Again there were regional variations with this tendency most marked in the southern area of the province and particularly in Metropolitan Toronto.

The spectacular record of the Diefenbaker Conservatives in the federal general election of 1958 provides a convenient way to determine the impact of a dramatic change in the standings of the federal parties on their provincial counterparts. The following table examines the federal swing between 1953 and 1958 — the 1957 election is here regarded as transitional — and the party results in the immediately succeeding provincial elections.

	Conservatives		Liberals		CCF		Social Credit	
	1953-58 federal swing	Provincial swing in election after '58 federal	1953-58 federal swing	Provincial swing	1953-58 federal swing	Provincial swing	1953-58 federal swing	Provincial swing
Newfoundland	+17.1	-6.7	-12.8	-8.3	-0.4			
Nova Scotia	+17.8	-0.3	-14.6	-5.6	-2.2	+5.9		
New Brunswick	+12.2	-6.0	-9.3	+7.3	-1.2			
Prince Edward Island	+14.0	+5.9	-13.6	-5.9	-0.5			
Quebec	+20.2	-5.2 (Union Nationale)	-15.3	+6.8	+0.8			
Ontario	+16.1	-2.4	-14.0	+3.4	-0.6	+0.3		
Manitoba	+29.7	+19.5	-18.6	-6.0	-4.0	+3.6	-4.5	-11.5
Saskatchewan	+39.7	+12.0	-18.1	+2.4	-15.8	-4.8	-4.9	-9.2
Alberta	+45.4	+14.7	-21.3	-17.2	-2.5	-3.9	-19.2	+9.9
British Columbia	+35.3	+3.6	-14.8	-0.9	-2.1	+4.4	-16.5	-7.0

The impact of the Diefenbaker victory on provincial political fortunes is inconclusive. In the three westernmost provinces the Conservatives made significant gains in terms of proportions of the popular vote but remained insignificant political forces after the succeeding provincial elections. It is plausible to attribute to the 1958 sweep some significance in the displacement of Liberal by Conservative governments in Prince Edward Island and Manitoba. Quebec's spectacular support for the Conservatives in 1958 was followed by the Liberal victory in the provincial election of 1960. Perhaps the most decisive permanent result of the Diefenbaker sweep was the destruction of Social Credit as an important federal political force in Alberta and British Columbia, although this seems not to have compromised the provincial standings of the party.

We still know very little about federal-provincial electoral behaviour. The balance theory is discredited. Laponce's hypothesis that ideological politics discourage voter migrations appears to be validated by the circumstance that the CCF/NDP and more latterly the Quebec Creditistes appear to gain provincial and federal support from the same groups, although this hypothesis might require modification in the light of the symbiotic relation between Conservative and socialist electoral support in Saskatchewan. It is significant on the basis of the Laponce and Perlin/Peppin studies that switchers appear not to fall into the usual demographic categories of sex, age, income, education, occupation and religion. The Wilson-Hoffman analysis of federal-provincial voting in Ontario points up significant differences in behaviour among voters in particular regions and areas of the province at a particular period in time. Such research as this should discourage easy generalizations about this kind of voting behaviour on a Canada-wide basis.

Despite our ignorance of the complexities of federal-provincial voting behaviour we do at least know the outer limits of electoral dependence. Some parties in some provinces have been able to dominate one level without dominating the other. Since he became Premier in 1952 W. A. C. Bennett has shown little disposition to commit the prestige and resources of his party to federal politics. In Alberta the virtual demise of Social Credit as a federal force seems not in itself to have significantly weakened the party at the provincial level.[28] The Conservatives dominate federal politics in Saskatchewan but are not a significant provincial force. The Conservative government of Ontario has survived the domination of federal politics in the province by the Liberals. Apart perhaps from the Atlantic provinces where the classic two-party system prevails, any federal or provincial party with serious hopes of electoral success must gain the support of voters who either support other parties or abstain in elections at the other level of government.

PARTY ORGANIZATION

Party organization in Canada is an almost unexplored field. The analysis below is thus based on fragmentary information.

Do the same local party activists participate at both federal and provincial levels? Or, alternatively, are large numbers of activists oriented exclusively or almost exclusively toward one level or the other? The three major parties appear to promote the idea that federal and provincial wings are members of the same team. To what extent is this mythology and to what extent a fairly accurate description of Canadian political behaviour? One might suppose, in the absence of evidence, that in provinces and constituencies where parties are strong federally and weak provincially, or vice versa, there are tendencies at work to encourage activists to participate at only one level rather than both. But is this the case?

In a study presented in 1970 Henry Jacek, John McDonough, Ronald Shimuzu and Patrick Smith examined the federal-provincial activity of 180 party officials in three Hamilton constituencies:[29]

High Activity	Liberal	PC	NDP	Total
Provincially only	0	8	2	10
Provincially and federally	36	30	38	104
Federally only	30	16	2	48
At neither level	11	4	3	18
Total	77	58	45	180[30]

This study indicated a very great variation among the parties in respect to integration on federal-provincial lines. The Liberal party is least integrated because the inducements to membership and activity are based largely on federal patronage and the NDP most integrated because of common ideological and policy commitments. The Conservatives are between the two in degree of integration with rather highly personalized patterns of allegiances among upper-status persons.

The most significant developments in the organizational structure of the two major parties in the past decade is the growth of extra-parliamentary machinery. While the movement is very uneven, the general trend of the democratization of the parties at both levels is at first an opening up of membership participation in the nominating function followed by partici-pation, or ostensible participation, of members in the formulation of party policy. In general, this development is in the direction of lessening the integration of the parties on federal-provincial lines as each develops extra-parliamentary machinery to a large extent independent of the party at the other level. Prior to the 1960s it was broadly accurate to describe the national Liberal and Conservative parties outside Parliament as federations of the provincial parties. This has in the main ceased to be so, although the constitution of the national Liberal party describes that group as a federation of provincial parties.

Beginning in 1919 with the Liberals and 1927 with the Conservatives the major parties have selected their leaders through representative party conventions.[30] At the most recent of these conventions in 1968 and 1967 respectively about 60 per cent of the delegates were chosen by federal constituency organizations while the rest were either *ex officio* delegates by reason of holding legislative or party offices or were nominees of provincial, women's and youth groups of the parties. Voting for leadership candidates proceeds through successive secret ballots until one candidate attains a clear majority. The important characteristic of the leadership conventions is that provincial leaders do not dominate such meetings as do their state counterparts in national nominating conventions in the United States. The secrecy of the ballot and the expectation in the two most recent conventions that more than one ballot will be required to choose a leader means that serious candidates must secure the support of aggregates of individual delegates rather than provincial blocs.

Both the major parties are now committed by their constitutions to hold periodic national conventions dealing with organizational and policy matters. It is still not clear what role such conventions will assume in designing policy-inputs for their respective parties in Parliament or for the Canadian political system as such. Whatever part such gatherings come to play in this as in leadership matters, it is reasonably certain that they will not be dominated by provincial parties or leaders.

The circumstances under which the Premiers of provinces commit their own prestige and organizational resources in federal elections is highly variable. Duplessis of Quebec and Frost of Ontario made such commitments to the Diefenbaker Conservatives in 1957 and 1958, although neither had given such support to the federal party in 1953. Robert Stanfield of Nova Scotia supported the Conservatives in 1965 while little help was given to the national party by Duff Roblin of Manitoba or John Robarts of Ontario. The late Ross Thatcher of Saskatchewan committed little of his support or that of his party organization to the federal Liberals when he was in power between 1964 and 1971. Quebec Liberals from 1960 onward appear to have given little assistance to their federal counterparts, particularly since the almost complete separation of the federal and Quebec wings of the party which was effected in 1964. From 1935 onward the national Social Credit movement was to a large extent the extension of the Alberta party. On the other hand, Premier Bennett of British Columbia has shown only a marginal and intermittent interest in federal Social Credit politics. Only in the CCF-NDP has there been a close integration of federal and provincial party organizations.

The support of provincial party organizations is undoubtedly of assistance to federal politicians but, as the results of the 1968 general elections demonstrate, it is by no means decisive. More perhaps than in elections of the two decades before, the provincial Conservatives and Liberal parties throughout Canada were mobilized behind their federal counterparts. The Conservatives had healed some of the internecine quarrels of the Diefenbaker years and the Liberals were riding on the wave of Trudeaumania. However, each of the two major national parties did well in those provinces where it was out of office provincially, with the exception of Nova Scotia. The Union Nationale and Ontario Conservatives supported the federal Conservatives but the latter party received 21.3 per cent and 32.0 per cent of the popular vote respectively in these two provinces. On the other hand with Liberal governments in power in Newfoundland, New Brunswick and Prince Edward Island the federal Conservatives won 52.8 per cent, 49.7 per cent and 51.8 per cent of the popular vote compared with 31.4 per cent nationally. As for the Liberals, their proportion of the popular vote in provinces with Liberal administrations was 42.8 per cent in Newfoundland, 44.4 per cent in New Brunswick, 44.9 per cent in Prince Edward Island and 27.1 per cent in Saskatchewan compared with 45.5 per cent nationally. Only in Nova Scotia where the Conservative proportion of the vote was the highest in the country, 55.2 per cent, was a provincial party able to "deliver," and this result was no doubt due largely to the continuing personal popularity of the Conservative leader and former Nova Scotia Premier, Robert Stanfield. In fact, the relatively poor showing of the Liberals in Saskatchewan and Newfoundland — and perhaps that of the Conservatives in Manitoba — may be attributed to the decreasing popularity of provincial governments of those parties.

On the basis of a detailed study of relations between the federal and provincial wings of the Conservative party in British Columbia during the period when George Drew was national leader Edwin R. Black has made several perceptive generalizations about party organization in Canada. These generalizations summarize most of what we now know about this matter:

> 1. Canada's major parties do not fit the model of unified country-wide parties with hierarchically inferior provincial subdivisions; major party supporters do not exhibit the necessary degree of commitment. 2. Both the structure and the internal operation of a major party resemble that of the Canadian system of government. The sovereignty of provincial party units is as real and extensive as that of the provinces with respect to Ottawa. 3. Just as the virtual independence of a provincial government's policy-making depends to a considerable extent on its provincial resources, so the effective control of provincial organization by the local officers depends upon the local unit's political resources in comparison with those of the central party; such resources are considered to be size and commitment of membership, financial capabilities, quality and appeal of leadership, and, of course, electoral success. 4. Party organizers must deal with three types of active members: those whose political interests are primarily oriented in provincial terms, those whose interests find primary expression in central-government goals, and those whose interests are multifaceted or else are concentrated on some aspect of political life comprehending both spheres of government — such as the attainment of ideological objectives or general governmental power for the party. 5. A party's policy objectives and organizational requirements in the federal and provincial arenas are often quite different, but both sets of leaders

must rely in large measure on the same relatively small group of people and on the same resources for their field work. 6. The interests and energies of the party machinery within one province cannot be converted readily and with equal efficiency to both federal and provincial objectives. Attempts to treat the party as if it were readily convertible impose almost intolerable stresses on the organization, stresses which may be expected to become manifest in difficulties between the party leaders. 7. The public or private character of the expression and resolution of internal party differences is a reflection of the leadership skills and institutional machinary with which the groups are endowed, and of the party's electoral morale. 8. Even where a provincial party organization is controlled by relatively ineffectual persons, if they are determined in their leadership, representatives of the central party can undertake "corrective" action only at considerable risk. 9. The provincial party is a highly-charged organism, with many internal stresses and tensions, which must be capable of frequent integration with as many as nine others of similar nature to produce a country-wide mechanism focussing its power on system-wide problems. 10. The pattern of authoritative relationships between central and provincial party groups will depend upon whether public office is held by one, neither, or both of the two party groups. These relationships will also be affected by the nature of any "rehabilitative" process through which an out-of-office party faction may be going and by the degree of ideological and policy solidarity between the central and the provincial units.[31]

It may well be that in federal politics perhaps more than in provincial the popularity of party leaders is more crucial than organization in determining levels of electoral support. Certainly this appears to have been so in the Diefenbaker and Trudeau victories of 1958 and 1968 respectively. If this is so, there is a profound influence toward autonomous federal and provincial parties and political systems since national leaders are likely to be neither willing nor able to mobilize their personal influence behind their provincial colleagues. Heath Macquarrie has said this of the leadership of Robert Borden:

> His close and continuing liaison with provincial leaders was an essential part of the process by which the Conservative Party slowly recovered from the disheartening defeats of 1896 and 1900. While the result of the 1911 election is generally attributed solely to reaction to the reciprocity proposals, it should be noted that the Conservative resurgence in the federal field followed the establishment of strong provincial Tory regimes in Ontario, British Columbia, Manitoba, and New Brunswick. With the premiers of these provinces Borden was always in frank and friendly contact. This political friendship took tangible form when the provincial party machines became totally involved in the 1911 campaign.[32]

Contemporary leaders of the two major parties rely much less on provincial party organization than did Borden. Their continuing task is to establish and sustain their own personal popularity with the aid of federal party machinery oriented to federal electoral success and largely autonomous of the provincial wings of the party.

PARTY CAREERS

According to the 1970 *Parliamentary Guide* 37 Members of the House of Commons had contested one or more provincial elections and of these 17 had sat in provincial legislatures. The party breakdown is this:

	Held provincial seats	*Unsuccessfully contested provincial elections*
Progressive Conservative	5	6
Liberal	6	4
New Democratic Party	6	6
Creditiste		3
Independent		1

Thus only 6.4 per cent of the 264 seats in the House were filled by former members of provincial legislatures while 14.0 per cent were held by those who had contested provincial elections successfully or unsuccessfully. The party breakdown is interesting — 54.5 per cent of N.D.P. Members had contested provincial elections while the corresponding percentages for the Progressive Conservatives and Liberals were 15.3 and 6.5 respectively.

Of 528 members of provincial legislatures about whom the *Parliamentary Guide* gives information, 37 or 7.0 per cent had contested federal elections while of these 17 or 3.2 per cent had been Members of Parliament.

In terms of contemporary federal-provincial relations it is significant to examine the membership of cabinets to determine the extent of the experience of their members at the other level. The three recent federal cabinets noted below are those constituted in 1957, 1963 and 1968 by incoming Prime Ministers:

The Diefenbaker cabinet of 1957. Of the sixteen ministers chosen by Prime Minister Diefenbaker in June 1957 only three (Nowlan, Brooks and Churchill) had ever sat in provincial legislatures.

The Pearson cabinet of 1963. Of the twenty-two ministers chosen by Prime Minister Pearson in April 1963 only one (Arthur Laing) had ever sat in a provincial legislature.

The Trudeau cabinet of 1968. Of the twenty-eight ministers chosen by Prime Minister Trudeau in 1968 only two (Laing, Kierans) had ever held seats in provincial legislatures.

Thus recent federal cabinets have been constituted almost entirely of ministers without provincial elective experience. Of the three cabinets mentioned above only the Honourable Eric Kierans had held cabinet office at both levels. (The former Premier of New Brunswick, the Honourable Hugh John Flemming, was federal Minister of Fisheries between 1960 and 1963.) The Liberal party during this century has developed a practice of coopting persons from outside federal politics and advancing them quickly to cabinet rank.[33] During the period prior to the leadership of Lester Pearson this process often involved bringing powerful provincial politicians directly into the Liberal cabinet. This older tradition has been terminated by the last two Liberal leaders.

Of 164 provincial cabinet ministers listed in the 1970 *Parliamentary Guide* only six had sat in the House of Commons. Of these, Thatcher and Schreyer were Premiers of Saskatchewan and Manitoba respectively, three were Quebec ministers who had formerly been Conservative M.P.s and the other an Alberta minister formerly a Social Credit Member of Parliament.

In general then, careers to elective office at federal and provincial levels are to a large extent separated — except for the New Democratic Party. So far as federal-provincial relations are concerned cabinet ministers deal with one another in the absence either of personal experience or ambitions at the other level.

PARTY FINANCE

Long-run trends in party finance in Canada work in the direction of the mutual independence of the federal and provincial wings of the Liberal and Conservative parties. The most astute student of this subject, K. Z. Paltiel, has argued that this development has had a crucial disintegrative effect on Canadian federalism. He wrote of the older system:

> The traditional methods of financing the two old Canadian parties, the Liberals and the Conservatives, helped overcome the splintering effect of the provinces and provincial party organizations. This was accomplished through a highly centralized system of party finance. This system rested on a common basis: the centralized corporate industrial and financial structures located in Montreal and Toronto. It is common knowledge that the two old parties were largely financed from the same sources. These corporate contributors numbered in the hundreds rather than in the thousands. Under this system, provincial and even municipal elections, as well as federal elections, could be and were financed from the central party funds and sources. The traditional system of party finance had important integrative effects which helped overcome the centrifugal forces in Canadian political life. This beneficial result was made possible by the highly concentrated nature of Canadian industry and finance.[34]

In the period since the end of the Second World War the older system has been attenuated. The rise of third parties has contributed to this trend. The increasing importance of natural resource development, primarily under provincial jurisdiction, has given corporate donors incentives to contribute directly to provincial parties. Paltiel has described the recent situation:

> . . . the British Columbia and Alberta wings of the federal Liberal and Conservative Parties have become largely self-supporting and contribute on occasion to the support of the Saskatchewan wing. Manitoba in the heyday of the Winnipeg Grain Exchange was self-supporting but now is a net importer of election funds. The rest of Canada, as far as the two major parties are concerned, are beneficiaries of transfer payments; they are in part political colonies except when some grass-roots movement has swept a minor party into power or the provincial wing of a traditional party can exploit the advantages of incumbency by using office to gain funds for organizational purposes by fair or foul means.[35]

The direct or indirect subsidy from the public purse either of parties or individual candidates for election works against federal-provincial integration by putting resources in the hands of parties quite independent of party decisions taken at the other level. Quebec in 1963 and Nova Scotia in 1969[36] enacted legislation providing for limits to the expenditure of parties and for subsidies to the candidates of recognized parties. It is significant that the Quebec law was enacted at the time that the dominant forces in the Quebec Liberal Federation were effecting an almost complete separation between the Federation and the federal Liberal Party. The Report of the federal Committee on Election Expenses published in 1966[37] recommended, among other things, a system of public subsidies to candidates and subsidized broadcasting for political parties. This Report has not as yet been acted upon. In general terms, the public subsidy of parties or candidates at either or both levels works against intraparty integration.

IDEOLOGY

As is well known, the national Liberal and Conservative parties in Canada are both ideologically inclusive in the sense that each comprehends persons of divergent ideological viewpoints and attempts to appeal to voters of widely varying ideological persuasions. The Conservative cabinet of Prime Minister Diefenbaker included ministers as diverse in their perspectives as Donald Fleming and Alvin Hamilton and within three weeks soon after the 1965 general election Prime Minister Pearson conferred important portfolios on Jean Marchand and the late Robert Winters. There are diversities at least as extensive as these in the caucuses and extra-parliamentary organizations of the two major parties. However, despite the lack of conformity on ideology the normal workings of cabinet and of caucus solidarity and of the requirements of future electoral success predispose parties at each level toward agreement on particular issues. Such influences are much weaker or exist hardly at all between federal and provincial wings of the same party. Particularly among the Liberals there have been wide variations. In economic matters Saskatchewan and Manitoba Liberals have been on the right of the political spectrum while when in office the Lesage and Robichaud governments put into operation in Quebec and New Brunswick respectively more comprehensive programmes of reform than those ever undertaken in Canadian provinces.[38] Interestingly, recent Progressive-Conservative governments in the provinces have been middle-of-the-road in social and economic matters. One might thus hypothesize that ideological diversities among Liberals are most clearly manifested in the orientations of the federal and provincial wings of the party and that the system provides few requirements that these be resolved. On the other hand, such differences among the Conservatives tend to take place within the national party and from time to time compromise the electoral success of that party. In general, a common and unifying ideology is not an influence toward federal-provincial integration among the major parties and the national and provincial wings conform to the ideological perspectives of their respective party activists and the perceived requirements of electoral victory among their respective electorates.

(The constitutional division of legislative powers between Parliament and the provinces as well as cultural dualism appears to have had a significant influence on the ideological inclusiveness of the two major parties. Many but by no means all of the subjects giving rise to left-right divisions among the electorate are within provincial rather than federal jurisdiction — the predominant aspects of health, social security and welfare; collective bargaining and industrial standards for most workers; municipal government; the exploitation of natural resources. Thus *within* particular provinces there are on occasion or permanently ideological cleavages between the major political contenders in those jurisdictions, cleavages much more clear-cut than those in national politics.)

PARTY SYMMETRY

Party symmetry in a sense is a residual category, as it is inextricably related to all the other dimensions of intraparty relations which have been analyzed above. In general terms, if the party system were symmetrical with the same parties the major competitors at both federal and provincial levels there would be important influences toward integration. Conversely, asymmetry contains predispositions toward the confederal form.

In late 1971 the Canadian party system had many elements of asymmetry. Parties other than the Liberals and Conservatives were in power in British Columbia, Saskatchewan and Manitoba. The federal party which dominated federal politics was in power only in Newfoundland, Nova Scotia, Prince Edward Island and Quebec and the official opposition in Saskatchewan, Ontario and New Brunswick. Two minor parties were the government and official opposition in British Columbia. In Quebec all three opposition groups with seats in the National Assembly were minor parties, and the Creditistes were the major opposition to the Liberals in federal elections. Thus only in the four Atlantic provinces existed the classic two-party system of Liberals and Conservatives.

(Although it does not relate directly to this analysis, Maurice Pinard's suggestive theory of the rise of third parties in Canada may be mentioned parenthetically here for the light it sheds on party asymmetry.[39] He presents an impressive array of evidence from federal and provincial political history leading to the conclusion that where one party dominates a political system effective opposition to that party is likely to find an outlet in a new party rather than a resurgence of strength in the weak opposition party. Thus ". . . the indications are that whenever the opposition party (or the strongest of many opposition parties) fails to return at least a third of the votes while in opposition, it tends to be replaced by 'third parties'."[40])

Asymmetry in Canada has direct consequences for intraparty relations, most of those consequences working in the direction of what I have called the confederal form. The existence in particular provinces of parties which are oriented exclusively or almost exclusively to competition at one level rather than both means that either large groups of voters switch party allegiances between federal and provincial elections or abstain from voting their characteristic allegiance at one or the other level. Those seeking party careers will be predisposed by asymmetry toward service at one level rather than both in succession: at the extreme, an ambitious Saskatchewan Conservative is unlikely to be attracted to provincial politics while a Social Credit careerist in British Columbia must perforce look to Victoria. If we assume, as is reasonable, that an important determinant of the success of a party in soliciting campaign funds is its prospects of electoral success, donors will be predisposed toward giving to one wing rather than both. Parties which are weak often tend toward ideological sectarianism and such circumstances embarrass the party at the other level which is stronger and more ideologically inclusive.

There are thus a group of pervasive influences at work in the direction of autonomous federal and provincial party systems in Canada, toward the confederal form. However, several qualifications to this generalization should be made:

First, in the Atlantic provinces where the two-party system is sustained there is a significantly higher degree of federal-provincial party integration than elsewhere in Canada.[41] Throughout the country, asymmetry works toward the confederal form and symmetry toward integration.

Second, the parties differ significantly in their degrees of integration. The Liberals are the most confederal, the Conservatives less so. However, in several dimensions the New Democratic Party is relatively highly integrated on federal-provincial lines. Where it has significant electoral strength, this strength has been manifested at both levels. Its traditions of party finance provide for regularized transfers of resources between federal and provincial wings.[42] Party activists from the level of the worker in the local constituency to the national leader characteristically participate in both provincial and federal electoral activity. Party careerists characteristically accept nominations for elective office at both levels in the course of their political service. The NDP includes a broad spectrum of ideological commitment, but ideological conflicts of a crucial nature seem to divide the party on other than federal-provincial lines.[43] It thus seems reasonable to expect that in the unlikely event of the NDP forming a national government intraparty relations would become a significantly more important instrument of cohesion in Canada than is now so.

Third, partisan-political activity involves complexes of interpersonal relations which can and no doubt do exert important influences on interactions between federal and provincial wings and on government-to-govermnent dealings. Of all important Canadian institutions, the two major parties are perhaps least subject to authoritative procedures regulating their internal workings. Despite the influences toward the confederal form, party leaders have important channels of access to their partisan counterparts at the other level. Again, despite the growing independence of federal and provincial party organizations, most active Liberals and Conservatives believe that they are in some general sense members of respective teams and in most parts of the country and under most circumstances the notion is propagated that there is one party rather than semi-autonomous federal and provincial wings. Partisan activity involves hates and fears, personal allegiances and policy commitments and in many circumstances these personal factors are important in the working of the federal system.

Despite these qualifications, the two major parties have increasingly manifested confederal forms. In doing so, these parties have almost ceased to be instruments of federal-provincial integration where the authoritative resolution of federal-provincial conflicts has become increasingly crucial for the stability if not the survival of Canadian federalism.

ELECTIONS AND FEDERAL-PROVINCIAL CONFLICT

If intraparty relations have a diminishing integrative capacity in the Canadian political system, it is conceivable that popular elections could be effective instruments to resolve disputes between the national government and dominant influences in particular provinces or regions. Perhaps the best available way to investigate this matter is to examine briefly four sets of elections in recent Canadian political history where federal-provincial relations have been of great salience.

1. *Alberta, 1935.* In the Alberta provincial election of August, 1935, the

Social Credit party under William Aberhart came to power with 54.2 per cent of the popular vote. The party was elected on a platform of monetary reform which challenged some of the most crucial elements of national economic policies. Six weeks later in the federal general election the Alberta voters gave Social Credit 46.2 per cent of the vote and all but two of the province's 17 seats in the House of Commons while on a country-wide basis the Liberals came to power with 44.8 per cent of the popular vote and 173 of 245 seats in the Commons. In the subsequent period the federal government was willing and able to obstruct Alberta's policies for monetary reform on a provincial basis.[44]

2. *Quebec 1939, 1940.* Premier Maurice Duplessis of Quebec un-expectedly called an election for October, 1939, with the alleged justification that Ottawa was illegitimately using the war-time emergency to encroach on provincial powers. Prime Minister King and Liberal cabinet ministers from Quebec took this challenge with the utmost seriousness. Two such ministers — Charles B. Power and Lucien Cardin — assumed direction of the provincial campaign, including raising funds from outside[45] and inside the province and participating in the selection of local candidates. The four Liberal mininsters from Quebec campaigned actively in the province and threatened to resign if the Union Nationale was sustained. The result was a decisive Liberal victory with 53.5 per cent of the popular vote and 69 of the 86 seats in the Legislative Assembly. In the federal election of March 1940 the Liberals received 63.3 per cent of the Quebec popular vote and all but four of the province's 65 seats in the House of Commons.

3. *Ontario 1940, 1943.* On January 18, 1940, Liberal Premier Hepburn of Ontario and the leader of the Conservative Opposition in the province jointly sponsored a resolution in the Provincial Parliament condemning the federal King government for not prosecuting the war effectively. The Prime Minister of Canada responded by requesting a dissolution of Parliament on January 25 and an election was held on March 29. Hepburn had in the recent past collaborated both with the Quebec Union Nationale and the federal and provincial Conservatives in attempting to displace Mackenzie King. In the 1940 election the federal Liberals increased their share of the popular vote in Ontario to 50.8 per cent from 42.4 per cent in 1935 and of seats from 56 to 57. Hepburn resigned as Premier in October 1942 and in August of the next year the Ontario Liberals sustained a disastrous defeat in the Ontario election, emerging with only 14 seats as against 38 for the Conservatives and 34 for the CCF.[46]

4. *Quebec 1968, 1970.* In the federal general election of June, 1968, Prime Minister Trudeau and the Liberal party campaigned in Quebec and throughout Canada on Trudeau's view of Canadian federalism. The party was sustained in Quebec with 53.6 per cent of the popular vote and 56 of 74 seats in the House of Commons. In the provincial general election of April, 1970 the Liberal party was returned to power in Quebec with 45 per

cent of the popular vote and 72 of 108 seats in the National Assembly. The party had campaigned on a federalist platform.

There is an inevitable arbitrariness in interpreting the situations outlined above. In the Alberta and Ontario cases the results were relatively unequivocal. After the federal election of 1935 Ottawa was willing and able to frustrate Alberta's plans for monetary reform and so a national majority imposed its will on a provincial majority. The 1940 national election sustained the war-time policies of Prime Minister Mackenzie King against the challenge posed by Ontario — as well as Quebec — and the subsequent provincial election resulted in the defeat of the Ontario Liberals. The Quebec results of 1939 and 1940 installed in office in the province a government under heavy political obligations to the federal Liberal leadership and rallied a provincial majority around that leadership and its policies. However, the Union Nationale was returned to power on a nationalist platform in 1944 and for at least 15 years afterward the provincial Liberals were seriously embarrassed by accusations that they were subservient to Ottawa. It is perhaps too early to assess the long-term results of the 1968 and 1970 elections in Quebec.

If general elections were to be a method of resolving federal-provincial conflicts two conditions would have to be met:

First, some crucial aspect of federal-provincial contention would be so central to electoral competition that the voting results could reasonably be interpreted as a mandate for one side or the other in such contention.

Second, in particular provinces the electorate would be consistent in giving its majority support in successive federal and provincial elections to parties whose policies in federal-provincial relations were not inconsistent.

These two conditions are not often fulfilled.

Most general elections at both levels of government centre on personalities and policies not directly connected with federal-provincial relations. The four circumstances described above were atypical.

However, even when federal-provincial relations are highly salient in federal or provincial elections voters often give their support to parties with quite inconsistent policies and objectives. Quebec voters returned the Duplessis nationalists in the provincial elections of 1944, 1948, 1952 and 1956 but gave overwhelming support to the federal Liberals, who were more centralist then any party in peace-time Canadian history in the elections of 1945, 1949, 1953 and 1957. During this period the Quebec electorate gave little effective support to the federal Conservatives who were significantly more solicitous of provincial rights. Similarly, in every British Columbia election since 1952, W. A. C. Bennett has campaigned against federal power and other allegedly alien influences but the same electorate who have responded to him have given majority support to other federal parties. Provincial autonomy is to a greater or less degree the electoral stock-in-trade of most provincial politicians seeking office. However, the electoral success of the most autonomist of these leaders has often little or nothing to do with resolving federal-provincial disputes in their favour.

More than any other federal election in Canadian history that of June 1968 may reasonably be regarded as conferring a mandate for a party and a leader to implement a particular view of Confederation. Pierre Elliott Trudeau ostensibly, and I believe actually, entered elective politics to make that view prevail. The view was explained with clarity before and during the campaign. The new Liberal leader made no other important election promises. However, despite the salience of the issue and the relative decisiveness of the electoral result several of the provinces — including all of the larger ones — continue to contest at several fundamental points the view of federalism on which Prime Minister Trudeau and his party were elected. It is improbable that the Prime Minister and his colleagues could devise any politically practical way to overcome such provincial opposition.

In general then, elections have a very limited capacity to effect the authoritative resolution of federal-provincial conflict.

THE PARTISAN-POLITICAL SYSTEM AND EXECUTIVE FEDERALISM

As we saw earlier in this chapter, Riker's attribution of the decisive role to political parties in federalism makes no analysis of the roles that parties actually play in these political systems. In Canada as in other western democracies parties appear to be of diminishing importance. John Meisel, in an article written in 1965, analyzed this phenomenon.[47] In his analysis, several of the factors at work in Canada are common to western nations. "Voluntary associations, interest groups, and private and semi-public organizations" have increased in numbers and wealth and rival parties in the processes by which public decisions are made. There has been a "gradual diminution in Europe and North America of the cleavages in attitudes toward social issues" and in such circumstances parties have become "bland" to maximize their electoral support and have thus surrendered their innovative role to groups with more specific concerns. The specialized nature of modern government has led to the partial eclipse of elected legislatures by "independent or quasi-independent boards, agencies, and commissions, by so-called advisory bodies and, to some extent, even by Royal Commissions" as well as by the expert civil service. The merit system in the civil service and more generally the regularization of public business have diminished the patronage available to politicians. These circumstances have challenged parties in all the western democracies to a greater or lesser extent but, according to Meisel, have been compounded by factors specific to Canada. The Liberal policy of coopting into positions of influence persons with little or no previous political experience has resulted in amateurism and the lack of adequate political skills in high places. Conversely, the Conservatives have failed to recruit able people into political life. The parties have become increasingly regionalized and have done badly in their vitally necessary role in Canadian integration in creating a "national political culture." Most importantly, from the point of view of this study, federalism itself has been significant in the decreasing role of political parties:

> Canada's federal system has imposed a particularly difficult task on the parties. To the extent that many of our major governmental decisions have resulted from intensive consultations between different levels of government, parties have to some measure been locked out of the most important decision-making processes. Dominion-provincial conferences, meetings of premiers, committees of experts representing the civil services of several provinces, and possibly two or three levels of government, working parties of various provincial ministers and experts, have all downgraded the role of parties who still bear considerable responsibility for the consequences of decisions but cannot always participate in their making. Canadian federalism has, therefore, been a major contributor to the decline in importance and effectiveness of political parties.[48]

Meisel is here referring to what in Chapter 3 was called "executive federalism."

Political parties are thus of decreasing importance in the Canadian federal system. Partisan politics have relatively limited capacities for effecting the resolution of federal-provincial conflicts either through intraparty relations or general elections. We have also seen in Chapter 1 the restricted role of constitutional amendment and evolving patterns of judicial review in bringing about successive redelineations of the powers of Ottawa and provinces as circumstances change. Thus very heavy burdens are thrown on intergovernmental relations in managing the federal system, on executive federalism.

The most obvious linkage between the partisan-political system and executive federalism is that the power of those who make the final and authoritative decisions in federal-provincial relations is legitimated by prior electoral success. Conversely, politicians in opposition at both levels are to an overwhelming degree "locked out," in Meisel's words, of effective influence in these matters; federal-provincial relations absorb a relatively small amount of time in the debates of Parliament and the provincial legislatures and under many circumstances these bodies have no real alternatives to ratifying decisions reached in intergovernmental negotiations. How then are electoral standings influenced by executive federalism?

Somewhat like sovereign states, Canadian provinces have fairly durable and persisting interests. Whatever administrations are in power, Ontario is a large and wealthy province and Prince Edward Island a small and poor one. New Brunswick is inevitably more preoccupied with bilingualism than is Alberta. Every Quebec administration since 1944 has put a higher priority on autonomy than have other provinces. It is safe to predict that despite their egalitarian commitments no potential NDP governments of British Columbia or Ontario would press for higher equalization payments to less favoured provinces. However, as is the case with sovereign states, these persisting interests do not prevent provincial leaders adopting different strategies in dealing with Ottawa and ideology in some circumstances is of considerable importance in federal-provincial relations. Ideology appears, for example, to have determined the opposition of the CCF-NDP government of Saskatchewan in the early 1960s toward an inflexible formula for constitutional amendment and such opposition was ended by the displacement of that party by the Liberals in the provincial election of 1964. The personalized and erratic style of W. A. C. Bennet has been of some consequence for federal-provincial relations. Premier Robarts of Ontario assumed a crucial role in attempting to reconcile conflicts between Quebec and the rest of Canada but his successor William Davis has up to now given this activity less importance.

Provinces have thus persisting interests and provincial politicians in power have of course a persisting concern to press these interests in such a way as to be re-elected. Future electoral success at the provincial level has come to depend in large part on appropriate federal policies, particularly in respect to fiscal matters. This rather than the partisan complexion of the government in power in Ottawa appears to be the crucial determinant of the stances of provincial leaders toward federal politics. For example:

1. In the 1957 federal election Mr. Diefenbaker and the Conservatives were perceived by several of the provincial administrations as being more sensitive to provincial interests than were the incumbent Liberals. This perception seems to have been important in winning for the new Conservative leader the organizational support of the governing parties in Nova Scotia, New Brunswick, Quebec and Ontario. This support, particularly of the two central provinces, appears to have been important in the Diefenbaker victory.

2. In the 1965 election campaign Premier Robert Stanfield of Nova Scotia threw the support of his organization behind the federal Conservatives and the party unexpectedly increased its share of the popular vote by 1.9 per cent and won three of the province's ten seats from the Liberals. In a perceptive article Murray Beck attributes part of the strong support of the Premier to Robert Stanfield's predispositions as "a strong party man." Beck goes on to describe other influences at work:

> Mr. Stanfield probably felt impelled to intervene all the more because of his recent relations with Ottawa. For most of his premiership up to 1963, he could expect sympathetic consideration from the federal government of the day, expecially since he had

been an architect of its initial victory. Certainly he had a direct pipe-line to the fountainhead of authority at Ottawa. That happy situation ended in April, 1963. He could not have expected the same solicitous attention from a Liberal government. Yet he had hoped for greater recognition of the fiscal incapacity of his province. The political maladroitness which characterized the Pearson government in this area, as in many others, provided him with more than enough ammunition for electioneering purposes.[49]

3. In the 1968 federal election the governments of Quebec and Ontario distrusted the policies of the Trudeau Liberals in respect to the provinces. As we have seen, the support of these two provincial organizations was thrown behind the federal Conservatives.

Provincial political parties, and most importantly those in power, have discretion in determining how much, if any, of their prestige and resources they will commit to their federal colleagues in federal elections. The outside limits of this discretion under the normal political rules are that provincial politicians will not do anything which aids the opposing parties. However, even these limits are sometimes exceeded. As we have seen, Liberal Premier Hepburn of Ontario in the early part of the Second World War openly cooperated with the Conservatives in an attempt to oust the Liberal government of Prime Minister Mackenzie King. Just a few days before the federal general election of April, 1963, Premier Lesage delivered publically what was widely interpreted as an ultimatum to both federal parties on future fiscal relations with the provinces; because the Liberals were expected to win the election this statement was a considerable embarrassment to Mr. Pearson and his colleagues. In most circumstances, however, provincial parties will be more solicitous of the interests of their federal counterparts.

Within the context of federal-provincial relations as such the partisan complexion of the governments involved is not crucial and it would indeed be unusual to see a Conference of Prime Ministers and Premiers divide on party lines. Both the permanent and occasional cleavages in this context are on axes other than partisan ones; between "have" and "have-not" provinces; between governments which put an urgent priority on bilingual and bicultural matters and those which do not; between Quebec and the other jurisdictions; between the heartland of Ontario and Quebec and the peripheral provinces. In recent years Ottawa's policies toward the provinces — most crucially in respect to fiscal matters and to regional economic development — have come to be based on rationalized criteria which do not take into account the partisan complexion of provincial governments. For example, in 1969 the Conservatives were displaced by the Liberals in Nova Scotia and in 1970 the Liberals by the Conservatives in New Brunswick but it is improbable that in its dealings with Ottawa the position of either province has been changed significantly. In broad terms, neither provincial electorates nor provincial parties can expect to enhance their influence to any marked degree by having governments of the same partisan complexion in power in the provincial capital as in Ottawa. From the federal point of view, whatever parties are in power provincially will press provincial interests. So far as policy matters are concerned, provincial administrations are not notably more or less compliant because of their partisan complexion and federal politicians have no urgent interest in ensuring that their colleagues are in power provincially. This latter generalization must, however, be qualified in the case of Quebec where there is an emergent polarization within the provincial party system on federalist-separatist lines. The polarization of Quebec politics on the continuance of Confederation means amost inevitably that federal leaders will be oriented differently towards this political arena than toward others where the choices facing provincial electorates are less crucial. Cultural duality is the subject of Chapter 6.

NOTES

[1] Oxford University Press, Editions of 1946, 1951, 1953, 1963.

[2] *Federalism and Constitutional Change*, Oxford University Press, 1956, Chapter 1, "The Character of Federalism" and "A Note on the Nature of Federalism," LXVII *Political Science Quarterly*, No. 1, March, 1952, pp. 81-95.

[3] The most influential of the integration theorists is Karl Deutsch. See his *Nationalism and Social Communications*, John Wiley and Sons, New York, 1953; with William J. Foltz (editors) *Nation Building*, New York, Atherton Press, 1966, and *The Nerves of Government*, The Free Press, New York, 1963.

[4] *New Federations: Experiments in the Commonwealth*, Oxford University Press, 1966.

[5] *Comparative Federalism: The Territorial Dimension of Politics*, Holt, Rinehart and Winston, New York, 1969, pp. 329-341.

[6] *Trends of Federalism in Theory and Practice*, Praeger, New York, 1968, particularly Chapter 5, "Federalism and Party System." As well as the book-length treatments of federalism by Watts, Duchacek and Friedrich the book of readings *American Federalism in Perspective*, Edited by Aaron Wildavsky, Little, Brown, Boston, 1967, has a long excerpt from Riker's book and of the other twelve articles four are devoted to federalism and the party systems of the United States, Canada and Australia.

[7] Little, Brown, Boston. Particularly Part I, "A Theory of Federalism," and pp. 135-136.

[8] Riker, like C. J. Friedrich, seems to me to make an unduly clear-cut distinction between federalism and imperialism. See the latter's treatment in *Man and His Government*, McGraw-Hill, New York, 1963, Chapter 31, "Empire: Coercive World Order," and Chapter 32, "Federalism: Consensual World Order." However, in the Canadian case a major impetus to the original federal bargain was the prospect of a vast hinterland to be peopled, developed and exploited by the Canadian heartland of Ontario and Quebec. On the Canadian prairies during the 1930s we were sometimes told that the region was in the most humiliating of all possible circumstances as "a colony of a colony."

[9] p. 136.

[10]In a study of political perceptions, attitudes and behaviour in Vancouver — Burrard Jean Laponce asserted that the electors operate within three political systems — federal, provincial and American. He found ". . . the greater one's involvement with Canadian politics, the greater is the intellectual involvement with American affairs." *People vs. Politics*, University of Toronto Press, 1969, p. 165.

[11]*New Federations: Experiments in the Commonwealth*, Oxford University Press, 1966, p. 338.

[12]"Canadian Liberal Democracy in 1955," *Press and Party in Canada*, G. V. Ferguson and Frank Underhill, Ryerson Press, Toronto, 1955, pp. 39-40.

[13]*The Government of Canada*, University of Toronto Press, 1946, p. 575.

[14]"Federal-Provincial Voting Patterns in Canada," in John C. Courtney, Editor, *Voting in Canada*, Prentice-Hall of Canada, Toronto, 1967, pp. 82-89.

[15]p. 84.

[16]"The Liberal Party in Contemporary Ontario Politics," III *Canadian Journal of Political Science*, No. 2, June 1970, p. 198. By permission of the authors and the Canadian Political Science Association. Emphasis in text.

[17]p. 199.

[18]p. 199.

[19]*Politics in Sudbury*, Laurentian University Press, 1966, p. 85.

[20]"Voting in a Provincial General Election and a Federal By-Election: A Constituency Study of Saskatoon City," XXXII *Canadian Journal of Economics and Political Science*, No. 3, August 1966, pp. 339-353.

[21]p. 344. By permission of the authors and the Canadian Political Science Association.

[22]p. 86. By permission of Jean E. Havel.

[23]"Variations in Party Support in Federal and Provincial Elections: Some Hypotheses" IV *Canadian Journal of Political Science*, No. 2, June 1971, pp. 280-286.

[24]p. 281. By permission of the authors and the Canadian Political Science Association.

[25]p. 286. However, the authors suggest that the importance of federal "affect" in Ontario politics is atypical and that provincial affect is relatively more important in the Atlantic provinces. By permission of the authors and the Canadian Political Science Association.

[26]*People vs. Politics*. On federal-provincial switching see pp. 168-176.

[27]p. 17.

[28]It seems reasonable to attribute the replacement of Social Credit by the Conservatives in the provincial election of 1971 almost entirely to factors other than those of federal politics.

[29]"Federal-Provincial Integration in Ontario Party Organization — The Influence of Recruitment Patterns," Paper presented to the 1970 meeting of the Canadian Political Science Association (mimeo). Table 2.

[30]Donald V. Smiley, "The National Party Leadership Convention in Canada: A Preliminary Analysis," I *Canadian Journal of Political Science*, No. 4, December 1968, pp. 373-397.

[31]"Federal Strains within a Canadian Party," in Hugh G. Thorburn, Editor, *Party Politics in Canada*, Second Edition, Prentice-Hall of Canada, Toronto, 1967, pp. 139-140. By permission of the author and *The Dalhousie Review*.

[32]From *Robert Laird Borden: His Memoirs*, Vol. 1, Carleton Library, No. 46, reprinted by permission of The Canadian Publishers, McClelland and Stewart Limited, Toronto.

[33]See John Porter, *The Vertical Mosaic*, University of Toronto Press, 1965, pp. 398-403 and pp. 405-415.

[34]"Federalism and Party Finance: A Preliminary Sounding," in *Studies in Canadian Party Finance*, Committee on Election Expenses, Queen's Printer, Ottawa, 1966, pp. 4-5. Reproduced by permission of Information Canada. This collection of studies is invaluable for the student of Canadian party organization as well as party finance, as is K. Z. Paltiel, *Political Party Financing in Canada*, McGraw-Hill Series on Canadian Politics, Toronto, 1970.

35"Federalism and Party Finance," p. 13. Reproduced by permission of Information Canada.

36See *Paltiel, Political Party Financing*, pp. 121-132.

37Queen's Printer, Ottawa.

38In an article published in 1961 Pierre Elliott Trudeau criticized the democratic socialists in Canada for what he regarded as over-rigid adherence to common policies and a common ideology throughout the country. He advised different policies to meet the varied needs and degrees of political maturity of the individual provinces. "Practice and Theory of Federalism," in *Social Purpose for Canada*, Michael Oliver, Editor, University of Toronto Press, pp. 371-393. One can assume that the Prime Minister finds the desired degree of ideological heterogeneity in the party of which he is now national leader.

39*The Rise of a Third Party: A Study in Crisis Politics*, Prentice Hall, Englewood Cliffs, N.J., 1971.

40p. 37.

41In Newfoundland according to S. J. R. Noel "Federal politics have been in practice an extension of provincial politics—a further test of the premier's popularity." *Politics in Newfoundland*, University of Toronto Press, 1971, p. 282. This might of course be less true if Premier Smallwood should pass from the political scene. The present leader of the Newfoundland Conservatives, Frank Moores, resigned his seat in the House of Commons to take that position and was formerly President of the Progressive Conservative Party of Canada. For an anecdotal account of Maritime politics pointing up among other things the complex relations of federal and provincial politicians see Dalton Camp, *Gentlemen, Players and Politicians*, McClelland and Stewart, Toronto, 1970. An unpublished article by Agar Adamson on the 1970 leadership contest in the Nova Scotia Progressive Conservative party has shown me the close interrelation of federal and provincial Conservative politicians in that party.

42"The Finances of the Cooperative Commonwealth Federation and the New Democratic Party," Khayyam Z. Paltiel, Howat P. Noble and Reginald A. Whitaker, in *Studies in Canadian Party Finance*, pp. 317-404.

43The revival of ideological conflict in the NDP occasioned by the rise of the Waffle group could see such conflicts partly on these lines and some at least of the Waffle perceive the government of Manitoba as the bastion of the party's right wing.

44See generally J. R. Mallory, *Social Credit and the Federal Power in Canada*, University of Toronto Press, 1955.

45See particularly *A Party Politician: The Memoirs of Chubby Power*, Edited by Norman Ward, Macmillan of Canada, 1966, pp. 120-132 and pp. 344-356.

46See Neil McKenty, *Mitch Hepburn*, McClelland and Stewart, Toronto, 1967, Chapters 13, 15 and 16.

47"Recent Changes in Canadian Parties" in *Thorburn, Party Politics in Canada*, pp. 33-54.

48p. 37. By permission of the author.

49"The Electoral Behaviour of Nova Scotia in 1965," in Courtney, *Voting in Canada*, p. 97. By permission of J. M. Beck and *The Dalhousie Review*. Since this Chapter was written Premier Davis of Ontario has publicly pledged the support of himself and his political organization to the federal Conservatives in the general election expected in 1972. Unlike his predecessor, Davis has participated actively in the national party and was Chairman of the party's policy committee at the 1967 national convention. The decision to support the federal Conservatives is congruent, however, not only with partisan predispositions but the very inharmonious relations between Queen's Park and Ottawa in respect to economic matters.

5

The Political Economy of Canadian Federalism

At the Federal-Provincial Constitutional Conference of February, 1969, Premier John Robarts of Ontario told this story: "Not too long ago at two o'clock in the morning my phone rang and a voice said, 'John, I want to discuss federal-provincial fiscal arrangements.' I said, 'It is two o'clock in the morning. Would you come to my office at nine-thirty?' The voice said, 'At nine-thirty tomorrow morning, I won't give a damn.' "[1]

Premier Robarts' friend may well have been able to retain both his emotional equilibrium and his faith in his country by refusing to think about fiscal relations in the daylight hours. In 1947 the late Robert MacGregor Dawson gave his assessment, "This world of Dominion-Provincial finance has, indeed, an air of grotesque unreality, untrammeled by logic and the ordinary restrictions and meanings of words."[2] Since Dawson wrote, the conflicts have continued and claims and counter-claims are made in terms of a whole vocabulary intelligible only to initiates: "tax abatements" and "tax room"; "fiscal capacity" and "fiscal need"; "contracting-out" and "fiscal equivalents"; "revenue equalization" and so on. This area is full of pitfalls for the unwary academic observer who must rely to a very large extent on the public statements of governmental leaders. Nowhere is the threefold classification of falsehoods as "lies, damned lies and statistics" more meaningful, and nowhere do Canadian politicians so embellish their pursuit of the crassest of purposes with appeals to the elegancies of economic analysis or what purport to be immutable principles.

Since Confederation Canadian political leaders have from time to time

attempted to forestall conflicts between the federal and provincial governments about financial matters by embodying fiscal settlements in the
constitution. Section 118 of the British North America Act of 1867
stipulated that the scale of subsidies to the provinces laid down in the Act
"shall be in full Settlement of all future Demands on Canada." Despite
what has been called the "finality clause," less than two years after the
Dominion was established the threats of Nova Scotia separatism led the
federal government to make an upward revision of the original schedule of
subsidies.[3] The subsidy question then evolved as a focus of continuous
federal-provincial conflict, and Section 118 became and remained until the
Second World War what J. A. Maxwell called "a flexible portion of the
British North America Act."[4] In 1907 Ottawa and all the provinces except
British Columbia agreed on a new scale of subsidies which was enacted as
an amendment to the B.N.A. Act as a "final and unalterable settlement."
This attempt at finality was no more successful than the one of four decades
before. Since then, the old impulses have not died. During the process of
constitutional review begun in 1968 the Conservative government of Nova
Scotia — an administration otherwise characterized by responsibility and
good sense in federal-provincial relations — pressed for the entrenchment
of an equalization formula in a revised constitution to remove conflicts
among Ottawa and the provinces about this matter. In a similar spirit,
Prime Minister Trudeau so stated his hopes for constitutional reform in a
document introduced into the Conference of February, 1969:

> What is required is a new orientation to intergovernmental
> cooperation — a clearer definition of the roles of the two orders of
> government may well help to achieve this — a new orientation
> which would focus the attention of governments on the whole
> complex of public services and on the whole of Canada's tax system,
> *as they affect the citizen.* This new orientation, this focus, is what
> federal-provincial relations must come to mean to the citizen,
> instead of the unhappy disputes which have persisted between
> governments during the postwar period as to the share of certain
> taxes which each government ought to get."[5]

Apart from embodying fiscal provisions in the constitution, there have been
proposals for eliminating or resolving conflicts between Ottawa and the
provinces about fiscal matters by establishing executive agencies to
adjudicate competing claims. The Royal Commission on Dominion-
Provincial Relations in its Report, published in 1940, recommended a
Finance Commission to advise the federal government on requests for
National Adjustment Grants whose objective, in the Commission's formulation, would be to place every province always in the position so that it
could provide services at national average levels without levying taxes at
rates above the national average.[6] In his 1964 attempt to rewrite the
Canadian constitution Peter J. T. O'Hearn visualized a Federal Council of

federal and provincial delegates with the power to make "a binding Allocation between the Government of Canada . . . and the Governments of the Provinces . . . for any period not exceeding Ten Years, of the Powers to tax and borrow and may determine the Limits of Rates or Amounts that shall apply to this Allocation. . ."[7] Similarly, Marcel Faribault and Robert M. Fowler in their outline of a "possible Canadian constitution" published in 1965 recommended a Fiscal Commission with members chosen partly by Ottawa and partly by the provinces and with a corporate responsibility for regulating a wide range of fiscal matters.[8] As we saw in Chapter 3, the Ontario government in 1971 suggested that the Conference of Prime Ministers and Premiers constitute itself as a Joint Economic Council "to review and determine, on a continuing basis, national economic goals of a strategic order."

It is wildly improbable that federal-provincial conflict in respect to economic matters will be or can be ended through either a new constitutional settlement or through those governments giving up their freedom of independent action to some kind of joint executive authority. Such conflict is inherent in the Canadian federal system. Those who place a high priority on rationality and coherence in public policy can easily demonstrate that this lack of federal-provincial articulation exacts a high price, and in 1969 one of Canada's most influential economists, Jacques Parizeau, after nearly a decade as adviser to successive Quebec governments, decided the price was too high and joined the Parti Québécois.[9] Yet the hope persists that Ottawa and the provinces will come to agreement on the most fundamental of economic matters. The federal Royal Commission on Taxation, for example, believed that the demonstrable benefits of effective policies for economic stabilization were so overwhelming that, with experience, the federal and provincial governments could progress from more effective consultation about economic matters to the "development of binding commitments and agreements" about stabilization.[10] After the establishment of the Tax Structure Committee in 1964 some of the provinces hoped that this group would be able to evolve federal-provincial agreement on tax-sharing and expenditure-priorities. The reality makes such solutions unlikely.[11] At the most elemental level, federal-provincial fiscal relations are shaped by the desire of provincial politicians to spend public revenues without levying taxes for these purposes and of course by the resistance of Ottawa to such pressures. There are inherent conflicts of interest between "have" and "have not" provinces and between the government with national responsibilities and those with provincial responsibilities. D. G. Hartle has come to this realistic assessment: ". . . *It is most unlikely that we will ever attain, under a federal system of government, the situation where all governments get together, agree on priorities for expenditures, and then parcel out the revenues among themselves in accordance with these agreed priorities.* There are major and unavoidable conflicts of interest between levels of government that can only be resolved through hard bargaining."[12]

In respect to economic matters then, Ottawa and the provinces are both interdependent and unwilling to give up their individual freedom of action either to the other level or to any kind of joint decision-making agency. J. A. Corry asserted in 1958, "Dominion-Provincial Conferences, notably those held to negotiate about tax agreements every five years, have become clearing houses for many disputed issues between the Dominion and the provinces. One can almost say that the various stresses and strains of the system are negotiated down to tolerable compromises in the course of hammering out the next tax agreements."[13] Since Corry wrote, the number of economic issues subject to joint federal-provincial action has markedly increased in scope and importance.

THE BASIS OF THE PRESENT FISCAL REGIME

The current patterns of fiscal and economic relations between the federal and provincial governments can be understood only against the background of a series of interrelated developments during and immediately at the end of the Second World War.

The Rowell-Sirois Report, published in 1940, recommended a very new distribution of tax sources, revenues and responsibilities between the federal and provincial governments.[14] The federal authorities were to be given exclusive responsibility for unemployment insurance and for a proposed system of contributory old age pensions and exclusive access to the taxation of personal and corporate incomes and of estates. The existing system of statutory subsidies to the provinces was to be eliminated and the federal authorities would assume the responsibility for provincial indebtedness. In place of the tangled web of subsidies as these had developed without coherent purpose there was to be a system of unconditional National Adjustment Grants paid so as "to enable each province (including its municipalities) without resort to heavier taxation than the Canadian average to provide adequate social, educational and developmental services."[15] Significantly, the thrust of the Commission's recommendations was toward the financial and administrative independence of the two levels and against the complex of joint arrangements which came to be described, with considerable inaccuracy, as "cooperative" federalism. The preoccupations of the Second World War and the opposition to the Report by the governments of Ontario, Alberta and British Columbia prevented serious negotiation about the new scheme for Canadian federalism recommended by the Commission.

In retrospect, the most significant and lasting contribution of the Rowell-Sirois Commission was its approach to interprovincial fiscal equalization based on a rational evaluation of fiscal need. The Commission investigated, and it must have taken great forbearance to do so, the claims of the individual provinces for upward revisions of their respective subsidies, claims in almost all cases based on the most tendentious accounts of the purportedly contractual nature of commitments incurred by Ottawa at various times and about the allegedly adverse effects of national economic policies on the maritime and western provinces. The Commission in rejecting these claims proposed that the subsidy system be replaced by grants based on provincial fiscal need. Such need was a great deal less subject to precise measurement than the Commission believed, and in particular its recommendations ignored the circumstance that the costs and needs of provincial and municipal services could not be evaluated without a great deal of subjectivity. On the other hand, the Commission's work proved successful in establishing in the postwar period an ever-increasing rationality in determining the scale of federal unconditional assistance to the provinces, and in putting behind Canada the older patterns of special pleading and short-run expediency which had characterized the previous history of the subsidy question.

In 1941 the federal government preempted the income tax and succession duty fields with compensating payments to the provinces. This action projected Canada into a system of tax and revenue sharing whose major elements still exist. The complexities of the various tax agreements from the Second World War onward have been described and analyzed elsewhere. This fiscal coordination has moved in three directions, in each case resulting in the interpenetration of federal and provincial interests and policies:[16]

1. Federal tax abatements have transferred revenue sources from Ottawa to the provinces. The procedure here is a reduction in the federal rates of direct taxation allowing the provinces to increase their levies at no political risk since the taxpayer's provincial obligation is offset by a reduction in his federal burden. The abatement system, which is now being ended, has led to the continual struggle between Ottawa and the provinces about "tax room," that is, pressures for and against decreases in federal rates of direct taxation.

2. Federal equalization grants transfer funds to the provinces to be expended as the latter wish. As we shall see, the major part of equalization grants has been related to the actual or imputed yields to the provinces from certain tax sources.

3. Federal-provincial tax collection agreements have been concluded for the convenience of taxpayers and the coordination of federal and provincial tax policies. Because Ottawa will collect income taxes for the provinces only on the condition that the latter make their levies on the federal tax base, this tax base becomes a matter of concern to both levels.

The so-called White Paper on Employment and Income, made public in April, 1945,[17] committed the government of Canada to maintaining "a high and stable level of income and employment." Fiscal policy, i.e., the adjustment of federal rates of taxation and expenditure in the interests of stabilization, was to be the chief instrument by which Ottawa would discharge this new responsibility:

> The Government of Canada will be prepared, in periods where unemployment threatens, to incur the deficits and increases in the national debt resulting from its income and employment policy, whether that policy in the circumstances is best applied through increased expenditure or reduced taxation. In periods of buoyant employment and income, budget plans will call for surpluses. The Government's policy will be to keep the national debt within manageable proportions and maintain a proper balance in its budget over a period longer than a single year.[18]

This was a decisive break from the older practices in which the federal government attempted to balance its budget each fiscal year and in which during the Depression declining public revenues were countered by increased rates of direct and indirect taxation. The White Paper established in Canada the situation where the federal government was held responsible for full employment and price stability, and most citizens still continue to look to Ottawa when inflation and/or unemployment occurs, although under the circumstances of the early 1970s it is plausible to argue that the federal authorities have no longer the capacity by themselves to discharge this responsibility in any effective way.

The White Paper was published just before the European war was terminated and had as a major focus of its concern the immediate problems which would face the Canadian economy when hostilities ended. The Federal-Provincial Conference on Reconstruction was convened in early August 1945 just at the time of Japan's surrender, and in its so-called "Green Book" proposals the federal government put forward a bold and comprehensive plan of reform for peace-time Canada.[19] The wartime tax rental agreements would be renewed with more generous payments to the provinces in exchange for their giving Ottawa exclusive access to taxation on incomes and estates. Through federal-provincial cooperation a national health insurance plan would be established, along with a system of health grants to the provinces for specific purposes. Ottawa would assume wider responsibilities for social security including old age pensions to all residents over 70, half the costs of provincial social assistance plans to persons between 65 and 69 and an extension of the coverage of the existing unemployment insurance scheme. There would also be cooperation with the provinces in the conservation and development of natural resources. During the War — and particularly in the Session of 1944-45 — Parliament had enacted several other measures asserting federal leadership. Among these were family allowances, price supports for agricultural products, assistance for technical education and for housing, the establishment of an Industrial Development Bank along with Departments of National Health and Welfare, Veterans' Affairs, and Reconstruction. Along with the Green Book proposals and the White Paper, these wartime measures may reasonably be regarded as a "New National Policy" giving Canada under Dominion leadership a set of objectives comparable in scope to those of the original national policy of the nineteenth century which had in the main been achieved by the beginning of the First World War.[20]

Federal-provincial agreement on the Green Book proposals proved impossible, and at its second set of Plenary Sessions the Conference on Reconstruction adjorned *sine die* on May 3, 1946. It was essential to the federal plan for post-war Canada that Ottawa's dominance in fiscal matters be secured. To this Ontario and Quebec would not assent. Despite this failure, almost from the day the Conference adjourned the federal authorities proceeded to implement the grand design of 1944-45 in a piecemeal fashion and by a decade later most of these objectives had been in large part achieved.

THE ATTENUATION OF FEDERAL DOMINANCE[21]

The Canadian federal system as it emerged from the Second World War and persisted for more than a decade afterward was dominated by the central government. As we have seen, Ottawa at the end of the War had committed the country to a set of objectives which was at the same time precise and comprehensive. In its pursuit of these objectives the political leadership was assisted by a sophisticated and aggressive federal civil service. Although federal dominance in taxation and public expenditures declined from wartime levels, in 1955 federal taxes were 16.9 per cent of Gross National Product compared with 6.9 per cent for provincial and local authorities combined. This structure of federal dominance was buttressed by the predisposition of an overwhelming majority of Canadians, outside Quebec at any rate, to look to Ottawa rather than to their respective provincial capitals for leadership in meeting urgent public needs. The provinces had never fully recovered from the difficulties of Depression and War, and the balance of both political and bureaucratic competence ran strongly in favour of the central government.

The story of Canadian federalism since the late 1950s is the story of the steady attrition of the power of the central government. It is tempting to date this development from the coming to power of the Diefenbaker administration as a result of the general election of June 10, 1957, although its predecessor had already destroyed an important element of the previous system by its decision to divorce tax rental from equalization payments to the provinces in the agreements which came into effect on April 1 of that year. According to John Meisel's analysis of the 1957 election,[22] the longevity in power of the Liberals had made both the political and bureaucratic leadership in Ottawa increasingly insensitive to regional needs and grievances, particularly those which had developed in the Prairie and Maritime Provinces. The Progressive Conservatives under their new leader were remarkably successful in exploiting these disparate regional grievances without in the process formulating any new and coherent set of national objectives.[23]

If we take the years 1955 to 1965 we can see the very great changes in the fiscal balance between Ottawa and the provinces in this decade:

— in 1955 federal expenditures on goods and services were 8.5 per cent of G.N.P. while provincial and local expenditures combined were 6.0 per cent. In 1965 the corresponding proportions were 5.1 per cent and 7.9 per cent.[24]

— classes of expenditure mainly within provincial and local control increased in importance. Health expenditures were 1.3 per cent of G.N.P. in 1955, 3.1 per cent in 1965; social welfare 3.7 per cent in 1955 and 4.6 per cent in 1965; and education 3.0 per cent in 1955 and 5.3 per cent in 1965. The major direct responsibility of Ottawa, defence and mutual aid, declined during the decade from 6.5 per cent to 3.0 per cent of G.N.P.[25]

— in terms of tax revenues, federal taxes were 74.3 per cent of total levies paid by Canadians in 1955, provincial and municipal taxes combined 25.7 per cent. The corresponding proportions in 1965 were 60.9 per cent and 39.1 per cent. Provincial tax levies in this period increased 5.3 times.[26]

— federal transfer payments to the provinces increased from $440.0 millions in 1955 to $1,569.5 millions in 1965.[27]

The most urgent of public priorities then came to be within provincial rather than federal jurisdiction. This was reflected not only in the new fiscal balance but in the increasing sophistication and aggressiveness of the provincial administrations and the increasing disposition of Canadians to look to their provinces and local governments rather than to Ottawa for meeting emergent social and economic needs.

The structure of federal dominance coming out of the Second World War could be legitimated only so long as the national government could demonstrate its capacity to manage the economy effectively. By the latter 1950s this ability was no longer apparent. In 1957 unemployment as a proportion of the civilian labour force increased from 3.4 per cent in the previous year to 4.9 per cent and to 7.1 per cent in 1958.[28] During these years Canada was experiencing a rate of economic growth lower than that of other industrialized nations, and in 1958 its per capita product at constant prices actually declined.[29] Contrary to the expectations of those who had accepted the Keynesian analysis, high rates of unemployment and inflationary pressures were experienced at the same time. Out of this inadequate record of economic performance came not only an attenuation of the legitimacy of Ottawa's dominance but, in varying degrees, more aggressive and deliberate provincial action to encourage economic develop-ment.[30] All of the provinces engaged in efforts to seek markets and developmental capital and most committed themselves to one version or another of economic planning.

The attenuation of federal dominance in fiscal and economic matters has been manifested in several developments:

— in the tax agreements which came into effect in 1957 equalization payments were made to the provinces whether or not they rented the direct tax fields to the central government.[31] It was a central presupposition of the New National Policy that Ottawa could ensure full employment and price stability only if it had exclusive access to taxation on incomes. Thus the federal government was very much constrained in moving toward the interprovincial equalization of revenues by the circumstance that its schedule of unconditional payments had to be designed to induce the provinces to surrender the direct tax fields. However, this unified tax-sharing system was shattered in 1954 when Quebec began to levy its own tax on individual incomes. The divorcing of tax rental from equalization in 1957 was a crucial element in the destruction of the centralized fiscal regime. The 1957-62 agreements also began the abatement system. Under this tax rental scheme the provinces were to receive the following shares of federal taxation or, at their request, an abatement of federal taxes of the same amount: 10 per cent of federal personal income tax, 9 per cent of corporation profits and 50 per cent of succession duties.

— in the tax agreements which came into effect in 1962 the tax rental system was ended.[32] The abatement of corporation income tax remained at 9 per cent, that of personal income tax was increased to 16 per cent to increase one percentage point annually to 20 per cent in 1966-67. Thus the provinces were to levy their own taxes of personal and corporate incomes, although the federal government offered at no charge to the provinces to collect these taxes on the condition that the levies were made on the federal tax base.

— in 1965 the Parliament of Canada enacted the Established Pro-grammes (Interim Arrangements) Act which permitted the provinces to contract out of certain established conditional grant programmes and receive fiscal equivalents in compensation. This procedure will be discussed later in the Chapter.

— in 1965 the Canada Pension Plan was established, giving the provinces access to capital funds built up by contributors to this plan and its Quebec counterpart.[33] The Liberal government when it came to power as the result of the federal general election of April, 1963 was committed to the inauguration of a compulsory plan of contributory retirement pensions with benefits paid from general revenues. Led by Quebec there was vigorous provincial resistance to the attempt of the federal authorities to establish such a scheme. What finally resulted was the Quebec Pension Plan and, outside that province, the Canada Pension Plan. Under the latter, the funds accumulated are made available to the provinces in proportion to the amounts paid into the funds by the contributors from each participating province. These funds are used to purchase the securities of the government of Canada and of the provinces. Between 1966 and 1969 securities to the amount of $2,023.0 millions had been so purchased.[34]

The Lesage government which came to power as a result of the Quebec general election of June, 1960, played a decisive role in attenuating the centralized fiscal and economic regime which had been built up during the War and perpetuated afterward.[35] With singleness of purpose and sophistication the Quebec government on issue after issue challenged both the presuppositions and the structures of the New National Policy. However, Quebec's pressures for autonomy were for the most part in harmony with the emergent aspirations of the other provincial governments.

As we shall see later in this chapter, the federal authorities from late 1966 onward have re-asserted the powers of Ottawa in fiscal and economic matters. However, these new directions have been a refusal to accede to the further attenuation of federal power rather than to commit Canada to a new set of national objectives.

ECONOMIC STABILIZATION

The White Paper on Employment and Income committed the federal government to ensuring full employment and price stability in the national economy. The formulation of the White Paper was an application of the analysis of J. M. Keynes in his *General Theory of Employment, Interest and Money*, published in 1936. In the broadest of terms, it can be said that the Keynesian theory demonstrated that the free movement of prices and interest rates could not be depended upon to bring about conditions of price stability with full employment. It was thus the responsibility of national governments to devise policies ensuring appropriate levels of aggregate demand.

As T. N. Brewis has pointed out, "One of the chief attractions of the Keynesian theory was its association with an analytical formula which lent itself to ready administration."[36] Canadian policy-makers, both elected and appointed, found very compelling at the end of the Second World War an analysis which purported to show how the federal government might effectively stabilize the national economy without either a significant increase in the extent of public ownership or the more precise planning of economic objectives. However, the Keynesian analysis did not take into account the constraints imposed on national governments from developments outside their own borders or, in the case of federations, from states or provinces with important and autonomous economic powers. These latter constraints seem not to have been very important in the perspectives of Ottawa officialdom as the War ended. In 1945 the national authorities made 83 per cent of all public expenditures in Canada, and while it was no doubt expected that this proportion would decline with the return to peacetime conditions, it was probably anticipated that federal spending would remain dominant. On the taxing side, it was an essential element of Ottawa's perspectives that it would retain the exclusive access to levies on individual and corporate income deemed to be necessary for effective fiscal management. The White Paper thus contained a very limited recognition of the need for intergovernmental collaboration in sustaining full employment and price stability. It was suggested that Ottawa cooperate with the provinces and municipalities in planning a "shelf" of public works to be undertaken when, in the federal view, general economic conditions made this appropriate, and there should also be cooperation with the provinces in Dominion expenditure programmes for the conservation and development of natural resources.[37]

As we have seen, national fiscal and economic policies showed themselves incapable of sustaining full employment, price stability and growth from the late 1950s onward. Out of this inadequate record of performance came two contradictory lines of criticism of national economic policies. According to the first, the federal government had failed to act effectively through the fiscal and monetary instruments available to it to ensure appropriate levels of aggregate demand. In a scathing analysis of post-war federal policy published in 1965[38] H. Scott Gordon argued that Keynesianism "has made little headway in advancing the analytical work in the bureaucracy that underlies the formulation of employment and other economic policies, and despite some brief periods of favour, it does not appear to have won its way to any appreciable extent as a sound principle of fiscal policy."[39] According to Gordon, federal fiscal policy for most of the time since the White Paper had been based on the "Gladstonian" principle that "the government should keep its expenditures low and always balance its budget or have a small surplus" and on what he called the "Ricardian" view which attributed unemployment to a "structural mis-matching of the demand for labour and the supply of labour" rather than, in Keynesian terms, a deficiency of aggregate demand. The contrary view had been put forward by Jacques Parizeau in 1964. Parizeau saw the problem in terms of the rigidities introduced into the thinking of the federal authorities by the Keynesian theory itself: "The framework of federal action upon the economy had to be quite general, or to put it differently, national in scope. The emphasis was on the variations in the total aggregate demand and on large aggregates. Regional discrepancies in growth and structural bottlenecks were hardly considered and, in fact, at times the federal authorities explicitly refused to consider them."[40] A similar note was struck by Maurice Lamontagne in his analysis of postwar economic policy delivered at the Study Conference on National Goals convened by the federal Liberal party in 1960:

> Stagnation, inflation and unemployment have a very important regional and industrial incidence, especially in Canada. Certain regions or industries grow rapidly while others are depressed. Certain industries may enjoy rising prices while others, at the same time, suffer from relatively low prices. Some industries or regions may experience heavy unemployment while others suffer from a scarcity of labour. Our national aggregates, such as the gross national

product, the cost of living index and the national percentage of unemployment, are frequently the result of conflicting tendencies prevailing in different industries and different regions. It is always unrealistic and dangerous to interpret these national aggregates without taking their regional and industrial components into account. It is even more dangerous to attempt to solve such economic problems as unemployment as if they had the same causes and intensity throughout the country and as if they could be effectively met by the same policies in all industries and all regions.[41]

Whatever the respective merits of the aggregate-demand and structural analyses, it has become apparent since the late 1950s that the incidence of both price stability and employment — as well as of federal fiscal and monetary policies — varies greatly among the provinces and regions of Canada. This is particularly striking in terms of unemployment, since whatever the national average rates there are consistently higher rates of unemployment in the Atlantic region, Quebec and British Columbia than in the prairie provinces and Ontario. The Report of the Royal Commission on Taxation published in 1966 recommended that as an objective Canada should adopt a short-term unemployment rate of 3.5 per cent, an objective compatible with what the Commission regarded as acceptable annual increases in the consumer price index of 1.5 to 2 per cent.[42] However, it was estimated that the national average rate of unemployment of 3.5 per cent would be accompanied by the following rates across Canada:

Atlantic Provinces	6.0 per cent
Quebec	4.6 per cent
Ontario	2.6 per cent
Prairie Provinces	2.2 per cent
British Columbia	4.0 per cent[43]

The extent to which it is possible for federal fiscal and monetary policies to be tailored to fit the different economic circumstances of the provinces and regions of Canada remains a matter of debate among specialists. The Economic Council of Canada in its Fifth Annual Review published in September, 1968, saw very restricted possibilities in a "regionally oriented stabilization policy" undertaken by the federal government.[44] One of the difficulties is that there appeared to be almost insurmountable obstacles in measuring the impact of expenditures in particular provinces or regions on other provinces or regions. However, even if this difficulty was in part overcome there were other limitations faced by Ottawa in implementing fiscal policies so as to meet regional needs. Federal expenditures make up a declining proportion of total public spending and ". . . federal expenditures cannot be quickly changed to deal with short-run changes in the national economy. A dominating proportion is devoted to contractual or statutory payments that cannot be easily or quickly raised or cut back in response to short-run changes in the economic situation." On grounds of equity, the Council rejected "regionally discriminating tax changes for stabilization purposes." It was also argued that monetary policy was an inadequate instrument of regional differentiation because of "the essential unity of the capital market," the difficulty of erecting safeguards against funds being re-lent elsewhere than as designated and the circumstances that access to borrowing was not the chief problem of slow-growth areas.

The Report of the Standing Senate Committee on National Finance on the subject of Growth, Employment and Price Stability published in November 1971 saw somewhat greater possibilities for regional discrimina-tion in national fiscal and monetary policies than had the Economic Council.[45] The Bank of Canada finds it possible to exercise a degree of moral suasion to induce the chartered banks "to take a particular (*sic*) tender view of applications for credit from the slow-growth regions". The federal government should decentralize its own decision-making and should try to persuade private corporations to do the same, although it was not made clear just what the impact of such decentralization would be on private and public policies. Service industries should receive more recognition in policies for regional development. Federal purchasing policies rely too heavily on services in Central Canada. Despite this qualified optimism of the Senate Committee about regionally discriminating economic policies toward stabilization and growth, the general tenor of the Report saw limited possibilities for national policy in this direction.

Whether or not the provinces should design and implement their own fiscal policies is a matter of dispute. A common viewpoint is that in the absence of such policies or federal-provincial collaboration in economic stabilization, provincial and municipal tax and expenditure policies will be "perverse" in the sense that these jurisdictions will raise taxes and/or cut back on spending in times of adversity and lower tax rates and/or increase expenditures in prosperous periods. In its examination of provincial and municipal spending between 1945 and 1961, the Royal Commission on Taxation found that this had not been so and that these expenditures "did not exercise a destabilizing influence on the economy . . . The changes in provincial and municipal expenditures are as cyclically stable or more stable than the combined private and federal expenditures they replaced."[46] In the Commission's judgment this "built-in" stability was in large part the result of the provinces and municipalities relying very heavily on revenues from indirect taxes which were "relatively insensitive to short-run fluctua-tions in the level of economic activity." The increasing reliance of the provinces on direct taxation gave the Commission cause for concern that this stability was being attenuated and it was recommended that the federal government resist pressures to withdraw further from the personal income tax field.[47]

The Royal Commission on Taxation opposed independent stabilization policies by the provinces.[48] It was argued that because of the effects of such policies outside the borders of the respective provinces "unless each province took into account what all the other provinces and the federal government were doing, and were going to do, the individual provincial efforts could be offsetting, too extreme, or ill timed." The alternative was federal-provincial cooperation in designing and implementing stabilization policies.

In a study prepared for the Ontario Committee on Taxation in 1967 Clarence L. Barber argued for independent provincial fiscal policies toward price stability, full employment and economic growth.[49] Barber pointed out that the larger provinces had both populations and incomes comparable to those of several industrialized nations. He examined the constraints on provincial policies which did not exist in the case of sovereign states — provinces cannot control their own monetary policies, exchange rates or immigration policies. These did not, taken together, make it impractical or undesirable for provinces to have individual fiscal policies. There are of course leakages in provincial expenditures where the effects of changes in spending are partly experienced outside provincial borders and this "does seriously limit the effectiveness of provincial fiscal policy unless all or a number of provinces act in parallel fashion." However, several of the smaller industrial nations have such leakages as great as the larger Canadian provinces, and again this limitation on the provinces is "a difference in degree rather than kind." In Barber's view, the key question was whether provinces had adequate borrowing capacity to sustain counter-cyclical policies. He was relatively optimistic that the provinces had such capacity in meeting cycles of "moderate amplitude." Thus the provinces, and in particular the larger ones, had the ability to carry out independent fiscal policies and Barber was convinced that it was appropriate they should do so. The control of expenditures in many important matters is within provincial rather than federal jurisdiction. There is regional variation in the need for policy measures and the federal government has a limited ability to meet these varying needs through its own policies. The most effective stabilization policies will of course be those carried out in cooperation between all levels of government. However, Barber was willing to regard as appropriate provincial pressure through fiscal policy to change federal policies deemed inadequate to the needs of particular provinces or regions.

There appear to be no published studies on the extent to which the various provinces have designed fiscal policies toward economic stability and growth. The Ontario government has recently directed its fiscal policies in terms of the "full employment budget" defined as "a measure of the government surplus or deficit that would occur if the target of full employment were attained."[50] According to a 1971 Ontario Budget Paper, "The most significant feature of the total public sector's fiscal impact on Ontario is a permanent full-employment surplus, implying a built-in tax drag on the provincial economy. This permanent tax-drag is due wholly to the financial operations of the federal government in Ontario."[51] It was estimated that this permanent federal surplus, more influenced by discretionary changes in tax rates than in expenditure policies, was rapidly increasing — from 2.6 per cent of potential Gross Provincial Product in 1962 to 4.5 per cent of potential GPP in 1969.[52] Thus, according to the Ontario analysis, the net effect of federal policies was permanently "contractionary" in Ontario and Ottawa's attempts to mitigate inter-provincial disparities had frustrated full employment and economic growth in that province. From the Ontario perspective, provincial and municipal fiscal policies were necessary to counter the effect of federal action.

From the mid- and late 1960s onward policies directed toward economic stabilization have become the focus of intense federal-provincial conflict. In terms of taxation, it is generally agreed by specialists in public finance that changes in the taxes levied on personal and corporate income are the most useful stabilization devices available to governments. Yet from 1957 until the new federal policies of late 1966 there was a headlong retreat from these tax fields until under the 1967-72 arrangements the individual income tax abatements in respect to Quebec were 50 per cent and the other provinces, which had not accepted contracting out 28 per cent, while corporate taxes were abated at 10 per cent. In its policies enunciated in the fall of 1966, and still in essentials maintained, the federal government announced its intention not to yield to further provincial pressures for tax room. This new firmness can in part be attributed to Ottawa's apprehension that such yielding would impair critically the federal capacity to undertake effective stabilization policies, and at that time and afterward it was a federal rule-of-thumb that the national government required at least 50 per cent of the personal income tax field throughout Canada. In terms of expenditures, those made for services and facilities provided by Ottawa are a constantly declining proportion of total public spending and it is likely this decline will continue. The provinces, it is true, are heavily dependent on federal transfer payments of both a conditional and unconditional nature. However, apart from certain developmental projects and winter-works programmes almost all of these transfers are of a contractual or semi-contractual nature and thus cannot be adjusted to short-run economic conditions.

The provinces with varying degrees of vigor protested the aggressive anti-inflationary policies undertaken by Ottawa from August, 1969. Under the existing circumstances the provinces are less willing than Ottawa to tolerate unemployment for the sake of controlling inflationary pressures.

In general terms, Ottawa's independent discretion in policies for economic stabilization has been very much restricted and there have not developed effective institutions and procedures for intergovernmental collaboration in these matters. The price in terms of the effective management of the Canadian economy arising from these deficiencies is high.

THE EQUALIZATION OF INTER-REGIONAL DISPARITIES

Canada consists of several regional economies rather weakly integrated with each other and providing widely differing standards of material welfare to their respective residents. Per capita incomes in the poorest province remain about half those in the most prosperous:

Per Capita Personal Income
1970 (est.)

Newfoundland	$1,769
Prince Edward Island	$2,000
Nova Scotia	$2,513
New Brunswick	$2,258
Quebec	$2,794
Ontario	$3,562
Manitoba	$3,066
Saskatchewan	$2,620
Alberta	$3,052
British Columbia	$3,322
All provinces	$3,091[53]

In its Fifth Annual Review published in September, 1968, the Economic Council of Canada concluded:

> Differences in both the levels of economic and social well-being and in economic opportunity among the various regions and provinces of Canada are large, and have persisted with only modest change for over 40 years. This persistence has been remarkable; neither strong national economic growth nor the strains and turbulences of depression and war have had lasting effects on the basic pattern of regional disparities. There is little reason to suppose that the historical mix of market forces and public policy is likely to lead in good time to a significant reduction in those disparities.[54]

It is as yet too early to judge whether the more integrated and more aggressive policies undertaken through the federal Department of Regional Economic Expansion established in 1969 will provide a significantly new "mix" in reducing regional disparities.

Equalization Transfers as a Per Cent of Gross Revenues from Own Sources, by Province, 1971-72

Province	Gross Revenues from Own Sources	Federal Equalization Transfers*	Equalization Transfers as Per Cent of Gross Revenues from Own Sources
	$000,000	$000,000	%
Newfoundland	168	110	65
Prince Edward Island	38	21	55
Nova Scotia	280	95	34
New Brunswick	249	94	38
Quebec	2,764	446	16
Ontario	4,291	—	—
Manitoba	425	50	12
Saskatchewan	423	55	13
Alberta	920	—	—
British Columbia	1,160	—	—
Equalization adjustments for previous years (unallocated)	—	140	—
Total	10,718	1,011	9

NOTES *The amounts shown for equalization transfers to individual provinces exclude adjustment payments in respect of previous fiscal years.

All figures on this table are based upon official estimates made by Statistics Canada. The revenue data for the Province of Quebec have been adjusted in order to be comparable with those for other provinces.[55]

The major procedure for reducing the federal disparities among the provinces is the system of federal equalization grants paid to all provinces except Ontario, British Columbia and Alberta. The accompanying Table shows the extent of such transfers and their impact on reducing the differences in expenditures between the provinces which receive them and those which do not.

Attempts to reduce regional disparities through payments to the provinces are usually rationalized in terms of fiscal equity. Fiscal equity has been defined by John Graham as a principle which, if implemented fully, "would require that an individual of given circumstances would receive the same level of public services and incur the same tax burden wherever he lived in the country".[56] The units among whom burdens and benefits are equalized according to this principle are individuals rather than political units. Thus the federal government could not fully discharge its responsibilities for fiscal equity unless it imposed rigid conditions on its payments to the provinces. Otherwise, these jurisdictions might use their discretion to maintain levels of taxes and/or public services deviating from the national averages. A rigid adherence to the equity principle would be incompatible with the requirement of federalism for the autonomy of provinces in taxation and expenditure policies. Within these limits, however, the federal authorities may influence a higher degree of country-wide fiscal equity than would otherwise exist by making unconditional payments to the provinces according to formulae based on either fiscal need or revenue equalization.

Douglas H. Clark has defined fiscal need grants as "intergovernmental payments to political units which, on the basis of capacity to raise revenues from their own taxpayers, are determined to be in need of financial assistance to enable them, without having to impose unduly high rates of taxation, to provide reasonable standards of public service in relation to other political units having the same expenditure responsibilities and the same revenue-raising authority".[57] Thus fiscal need involves two elements — the capacities of governments to raise revenues and the costs and needs of the public services for which they are responsible.

As an alternative to grants based on fiscal need, there can be payments based on revenue equalization which is itself a measure of fiscal capacity. Clark defines revenue equalization grants as "intergovernmental payments to political units which, on the basis of their capacity to raise revenues from their own taxpayers, are determined to be in need of financial assistance in relation to other units having the same revenue raising authority".[58] Unlike fiscal need, payments based on fiscal capacity embodied in revenue equalization do not take into account the needs and per capita costs of providing services in the recipient political units.

Despite the recommendations of the Rowell-Sirois Commission for a system of subsidies to the provinces based on fiscal need, the tax arrangements from the Second World War onward have been based on revenue equalization. Thus the major elements of unconditional transfers have been based under the varying terms of successive agreements on the actual or imputed yields to the provinces from defined tax sources. On grounds of principle, fiscal need is clearly superior to revenue equalization in that it combines the capacity of provinces to raise revenue with the costs and needs of public services within their respective boundaries. However, even with vastly better tools of measurement than we now have it would be impossible to quantify the relative per capita costs and the needs for public services in the provinces without a great deal of subjectivity. Revenue equalization has the overwhelming advantage of lending itself to precise measurement. This principle was given explicit recognition beginning in the 1957-62 tax agreements which paid the provinces equalization whether or not they rented the direct tax fields to the federal government. As we shall see later in this chapter, it has received a much fuller embodiment in the arrangements in effect from 1967 onward according to which payments are determined with reference to virtually all the kinds of taxes which provinces levy.

Grants paid to the provinces conditional on the latter providing services according to stated standards have also had an equalizing effect in Canada:

Conditional Grants as a Percentage of Provincial Net General Revenue 1970

	%
Newfoundland	32.0
Prince Edward Island	43.6
Nova Scotia	33.3
New Brunswick	25.2
Quebec	18.3
Ontario	16.6
Manitoba	22.9
Saskatchewan	24.9
Alberta	18.5
British Columbia	19.2
Canada	19.3[59]

In terms of the range of public services, it is reasonable to suppose that federal inducements under conditional grant programmes encourage the less prosperous provinces to provide services that would otherwise be available in only the more fortunate ones. Federal conditions also work toward ensuring country-wide minimum standards, and several of the conditional grant programmes put specialized federal skills at the disposal of the provinces, skills which can economically be provided only in the larger ones. Further, three of the major shared-cost programmes — those related to medical care, hospital insurance and post-secondary education — embody what the Ontario authorities have objected to as "implicit equalization" by paying those provinces which spend less per capita on those services a higher *proportion* of total costs incurred than is paid to the higher cost provinces. Despite this equalizing direction of conditional transfers, there are countervailing influences. The poorer provinces, to participate in these joint arrangements, often find themselves spending more of their own revenues on the aided service than they would otherwise do. Thus it may plausibly be argued that provincial and local services such as general elementary and secondary education and intraprovincial highways for which no federal money is available are subject to more interprovincial disparity than if there were no conditional grants for other programmes.[59] Further, the pressures on the poorer provinces to raise their own revenues for conditional grant programmes may explain in part that their rates of taxation are higher than those in the more prosperous jurisdictions.

It remains a matter of contention whether conditional programmes of federal assistance should embody equalization. The more prosperous provinces argue that equalization should be confined to unconditional subsidies, although none has made positive proposals for further equalization by such formulae as would take into account municipal as well as provincial revenues if the implicit equalization of some of the conditional programmes were ended. According to this perspective, the norm should be an arrangement like that of the Canada Assistance Plan in which Ottawa pays the same proportion of costs incurred to all the provinces.

Apart from conditional and unconditional transfers to the provinces, the direct provision of federal services and uniform rates of federal taxation throughout Canada contribute toward reducing interregional disparities in respect to these matters. In examining the Canadian experience from 1929 to 1964 S. E. Chernick found that the effect of *all* direct taxation by government and of government transfer payments — both to other levels of government and to individuals — reduced the interregional dispersion of income.[60]

The equalizing policies described above have not been directed explicitly at reducing the intractable regional disparities in economic development. Yet from the late 1950s onward it became increasingly apparent that generalized fiscal and economic policies undertaken by the federal government could not by themselves alleviate the circumstances of disadvantaged regions, provinces and smaller areas and in a relative sense may even make these circumstances less favourable than otherwise. The difficulties have been lucidly summarized by L. E. Poetschke:

> Fiscal and monetary policies and special sectoral development programs and policies of the federal government in the Canadian context are by necessity national in scope. They are designed for, and are effective in, sectors and regions where the responses are the most sensitive. To do otherwise would seriously impair the nation's competitive position — a factor which a major trading

nation such as Canada can ignore only at its peril. In addition, even in those sectors falling solely within provincial jurisdiction — and these comprise a substantial and important range of economic and social activities — the provinces encounter serious economic and political obstacles to other than province-wide programs.

This then is the dilemma. On the one hand, large areas in Canada are unresponsive or marginally responsive to national and province-wide policies and programs directed to various sectors but on the other hand, to gear such national policies and programs to the special needs of depressed areas would be tantamount to economic suicide. In addition to this economic problem, there are other well known barriers to regionally directed action. Providing special attention to selected areas of the country requires substantial political courage. Also there is the difficulty of working around the departmentalized sector-oriented government structure — a feat which in our experience cannot be accomplished by legislative fiat or by building another bureaucratic structure.[61]

From the coming to power of the Diefenbaker government in 1957 there has been a steadily increasing recognition of the special needs of depressed areas in Canada. Special Atlantic Provinces Adjustment Grants above the regular equalization payments were paid to the Atlantic provinces from 1957-58 onward and in the same year was enacted legislation providing for federal assistance to those provinces for hydro-electric development. In 1961 Parliament enacted the Agricultural Rehabilitation and Development Act, the forerunner of later federal schemes for economic development.[62] The aim of the Act was to raise farm income by finding more profitable uses for marginal and sub-marginal agricultural lands, by encouraging employment opportunities in agricultural areas and by increasing the productivity of agricultural lands through soil conservation and the development of water supplies. The Minister of Agriculture was empowered to enter into agreements with the provinces to accomplish these objectives and in most cases the federal government paid half the costs of approved projects. In 1966 a Fund for Rural Economic Development of $50 millions was established. As the ARDA and FRED programmes progressed the emphasis shifted from land improvement toward education, training and employment in non-primary industry for residents of depressed areas.

In 1963 the recently-elected federal Liberal government sponsored legislation providing for the encouragement of "industrial development in areas of chronic unemployment on a planned basis." This programme as it developed provided for both tax relief incentives[63] and cash grants to industry in such areas as were designated by the federal Area Development Authority. According to T. N. Brewis, such designations were made on the basis of the most inadequate statistics, and incentives were given to industry without any effective attempt to specify what objectives were being pursued.[64]

The Trudeau government has given a higher priority than did any of its predecessors to efforts to narrow regional disparities in economic development. In 1969 the Department of Regional Economic Expansion was established under one of the most powerful ministers in the cabinet, Jean Marchand, with the responsibility of coordinating the various programmes of regional economic development which had been established. These activities are regarded by Ottawa as having a particularly crucial impact on national unity because Quebec is the most populous of the "have not" provinces. Even in its strenuous attempts to control inflation and hold down government expenditures begun in August, 1969, the federal authorities decided to increase spending on regional economic development — from a forecast of $263.2 M. in 1970-71 to a proposed $333.3M. in 1971-72.[65]

The Regional Incentives Development Act[66] which came into effect on July 1, 1969, has become the federal government's major instrument for encouraging economic development in the less favoured areas of Canada. Under the Act tax-free grants are made to businesses developing new facilities or expanding or modernizing existing facilities in areas designated in consultation with the province concerned.The combined incentives to a business may not exceed $30,000 for each job created directly, $12 millions or one-half the capital employed in the project, whichever is the least amount. The following areas were designated and fixed to July 1, 1972: all three Maritime provinces; all Newfoundland except Labrador; all of eastern and northwestern Quebec; and specified areas in the other provinces.[67] Designated areas are at least 10,000 square miles in extent and included in these areas are the "growth centres" in which development is to be stressed.

In direct efforts to stimulate economic development, governments in Canada have embarked on an almost uncharted sea. Specialists differ on the relative importance of the various determinants of economic growth and how to stimulate such growth most effectively, for example, in the relative emphasis which should be given to increasing investment expenditures on machinery and equipment in depressed areas as against enhancing the occupational skills of the labour force. Another disputed matter is the appropriateness or otherwise of public policies to encourage the emigration of population from these areas. Certainly the plethora of federal, provincial and local programmes to encourage economic development does not now make possible any informed specification or ranking of what objectives are being pursued or the economy with which these are being attained. Within each level of government developmental policies suffer a profound lack of coordination particularly, as Poetschke points out, between departments or agencies oriented toward sectors (agriculture, welfare, transportation, etc.) and those toward geographical areas.

The provinces and local governments are deeply committed to their own plans for encouraging economic development, including regional development. The price paid for competition between governments in this activity is high, whether this price is measured in terms of its frustration of the attainment of national economic objectives or the enhanced bargaining power of businesses, often American corporations, attendant on this competition. Of this latter Philip Mathias has written:

> Before it settled in Manitoba, the Churchill Forest Industries group was holding talks with the government of Quebec over the possibility of building a paper mill there. Undoubtedly, the price Manitoba paid for the Churchill Forest Industries complex was affected by the need to attract it away from Quebec. In early 1970, the Michelin tire group of France decided to build three plants costing $100 million in Nova Scotia, but only after a period of fierce competition between Nova Scotia and Quebec. The intrigue behind the scenes even involved pressure by Charles de Gaulle on the Michelin company in favour of a Quebec location. Michelin stuck stubbornly to its decision to locate the plants in Nova Scotia, and is receiving $50 million assistance.[68]

Municipalities often compete to attract industry so they can increase their tax base to meet rising education and other local costs with little or no heed of the other consequences of such action.[69] Ontario and Quebec have aggressive programmes to stimulate economic development and decrease regional disparities within these provinces, and these programmes obviously have important effects outside provincial boundaries and affect federal efforts to reduce regional disparities elsewhere in Canada.[70]

The increasing aggressiveness of all major jurisdictions in Canada to stimulate economic development through various kinds of incentives leads inevitably to intergovernmental conflict. Such conflict becomes increasingly intense in a prolonged period of high unemployment and one in which there is an increasing awareness of depressed areas where unemployment will seemingly not yield to national fiscal and monetary policies, at least within the limits of inflation deemed tolerable by the federal government if not most of the Canadian people. At Canada's present stage, incentive programmes involve a very high degree of executive discretion — a discretion which is inevitably exercised in a somewhat arbitrary way because developmental objectives are not as yet precisely specified and ranked.

It is characteristic of governments that the recognition of a need for public action is often succeeded by a period in which such needs are met by haphazard, indiscriminate and somewhat uneconomic measures. Later comes rationalization, the more exact ranking of objectives and the design of more precise policies for achieving them. So it may be in efforts to reduce the intractable economic disparities among the provinces and regions of Canada.

SHARED-COST PROGRAMMES

Shared-cost programmes involve financial concessions made available by one level of government to compensate another level for part of the costs incurred in providing particular services or facilities. One form of this device is the conditional grant[71] in which the recipient government receives funds for performing functions according to standards which are determined either unilaterally by the donor government or by the two levels in collaboration. The other variant provides the recipient jurisdictions either with grants or tax abatements, or a combination of the two, but does not involve any regulation of the standards or procedures imposed by the government which makes these concessions available.[72]

In Canada, as elsewhere, shared-cost arrangements help governments to meet certain basic circumstances faced by contemporary federations. There are insistent pressures toward the central government ensuring country-wide standards in the range and quality of public services and taking measures to improve the productive capacities of less prosperous regions. The central authorities have a fiscal capacity superior to that of the provinces or states in responding positively to these pressures. Yet the constitution as judicially interpreted provides a relatively stable and inflexible allocation of responsibilities between the two levels. The shared-cost arrangement is of crucial importance in allowing some reconciliation of stability and change.

In 1912 Ottawa inaugurated the first of the conditional grant programmes in providing $10,000,000 of assistance to the provinces in agricultural education over a ten-year period and in 1927 the first of the permanent grant-in-aid programmes was established with federal support of provincial schemes of old-age pensions. It was not, however, until after the Second World War that conditional grants became a central element of the federal system. From 5.3 per cent of gross provincial expenditure in 1954 conditional grants grew to 15.7 per cent in 1962 and appear to have levelled off as about a sixth of the total provincial spending.[73] In 1969-70 conditional grants to the provinces were so distributed:

	Gross provincial Expenditures*	Federal Conditional Grants*	Per Cent
Health	3,045.1	1,210.4	39.7
Welfare	1,063.1	475.9	44.8
Education	3,617.7	100.8	3.9
Transportation & communications	1,353.6	28.8	2.1
Natural resources and primary industry	530.8	87.5	16.5
Other	2,223.6	3.0	1
	11,833.9	1,906.4	16.1[74]

*Millions of dollars

The bulk of conditional grants is devoted to health and welfare, 88.5 per cent of the $1,906.4 millions so distributed by Ottawa in 1969-70. Three major schemes make up together 96.0 per cent of this federal contribution to health and welfare:

— under the Hospital Insurance and Diagnostic Services Act of 1958 the federal government contributes to provincial hospital insurance plans on the basis of 25 per cent of the national per capita cost plus 25 per cent of the provincial per capita cost in each province.

— under federal legislation enacted in 1966 Ottawa pays half of the national average per capita costs in aid of provincial medical insurance schemes.

— under the Canada Assistance Plan of 1966 the federal government pays 50 per cent of the provincial costs incurred in social assistance.

Until 1960 there was, apart from Quebec, little principled provincial resistance to conditional grant programmes although from time to time provinces complained that certain costs related to such programmes were not reimbursable. The Duplessis administration had opposed grants-in-aid on ideological grounds and, at considerable financial cost to the province and its residents, had remained outside several of these arrangements, although it had participated in others. The other provinces were for the most part content to accept such federal assistance and its accompanying conditions. At the 1960 Dominion-Provincial Conference, however, several of the provincial leaders launched attacks on the principle and operation of conditional grants.[75] The newly-elected Premier of Quebec announced that his government would accept on a temporary basis the grants that the province was not then receiving but would engage in a principled opposition to the encroachment on provincial autonomy inherent in the grant-in-aid device. The leaders of the less prosperous provinces complained that the existing programmes did not take into account the respective fiscal capacities of the recipient governments. There was a good deal of criticism of the effects of conditional grants in limiting the budgetary and programme discretion of the provinces. During the previous periods grants-in-aid had been discussed, apart from Quebec, almost entirely within the perspective of particular services and facilities. From 1960 onward this device became a central element in the evolving relations between Ottawa and the provinces.

In 1965 Parliament enacted the Established Programs (Interim Arrangements) Act as a positive response by the federal Liberal government to Quebec's objections to conditional grants as unwarranted encroachments on provincial autonomy.[76] Under the Act the provinces were given the opportunity of contracting out of five established programmes. The federal government in compensating provinces which had accepted this alternative would lower its individual income tax rates up to 20 per cent, with cash transfers between the two levels to make up the differences between the yields of such taxes and the amount the non-participating provinces would have received as conditional grants. The abatements were to be as follows:

Hospital insurance	14 points
Assistance for old age, blind & disabled persons	2 points
Unemployment assistance	2 points
Vocational training	1 point
Health grants	1 point

During varying transitional periods specified in the Act, non-participating provinces were to provide the specified services under the same conditions as had prevailed under the previous arrangements.

Only Quebec accepted the alternatives made available under the 1965 enactment. As we shall see later in this chapter, the new fiscal policies announced by Ottawa in the fall of 1966 were in the direction of a uniform division of responsibilities and uniform rates of federal taxation throughout Canada. However, none of the other provinces acceded to Ottawa's desire that they should accept the contracting-out option. In the federal White Paper on Taxation, issued in 1969, the Minister of Finance announced that the offer of 1966 had lapsed and would be revised "after the reform of the income tax is implemented and the relative value of 'tax points' and the costs of the major, continuing joint programmes can be better appraised."[77] Since the 1966 offer was withdrawn the governments of Alberta and Ontario have announced their desire to withdraw from the established programmes in exchange for fiscal equivalents. Contracting-out was a subject of discussion at the Federal-Provincial Conference of November, 1971, and it is possible that Ottawa will make a new offer based on the federal tax reforms which came into effect on January 1, 1972.

During the discussion on revision and review of the Canadian constitution begun in 1968 the federal authorities came forward with a proposal which would impose constitutional limitations on Ottawa's unilateral power to inaugurate conditional grant programmes.[78] According to this scheme a general conditional grant arrangement could be established only if a "national consensus" had been obtained for this action. The consensus would be determined by the federal plan receiving the approval of the provincial legislatures as these provinces were divided into the four divisions of the Senate of Canada, i.e., the Atlantic provinces, Quebec, Ontario and the four western provinces. "The affirmative vote of the legislatures in at least three of these Senate divisions would be required before Parliament could proceed with the proposed shared-cost programme. The vote of the legislatures in the Atlantic region would be considered to be in the affirmative if the legislatures of provinces having at least 16 of the 30 Senate seats of that region were to vote for the resolution (two of Nova Scotia, New Brunswick or Newfoundland). The vote of the legislatures of the Western region would be considered to be in the affirmative if the legislatures of provinces having 12 of 24 Senate seats of that region were to vote for the resolution (two of the Western Provinces)."

If a national consensus was so obtained and a province did not participate in the conditional grant plan, its individual citizens would be compensated by Ottawa, through procedures not specified in the federal proposal, by the aggregate amount that would have been paid to the provincial government if it had so participated. This ingenious proposal was debated at the Constitutional Conference of December 1969. Like other such "propositions" introduced into this process of review by Ottawa and the provinces, no agreement was sought in anticipation of the eventual renegotiation of a new constitutional package.

By the early 1970s severe anxieties about the conditional grant device have developed among the provinces. These anxieties were brought into focus by the hostility of most of the provincial governments to the federal plan for support to medical insurance which came into effect in 1968. While it is not completely clear just what was the nature of the consultation with the provinces prior to enactment of the federal legislation, it appears that the national government had entered into these discussions after having taken firm and unilateral decisions about the general conditions provincial medical insurance plans would have to meet to qualify for federal assistance. Several of the provinces did not regard medical insurance as a high priority in a time of relative financial stringency and some would have preferred to supplement private insurance schemes, a device that did not meet Ottawa's conditions. There were no provisions for paying a fiscal equivalent to non-participating provinces. Despite these provincial objections, the financial penalties incurred for not meeting the federal conditions for eligibility were so high that by the end of 1970 all ten provinces had enacted schemes qualifying for federal assistance. Federal-provincial tensions were compounded by the action of the federal government in its 1968 Budget in levying a Social Development Tax which was a 2 per cent surcharge on the taxable incomes of individuals up to a maximum of $120 a year. In defending this tax the Minister of Finance pointed to rapidly increasing federal expenditures on post-secondary education and hospital insurance and the heavy anticipated costs of assistance to provincial medical insurance plans. Ottawa's action in forcing its medicare plan on most of the provinces and then in preempting a new portion of the income tax field to raise a part of the costs for this and other services within provincial jurisdiction has led to more anxiety and anger about the use of the federal spending power than has ever existed in the past.

The provinces are continually apprehensive that Ottawa will terminate or limit its contribution to established conditional grant programmes. The federal authorities have already ended their participation in some programmes and limited their assistance to others. The root of the difficulty is that in a sense the federal government views its contributions to matters within provincial jurisdiction as being *ex gratia* and thus to be determined unilaterally from time to time in terms of Ottawa's policies and priorities.

As we have seen, the "have" and "have not" provinces complain about the financial implications of conditional grants from contradictory viewpoints. The more prosperous jurisdictions object to the implicit equalization of certain grants-in-aid which pay a higher proportion of total costs incurred in the poorer provinces. The "have not" provinces complain of the burdens imposed by conditional grant programmes on their own limited revenues.

Conditional grant programmes by their very nature restrict the autonomy of the provinces in matters within their jurisdiction. The standards for eligibility are sometimes other than those which provinces deem appropriate. For example, Ontario objected vigorously to the condition attached to medical insurance that only publicly-administered plans were eligible for federal assistance and there was a recent dispute with British Columbia over the province's refusal to grant social assistance to striking workers and their families. Other conflicts occur about Ottawa's definition of what provincially-incurred costs are shareable. Under the hospital insurance arrangements the federal government has refused to share in the costs of institutions devoted to the care of the mentally ill and those with tuberculosis, and in the building of the Trans-Canada Highway did not assume any part of the costs incurred in purchasing rights-of-way. In recent years the major provincial complaint is that conditional grants distort expenditure-priorities and this complaint has become more widespread as provincial procedures for determining these priorities have become more rationalized.

Ottawa has itself come to develop hesitations about some of the shared-cost arrangements. All but a few of the smaller of these arrangements are open-ended in the sense that total federal contributions are determined entirely by the costs incurred by the provinces in providing the aided service or facility. Late in 1971 the federal government put forward proposals designed to limit its assistance to three provincial functions in respect to which costs were growing at what were regarded as alarming rates — post-secondary education, medical care and hospital insurance. In respect to the first Ottawa proposed to continue its contributions of 50 per cent of the operating costs of post-secondary institutions for a further two years, with the proviso that in no year would the federal commitment increase more than 15 per cent over the last. The federal proposal related to hospital insurance and medical care was a block grant arrangement for health. A $640 millions federal "thrust fund" would be established for the rationalization and improvement of health services. Starting in 1973-74 Ottawa's contributions to the then existing hospital and medical insurance plans would be determined by a new formula limiting federal assistance to proportionate increases in the Gross National Product plus an escalation factor of 0.75 per cent declining progressively to zero in 1977-78. It is implicit in these proposals that there will be federal-provincial cooperation in controlling the costs of the aided services. The provinces have understandably reacted strongly against Ottawa's attempts to impose limits on its financial commitments.

THE FEDERAL PROPOSALS OF 1966 AND THE
NEW DIRECTIONS OF FEDERAL POLICY

At the meeting of the Tax Structure Committee in September, 1966, the federal government announced new directions in its fiscal relations with the provinces. These new directions were incorporated in the tax arrangements which came into effect in the 1967-68 fiscal year. The principles underlying these policies were thus enumerated by the Minister of Finance and this statement was often referred to by federal representatives in subsequent dealing with the provinces:

(1) The fiscal arrangements should give both the federal and provincial governments access to fiscal resources sufficient to discharge their responsibilities under the constitution.

(2) They should provide that each government should be accountable to its own electors for its taxing and spending decisions and should make these decisions with due regard for their effect on other governments.

(3) The fiscal arrangements should, through a system of equalization grants, enable each province to provide an adequate level of public services without resort to rates of taxation substantially higher than those of other provinces.

(4) They should give to the Federal Government sufficient fiscal power to discharge its economic and monetary responsibilities, as well as to pay its bills. In particular they should retain for Federal Government a sufficient part of the income tax field in all provinces — both personal and corporate — to enable it to use variations in the weight and form of that tax for economic purposes and to achieve a reasonable degree of equity in the incidence of taxation across Canada.

(5) They should lead to uniform intergovernmental arrangements and the uniform application of federal laws in all provinces.

(6) The fiscal arrangements should seek to provide machinery for harmonizing the policies and the priorities of the federal and provincial governments.[79]

The embodiment of these principles involved the following changes:

1. *A new basis for equalization payments.* The new formula rationalized and extended the principle of revenue equalization.[80] Under the arrangements in effect from 1962 to 1967 payments were made on the basis of national average revenues from the individual and corporate income tax fields plus half the revenues from provincial natural resource levies. The new formula took into account the yields from 16 standard taxes, virtually all the kinds of levies made by the provinces, and equalization was again paid to the national average. There was also a provision for stabilization which guaranteed that no province would receive less than 95 per cent of all unconditional grants it had been paid in the previous year.

2. *Shared-cost programmes.* As we have seen, the federal government in 1966 proposed that all provinces avail themselves of the contracting-out alternatives provided for under the Established Programs (Interim Arrangements) Act of 1965.

3. *Post-secondary education.* At a Federal-Provincial Conference in October, 1966, the federal authorities announced a very new plan for sharing the financial responsibilities for post-secondary education with the provinces.[81] This scheme replaced the existing arrangements under which Ottawa had assisted the provinces in meeting the capital and operating costs of technical and vocational education through a system of grants and had paid $5 per capita of provincial population in aid of universities. Under the new arrangements the provinces would receive, as each chose, either $15 per capita or 50 per cent of the operating costs of post-secondary institutions. Such compensation would be paid in terms of an equalized tax abatement of 4 per cent of the individual income tax and 1 per cent of the corporate income tax. At the same time, the federal government assumed the exclusive administrative and financial responsibilities for providing adult manpower training. This ingenious plan, devised it appears without prior consultation with the provinces,[82] met several federal objectives.[83] It made uniform the financial and administrative relations between Ottawa and all the provinces; under the former arrangements Quebec had contracted out of the conditional grant arrangements for technical education and had received compensation for university costs through equalized tax abatements rather than, as in the case of the other provinces, per capita grants. The new plan was in effect a block grant which met provincial objections that the previous arrangements curtailed their discretion, both as grants-in-aid for technical education were paid only according to federal conditions and as provincial expenditure-priorities were distorted by the differing provisions related to technical and to university education. The assumption by Ottawa of exclusive responsibilities for adult manpower retraining allowed the federal government to integrate its operations in respect to manpower placement with the retraining of workers for the labour market.

The new policies announced by Ottawa in the fall of 1966 reflected very different emphases in federal policies toward the provinces than had come to prevail in the recent past.[84] Through piecemeal development since the Second World War, the Canadian fiscal system had become so integrated that pressures on the provinces for increased spending became almost immediately converted into provincial demands on Ottawa for enhanced tax room. From the divorce of tax-sharing from equalization under the 1957 arrangements onward the federal government had yielded time after time to these provincial pressures. There was a new determination in Ottawa that, on the basis of a more generous system of equalization grants, this yielding should end and the provinces be required to look to their own revenue sources to meet rising expenditures. Further, as made explicit in principle (5) enumerated by the Minister of Finance, the federal authorities had become concerned about the *de facto* special status that Quebec had come to assume under the existing arrangements and wished to restore a common system of financial and administrative relationships between Ottawa and all the provinces.

The fiscal arrangements coming into effect in 1972 will be basically the same as those prevailing in the previous 5-year period with the following exceptions:

— the stabilization guarantee has been increased from 95 to 100 per cent. No province has yet been in such an unfortunate position as to take advantage of the 1967 provision for stabilization, although in some cases the federal guarantee is said to have improved the credit-worthiness of provincial securities. The new scheme means that no province will receive less in equalization grants than it was paid in the previous year.

— the federal estate tax is ended. Under the previous arrangements Ottawa returned to each province 75 per cent of the yield from this tax in that province. The federal rationale for discontinuing the tax was that it was inequitable that Ottawa should levy taxes both on estates and, under legislation coming into effect in 1972, on capital gains at death. The federal government has offered to collect estate taxes and refund the proceeds to such provinces as agree to some uniformity in their legislation. Ontario, Quebec and British Columbia imposed their own estate taxes prior to federal departure from this field. On December 29, 1971 the four Atlantic provinces, Saskatchewan and Manitoba announced they would levy comparable gift and estate taxes and try to avoid double taxation by entering into reciprocal agreements with other provinces having estate taxes. Only Alberta remains without such a tax, although the government of Ontario has indicated its intention to move away from such a levy once the new taxation of capital gains is integrated into the tax system. It is at least likely that differing provincial provisions related to the taxation of estates will come to mean that no province has the real alternative of levying such taxes at significantly high levels.

— Ottawa appears determined to limit its total commitments in aid of health services and post-secondary education.

— the federal government is ending the former system of tax abatements. The federal view is that this will "remove any suggestion that the standard rate of abatement (of the personal income tax) signified the federal government's view as to the appropriate rate of provincial tax. While there has been no legal barrier to establish provincial income tax rates higher than the standard abatement (of 28 per cent) . . . and indeed the majority of the provinces have in fact set higher rates — the abatement system may have imposed a practical barrier. This will no longer be the case, and provinces will be able to determine and justify their own tax rates, in the light of their own requirements."[85] Under the new arrangements the federal government in determining its own rates of income taxation will take into account in advance the scales of provincial levies. The ending of the abatement system is a corollary of Ottawa's determination not to yield to provincial pressures for tax room.

THE CONTINUING STRUGGLE

In February, 1970, the Tax Structure Committee made public a Report[86] which showed with great clarity some of the more fundamental influences conditioning the continuing struggle between the federal and provincial governments about fiscal matters:

1. There was a long-term increase in the proportion of the Gross National Product devoted to public spending. Throughout the 1950s this proportion remained relatively constant at 25-26 per cent but increased in the early 1960s to 28 per cent in 1964 and an estimated 33.4 per cent in 1969 and a projected 34.7 per cent in 1971-72.

2. There had been significant changes in the distribution of public revenues and expenditures among the three levels of government:

	1952	1956	1960	1964	1968	1971
Federal						
(percentage of all government total)						
Revenues (own Sources)	73	69	63	57	52	52
Revenues (after transfers)	67	62	52	48	42	40
Total Expenditures (less transfers paid)	66	59	50	46	42	37
Total Debt Outstanding	78	72	69	65	61	n.a.
Provincial						
(percentage of all government total)						
Revenues (own Sources)	15	18	21	28	33	35
Revenues (after transfers)	20	22	28	32	37	40
Total Expenditures (less transfers paid)	19	22	28	32	26	42
Total Debt Outstanding	14	17	18	22	26	n.a.
Municipal						
(percentage of all government total)						
Revenues (own Sources)	12	13	16	15	15	13
Revenues (after transfers)	13	16	20	20	21	20
Total Expenditures (less transfers paid)	15	19	22	22	22	21
Total Debt Outstanding	8	11	13	13	13	n.a.

(n.a. — not available)[87]

There is thus a long-term proportionate increase in provincial and municipal revenues both from their own sources and from transfers, and a corresponding decrease in federal revenues. On the expenditure side, excluding transfers, provincial spending has risen dramatically while that of the federal government, in relative terms, has decreased with municipal expenditures being relatively constant from 1960 onward.

3. The Committee estimated that there would be a consolidated public deficit of $1.7 billion in 1971-72 on the assumption that there was no change in existing tax policies or expenditure programmes. It was forecast that in the period 1969-70 to 1971-72 the federal government would run a surplus, and that the net position of the municipalities would be unchanged. However, it was estimated that the total provincial deficit would double in 1969-70, double again in 1970-71 and increase by a further 20 per cent in 1971-72. Significantly, from 1952-53 to 1969-70 the per capita deficit was higher in the provinces which did not receive equalization payments but as projected the deficit per person in Ontario, Alberta and British Columbia would exceed that of the other provinces in 1971-72.

4. The personal income tax had assumed a steadily increasing importance as a source of public revenues. In 1952 this tax accounted for about 20 per cent of all public revenues and 25 per cent of federal revenues. The Committee estimated that in 1971-72 personal income taxes would constitute one-third of total public revenues, and 45 per cent of federal and provincial revenues combined.

5. There had been a long-term increase in the proportion of total public revenues spent on health, education and welfare and it was predicted that this increase would continue, from about one-third in 1952 to 50 per cent when the Committee made its study. It is of course significant that these are for the most part within the constitutional jurisdiction of the provinces.

In the early 1970s federal-provincial conflict in the field of fiscal and economic policy is as intense as at any time in the history of Confederation and has come to be extended over a progressively wider range of matters than ever before. The conflict is not to be completely deplored. A strong case can be made that the progress that Canada has made toward tax integration and interprovincial equalization has been developed and can be sustained only through a continuing process of federal-provincial bargaining. The price of such conflict is, however, high whether measured in terms of the demands on the time and energies of governments, the frustration of rationalized and coherent public policies or the diminishing accountability of governments to their respective legislatures and electorates. Further, as we saw in Chapter 3, there has been little progress made in developing procedures to give authoritative resolution to these conflicts.

The tension between Ottawa and the "have" provinces is at a very high level because of federal determination not to yield to pressures for more, extended tax room and federal efforts toward interprovincial equalization. At the root of the complaints of the more prosperous provinces is the view that the national government has failed to take into account the special revenue needs attendant on development and has neglected and restricted growth in those parts of Canada whose endowment of human and material resources permits them to contribute most to the country's total material product.

There are of course counter-pressures on Ottawa from the less prosperous provinces, pressures to which the incumbent federal government has responded in fuller measure than did any of its predecessors. As we have seen, regional disparities in personal income have remained relatively constant over several decades and the poorer provinces have in general both higher tax rates and lower standards of provincial and local services than do the more prosperous ones. Demands for further revenue equalization are characteristically expressed in terms of a new formula which will take into account all or part of municipal revenues. There are of course pressures for an intensification of direct federal efforts toward economic development in the less-favoured provinces.

Ottawa's current emphasis on economic development has led to varying degrees of conflict with all the provinces. One element of this conflict is the view of the "have" provinces that in the less prosperous areas of Canada the federal authorities are supporting development which cannot be justified by economic criteria. However, both rich and poor provinces are to a greater or lesser degree involved with the federal authorities in conflicts about development. Left to itself, every province will work in the directions of a more diversified and more industrialized material base than even the loosest application of economic criteria would justify; no more than Canadians as a whole do residents of Newfoundland or Saskatchewan or British Columbia wish to be restricted to being "hewers of wood and drawers of water." Any conceivable industrial strategy adopted by Ottawa devoted to lessening the degree of foreign control of the Canadian economy and other national objectives will inevitably be in conflict with provincial economic particularisms. Federal, provincial and local plans for economic development are in the early stages. In their early phases at least it is understandable that such measures will involve a very broad scope of executive discretion if not arbitrariness. The exercise of such discretion leads directly to intergovernmental conflict.

There are of course continuing conflicts about economic matters between Ottawa and Quebec. Quebec is at the same time the largest of the "have not" provinces and the province with more urgent reasons than the others to safeguard its autonomy in economic as well as other matters. The problem, or challenge, of cultural duality in the Canadian Confederation is the subject of the next chapter.

NOTES

[1]Queen's Printer, Ottawa, 1969, p. 191.

[2]*The Government of Canada*, University of Toronto Press, Toronto, p. 120.

[3]Donald Creighton, *John A. Macdonald: The Old Chieftain*, Macmillan of Canada, Toronto, 1955, Chapter 1 "The Pacification of Nova Scotia."

[4]"A Flexible Portion of the British North America Act," *Canadian Bar Review* (1933), pp. 148-157. For a history of the subsidy question see Maxwell's *Federal Subsidies to the Provincial Governments in Canada*, Harvard University Press, 1937.

[5]The Right Honourable Pierre Elliot Trudeau, *The Constitution and the People of Canada*, Queen's Printer, Ottawa, 1969, p. 12. Emphasis Mr. Trudeau's. Reproduced by permission of Information Canada.

[6]Book II, pp. 83-84.

[7]Peace, Order and Good Government, Macmillan of Canada, Toronto, p. 45.

[8]*Ten to One: The Confederation Wager*, McClelland and Stewart, Toronto/Montreal, pp. 144-145.

[9]For Parizeau's analysis of federal-provincial financial relations made near the time this political decision was made see "Federal-Provincial Economic Coordination," in *Canadian Economic Problems and Policies*, Lawrence H. Officer and Lawrence B. Smith, Editors, McGraw-Hill of Canada, Toronto, pp. 81-92.

[10]Vol. II, Queen's Printer, Ottawa, p. 104.

[11]The government of Manitoba pressed persistently for agreement on expenditure priorities. See also the statement of Premier Robarts of Ontario in *Proceedings, Federal-Provincial Tax Structure Committee*, Sept. 14-15, 1966, Queen's Printer, Ottawa, pp. 33-46.

[12]"The Impact of New Tax Policies on National Unity," Institute for the Quantitative Analysis of Social Economic Policy, Research Paper No. 1, 1968, Quoted in *In Search of Balance — Canada's Intergovernmental Experience*, Advisory Committee on Intergovernmental Relations, Washington, D.C., 1971, p. 103. Hartle's emphasis.

[13]"Constitutional Trends and Federalism," Reprinted in *Canadian Federalism: Myth or Reality*, J. Peter Meekison, Editor, Methuen of Canada, Toronto, 1968, p. 62.

[14]*Report of the Royal Commission on Dominion-Provincial Relations*, King's Printer, Ottawa, *Book II, Recommendations*.

[15]p. 126.

[16]*In Search of Balance, op.cit.*, p. 4.

[17]*Employment and Income with Special Reference to the Initial Period of Reconstruction*, King's Printer, Ottawa, 1945. For a fascinating account of the origins of the White Paper by its original author see W. A. Mackintosh, "The White Paper of Employment and Income in its 1945 Setting," in *Canadian Economic Policy Since the War*, S. F. Kaliski, Editor, Canadian Trade Committee, Ottawa, 1966, pp. 9-21.

[18]p. 21. Reproduced by permission of Information Canada.

[19]*Dominion-Provincial Conference (1945), Dominion and Provincial Submissions and Plenary Conference Discussions*, King's Printer, Ottawa, 1946. See particularly the Summary of Dominion proposals as amended, pp. 382-391.

[20]Donald V. Smiley, *Constitutional Adaptation and Canadian Federalism since 1945*, Documents of the Royal Commission on Bilingualism and Biculturalism, Queen's Printer, Ottawa, 1970, Chapter II, "Postwar Canadian Federalism: The 'New National Policy'."

[21]See *Constitutional Adaptation and Canadian Federalism*, Chapter III, "Postwar Canadian Federalism: The Attenuation of Federal Dominance."

[22]"The Formulation of Liberal and Conservative Programmes in the 1957 General Election," XXVI *Canadian Journal of Economics and Political Science*, November 1960, pp. 565-574.

[23]Peter Newman, *Renegade in Power: The Diefenbaker Years*, McClelland and Stewart, Toronto/Montreal, 1963, for an account which emphasizes this failure.

[24]From Richard M. Bird, *The Growth of Government Spending in Canada*, The Canadian Tax Foundation, Toronto, 1970, p. 246.

[25]*Bird, op.cit.*, p. 256.

[26]*Bird*, p. 289.

[27]*Bird*, p. 281.

[28]Canada: Dominion Bureau of Statistics, *Canada Year Books*, 1962 and 1963-64.

[29]United Nations, Department of Social and Economic Affairs, Statistical Office, *Statistical Year Book*, 1963, New York, 1964, Table 170. In the period 1955-62 Canada's per capita product grew more slowly than that of any of the other industrialized countries compared — Denmark, France, West Germany, the United Kingdom, the United States and Japan.

[30]See Hugh Whalen, "Public Policy and Regional Development: The Experience of the Atlantic Provinces" in *The Prospect of Change: Proposals for Canada's Future*, Abraham Rotstein, Editor, University League for Social Reform, McGraw-Hill of Canada, Toronto, 1965, pp. 133-142 and T. N. Brewis, *Regional Economic Policies in Canada*, Macmillan of Canada, Toronto, 1969, Chapter 10, "The Role of the Provinces in Regional Development."

[31]For an account of these circumstances see A. Milton Moore, J. Harvey Perry and Donald I. Beach, *The Financing of Canadian Federation: The First Hundred Years*, Canadian Tax Foundation, Toronto, 1966, Chapter III.

[32]*Moore, Perry and Beach, op. cit.*, Chapter IV.

[33]For a journalistic account of the pension plan negotiations in April 1964 see Peter C. Newman, *The Distemper of Our Times*, McClelland and Stewart, Toronto/Montreal, 1968, Chapter 22. For another account by one of the major participants see Judy La Marsh, *Memoirs of a Bird in a Gilded Cage*, McClelland and Stewart, Pocket Book Edition, Toronto, 1970, Chapter 5.

[34]*The National Finances, 1969-70*, Canadian Tax Foundation, Toronto, 1970, p. 116.

[35]Donald V. Smiley, *The Canadian Political Nationality*, Methuen of Canada, Toronto, 1967, pp. 59-78.

[36]"Employment Policy," in *Canadian Economic Policy*, T. N. Brewis, H. E. English, Anthony Scott and Pauline Jewett, Macmillan of Canada, Toronto, 1961, pp. 150-151.

[37]The late Dr. Mackintosh asserted that in 1945 the idea of grants for public investment was not attractive to the Ottawa politicians and bureaucrats as a device for countering cyclical fluctuations in employment. *Op. cit.*, p. 20. The intergovernmental planning of a "shelf" of public works was never undertaken.

[38]"A Twenty Year Perspective: Some Reflections on the Keynesian Revolution in Canada," in *Canadian Economic Policy Since the War, op.cit.*, pp. 23-46.

[39]p. 46.

[40]"Federal-Provincial Fiscal Developments," in Canadian Tax Foundation, *Report of the 1964 Conference*, Toronto, 1965, p. 223. There has been an element in political and economic thought in Quebec which sees the roots of centralization in Canada in the acceptance by Ottawa of the Keynesian analysis. See François-Albert Angers, *Essai sur la Centralisation*, Éditions Beauchemin, Montréal, 1960 and *Report of the Royal Commission of Inquiry on Constitutional Problems*, Quebec, 1956, Vol. II, pp. 294-305.

[41]"Growth, Price Stability and the Problem of Unemployment," mimeo., p. 5.

[42]Vol. II, p. 29.

[43]*Op. cit.*, p. 29.

[44]Queen's Printer, Ottawa, Chapter 7 "Regional Aspects of Federal Economic Policies."

[45]Information Canada, Ottawa, Chapter VIII "National Policy-Making in a Regional Country."

[46]Vol. 2, p. 93. See also Clarence L. Barber, *Theory of Fiscal Policy as Applied to a Province*, A Study Prepared for the Ontario Committee on Taxation, Queen's Printer, Toronto, 1967, Chapter 3 "Fiscal Policy at the Provincial and Municipal Level: the Historical Record."

[47]pp. 96-99.

[48]pp. 102-103.

[49]Chapter 2.

[50]The Honourable W. D'arcy McKeough, *1971 Budget Ontario*, Queen's Printer, Toronto, 1971, Budget Paper A, "New Directions in Economic Policy Management in Canada," p. 45.

[51]*Op.cit.*, p. 47.

[52]p. 49.

[53]From *In Search of Balance, op.cit.*, p. 14.

[54]Queen's Printer, Ottawa, p. 141. Reproduced by permission of Information Canada.

[55]Federal-Provincial Conference of Prime Ministers and Premiers, Ottawa, Nov. 15-17 1971, *Notes for Remarks by Prime Minister Trudeau on Fiscal Arrangements*, mimeo, p. 15.

[56]"Fiscal Adjustment in a Federal Country," in John F. Graham *et al., Inter-governmental Fiscal Relationships*, Canadian Tax Paper No. 40, Canadian Tax Foundation, Toronto, 1964, p. 7.

[57]*Fiscal Need and Revenue Equalization Grants*, Canadian Tax Foundation and Institute of Intergovernmental Relations, Toronto, 1969, p. 3.

[58]p. 3.

[59]By what is to me a very unconvincing argument J. C. Strick has maintained that conditional grants to the provinces have not distorted provincial expenditure priorities to a significant degree. The bulk of such grants are for health and welfare. Between 1953 and 1970 when such grants increased markedly, the net proportion of provincial expenditures on those functions remained relatively constant. Thus those grants "have not caused substitution effects between these two functions and the other functions of government." The assumption is of course that the provinces desired to keep the proportions of next expenditures on health and welfare constant, an assumption for which no evidence is given. "Conditional Grants and Provincial Government Budgeting." XIV, *Canadian Public Administration*, Summer 1971, pp. 217-235.

[60]*Interregional Disparities in Income*, Staff Study No. 14, Economic Council of Canada, 1966, p. 23.

[61]Regional Planning for Depressed Rural Areas — the Canadian Experience," by permission of *Canadian Journal of Agricultural Economics*, February 1968.

[62]For an account of the ARDA programme see T. N. Brewis, *Regional Economic Policies in Canada, op.cit.*, Chapter 6.

[63]In 1961 the first tax incentive was begun when firms were permitted accelerated depreciation of their assets if they manufactured a product "not ordinarily" made in Canada or if they located in an area of surplus manpower and made a product "not ordinarily" produced in that area.

[64]*Regional Economic Policies in Canada*, pp. 162-163. Chapter 7 gives an analysis of the designated area programme under the federal Area Development Agency.

[65]*How Your Tax Dollar Is Spent*, Treasury Board, Information Canada, 1971, p. 23.

[66]17-18 Elizabeth, 1969, Ch. 6.

[67]*The National Finances 1969-70*, Canadian Tax Foundation, Toronto, p. 34.

[68]*Forced Growth*, James Lewis and Samuel, Toronto, 1971, p. 11.

[69]*Brewis*, p. 250.

[70]Brewis points out that because of its location eastern Ontario has better prospects for attracting profitable secondary manufacturing than such depressed areas as eastern Quebec or Newfoundland; p. 214.

[71]For accounts of federal conditional grants to the provinces at different periods of time see Luella Gettys, *The Administration of Canadian Conditional Grants*, Chicago, Public Administration Service, 1938; Donald V. Smiley, *Conditional Grants and Canadian Federalism*, Canadian Tax Foundation, Toronto, 1963 and George E. Carter, *Canadian Conditional Grants since World War II*, Canadian Tax Foundation, Toronto, 1971.

[72]The major instance of this in Canada is the arrangement by which Ottawa pays half the operating costs of institutions of post-secondary education.

[73]J. C. Strick, "Conditional Grants and Provincial Government Budgeting", p. 224.

[74]From J. C. Strick, "Conditional Grants and Provincial Government Budgeting", p. 223. By permission of the author and the Institute of Public Administration of Canada.

[75]Queen's Printer, Ottawa, 1960.

[76]For accounts of the opting-out arrangements see J. S. Dupré "Contracting Out: A

Funny Thing Happened on the Way to the Centennial," *Report of the Proceedings of the Eighteenth Tax Conference, 1964* and *Carter, Canadian Conditional Grants, op.cit.,* Chapter 5 "The Development of Contracting Out and Tax Abatements."

[77]The Honourable E. J. Benson, *Proposals for Tax Reform,* Queen's Printer, Ottawa, 1969, p. 81.

[78]The Right Honourable Pierre Elliott Trudeau, *Federal-Provincial Grants and the Spending Power of Parliament,* Queen's Printer, Ottawa, 1969, pp. 38-48. For a critique of the federal proposal see Donald V. Smiley and R. M. Burns, "Canadian Federalism and the Spending Power: Is Constitutional Restriction Necessary?" XVII *Canadian Tax Journal* (November-December, 1969), pp. 467-482.

[79]*Federal-Provincial Tax Structure Committee,* Ottawa, September 14 and 15th, 1966, Queen's Printer, pp. 13-14. Reproduced by permission of Information Canada.

[80]See Clark, *Fiscal Need and Revenue Equalization Grants, op.cit.,* pp. 38-56.

[81]*Federal-Provincial Conference, Ottawa, October 24-28, 1966,* Queen's Printer, 1968. For Prime Minister Pearson's proposals see pp. 3-21.

[82]*Report: Intergovernmental Liaison on Fiscal and Economic Matters,* Institute of Intergovernmental Relations, Queen's University, Ottawa, 1969, p. 127.

[83]I am indebted to J. S. Dupré for letting me read a Chapter on this issue from his forthcoming study on adult retraining programmes.

[84]Peter Newman calls the 1966 policies the replacement of "cooperative federalism" through federal-provincial conferences by "a tough and explicit policy of decentralization." *The Distemper of Our Times, op.cit.,* p. 324.

[85]Federal-Provincial Conference of First Ministers, *Statement on Federal-Provincial Taxation Arrangements by Finance Minister E. J. Benson,* mimeo, pp. 10-11. Despite Mr. Benson's contention that the abatement system may have created inhibitions on the provinces in raising provincial income tax rates above the federal abatement rate, by 1971 six provinces had in fact exceeded the standard abatement of 28 per cent (Prince Edward Island, 30.5 per cent, Newfoundland and Alberta 33 per cent, Saskatchewan 34 per cent, New Brunswick 38 per cent, Manitoba 39 per cent).

[86]Ottawa, 1970, mimeo.

[87]p. 11.

6

Cultural Duality and Canadian Federalism

Canada was established as a federation in 1867, albeit of a somewhat attenuated form, predominantly because of cultural duality. Most of the English-speaking Fathers of Confederation from Canada and the Maritime colonies would have preferred a unitary system — in the language of the day, a "legislative union" — but the French-Canadian Conservatives were unwilling to agree to any political settlement which would have placed those powers they deemed necessary to the integrity of their cultural and linguistic community in the hands of the majority in the new Dominion. However, among the Fathers from Upper Canada there were those too who wished to separate out some of those matters where the two historic communities had come into conflict since the Act of Union. Although such leaders as George Brown seem not to have wanted a coordinate division of legislative powers between Parliament and the provincial legislatures, they clearly anticipated the benefits of removing certain matters of previous English-French contention from the jurisdiction of the projected Dominion government.[1] Provincialist influences were also at work in the Maritime Provinces.

Cultural duality was at the first and is now the major *raison d'être* of Canadian federalism and the most powerful threat to its stability. Within the French-speaking community in Quebec there have been from the beginning conflicting influences toward autonomism and toward orientations which sought the objectives of that community within the wider Canadian framework. The early 1970s are characterized by a sharpening of this conflict and the polarization of Quebec politics around federalist and separatist alternatives.

STABILIZING FACTORS IN ENGLISH-FRENCH RELATIONS
BEFORE 1960

In the period between the Conquest and the death of Premier Maurice Duplessis of Quebec in 1959 there developed certain patterns of relations between Anglophone and Francophone communities in Canada and after 1867 these circumstances contributed to the stability of the federal system:

1. *Institutional self-segregation.* From 1759 onward there was sustained in Quebec what one might call a counter-culture with its justifying system of political, economic and religious thought. Pierre Elliott Trudeau wrote in 1954, ". . . against the English, Protestant, democratic, materialist, commercial and later industrial world, our nationalism worked out a defensive system in which all the opposite forces were stressed: the French language, Catholicism, authoritarianism, idealism, rural life and later the return to the soil."[2] The historian Michel Brunet has seen as the dominant currents of French-Canadian thought "l'agriculturisme, l'anti-étatisme et le messianisme."[3] These institutions and their justifying values did not in any direct way challenge Anglo-Saxon political and economic power either in Quebec or in Canada as a whole, and at the individual level most Anglophones and Francophones could pursue their occupational and other objectives largely without opposition from members of the other group.

2. *Mediation "at the summit."* Traditionally, the most important of Anglophone-Francophone political relations have been mediated by leaders of the elites of the two communities. In federal politics Anglophone party leaders have either had their Quebec lieutenants or — as has been the case with the Conservatives for most of the time since the death of George-Étienne Cartier in 1873 — have been trying with some urgency to find someone to play this role effectively. Although the Quebec lieutenant was by no means a co-Prime Minister when the party was in power, he had characteristically a wider scope of discretion in Quebec affairs than did ministers from the other provinces in respect to the areas they represented.[4] In the Quebec cabinet there was usually a cabinet minister from the English-speaking community — often the Minister of Revenue — representing Anglophone business interests.

3. *The traditional French-Canadian distrust of the state.* French Canadians have traditionally distrusted government, even governments in which they themselves have had a numerical dominance. According to Trudeau's analysis, because French Canadians received democratic institutions not through their own efforts but by the will of the English-speaking community they came to value democracy not for itself but as an instrument of ethnic survival.[5] The Church remained jealous of its privileges and erected a system of social and religious thought which was both authoritarian and anti-statist. Although successive Quebec governments mounted a stubborn defence of provincial autonomy against real or alleged federal encroachments, there was little disposition to use these

provincial powers imaginatively. A doctrinaire adherence to anti-statist values became a justification for French-Canadian political and religious leaders to cooperate in the economic domination of Quebec by Anglo-Saxon capital.

4. *The defence of historic, prescriptive rights.* Prior to the 1960s, French-Canadian leaders saw the welfare and integrity of their community primarily in terms of an unyielding defence of historic and prescriptive rights, particularly as these rights were embodied in the Confederation settlement. From the 1880s onward such interests were often defined in terms of the theory of Confederation as a compact either among the provinces or between the English and French communities.[6] The corollary of course was that the terms of Confederation could not legitimately be altered without the consent of the original partners.

These circumstances, taken together, gave a degree of stability to Anglophone-Francophone relations and to Canadian federalism. Institutional differentiation based on contrary value-systems made the individual and group objectives of members of the two communities relatively compatible. The mediation of community relations through the elites provided a regularized procedure for managing the demands of each group on the other. Anti-statism in Quebec facilitated both the domination of the province by English-speaking business interests and, particularly in the period between 1945 and 1960, the extension of federal powers in harmony with the preferences both of Canadians outside Quebec for national leadership and inside Quebec for public action to meet emergent social needs. Adherence by French Canadians to one version or other of the compact theory was an affirmation of the continuing legitimacy within Quebec of the federal system.

THE QUIET REVOLUTION IN QUEBEC
AND CANADIAN FEDERALISM

Each of the stabilizing elements which has been discussed in the preceding section was abruptly attenuated in the so-called Quiet Revolution of Quebec in the 1960s. Despite the speed and the comprehensiveness of change, these developments had their roots in the past. Many years before the death of Maurice Duplessis in 1959 the traditional institutions of Quebec and their justifying ideologies had become progressively less relevant to the circumstances of an industrialized community exposed to a modern and modernizing world. The formulations of the Duplessis era and later Quebec nationalism differed in many important respects but were similar in that they tended to equate Quebec with French Canada and were for the most part indifferent to the recognition of cultural and linguistic duality in federal institutions or in provinces and areas of Canada outside Quebec where there were significant concentrations of French-speaking people. On the other hand, the older nationalism was primarily defensive and the new currents of thought and policy much less so.[7] In turning from "survivance" to "épanouissement" the Quebec leadership decisively altered the older patterns of relations between Anglophones and Francophones.

1. *An attentuation of institutional self-segregation.* What the sociologist Hubert Guindon has called "a new middle class" had developed in Quebec in response to urbanization and industrialization.[8] During the Duplessis period this emergent class had been rendered impotent both by the traditional political and religious leadership and by the Anglophone centres of corporate power. The new groups were committed both by ideology and class interest to the rationalization and modernization of Quebec society. Their frame of reference was secular, materialistic and democratic. Because corporate business was in the main an Anglo-Saxon preserve, the new middle class turned to public institutions and in the main to the government of Quebec. This kind of development inevitably brought about new conflicts between the French-Canadian elites and centres of business and governmental power dominated by English-speaking Canadians.

2. *An end to anti-statism.* After the election of the Lesage administration in 1960 dominant currents of thought and policy in Quebec turned away from the older suspicion of the state and came to see the provincial government as the major instrument by Quebec society might be reformed. The interests of the new middle class lay in the expansion of the public sector and in the bureaucratization of public and private institutions. This led inevitably to the displacement of the Church from its dominance in health, education and welfare — as well as to the bureaucratization of the Church itself and the declining political influence of its leaders — and to more intervention than before in the private sector by the provincial authorities.

3. *An attenuation of elite accommodation.* From 1960 onward there was overt conflict among the Quebec elites which inhibited the older kinds of elite accommodation between Francophones and Anglophones both within Quebec and outside. During the early 1960s a frequent question asked by English-speaking Canadians was "what does Quebec want?" The meaning was undoubtedly "who speaks for Quebec?" and confusion was made worse because as one French-Canadian scholar pointed out in 1968, "Actually too many individuals among the elite are speaking in the name of the whole French-Canadian population."[9] The overt and vigorous conflicts within Francophone Quebec undoubtedly became more salient for relations between the two communities as an increasing number of Anglophone Canadians came to interest themselves in Quebec affairs. In the federal political parties, the new currents in Quebec were weakly manifested through the Progressive Conservatives[10] and the NDP and between the retirement of the Right Honourable Louis St. Laurent in 1958 and after the general election of 1965 no authoritative spokesman for Quebec emerged from the federal Liberal caucus. The results of the federal election of 1962

further confused the situation as the Creditistes displaced the Progressive Conservatives as the major opposition to the Liberals in Quebec federal politics on a programme which was at the same time federalist, anti-elitist and based on traditional French-Canadian values.[11] In the redefinition of Quebec's relations with the rest of Canada alternatives from revolutionary separatism to cooperative federalism were proposed and vigorously expounded. By the mid-1960s the older patterns of elite accommodation between the Francophone and Anglophone communities appeared in retrospect to have been relatively tidy and straightforward.

4. *The turning away from historic, prescriptive rights.* There was little disposition in the 1960s to defend Quebec's rights in terms of the compact theory of Confederation. Pierre Carignan said of prevailing constitutional attitudes in 1966, ". . . il semble que la majorité des Québecois d'expression française sont prêts a rejeter la constitution dans sa forme actuel. N'ayant pu convaincre leurs compatriotes que la constitutions constitue un pacte, ils ont eux-mêmes cessé de la croire: en consequence, ils ne se sentent plus liés par elle et remettent tout en question."[12] As we saw in Chapter One, in their acceptance and later rejection of the Fulton-Favreau formula for constitutional amendment, the Lesage Liberals were caught in the crossfire of changing attitudes. Interestingly, the direct challenge to the Fulton-Favreau formula, whose rigidities were a manifestation of constitutional conservatism, was made by the Union Nationale. Writing in 1965 when he was Leader of the Opposition Daniel Johnson pointed out that Canadians had lived under five constitutions — those of 1763, 1774, 1791, 1841 and 1867 — and said, "Les constitutions sont faites pour les hommes et non les hommes pour les constitutions. *Quand les conditions changent, c'est aux structures juridiques de s'adapter aux circonstances nouvelles. . .* Et les conditions ont changé depuis 1867."[13] In harmony with the new circumstances Johnson defined Quebec's position not in terms of historically-acquired rights but on the basis of the inherent right of nations to self-determination.[14]

The changes effected by the Lesage government were in the direction of reform of both the private and the public institutions of Quebec. Progress was made in creating a merit civil service and the assistance of some of the most able persons in the province was secured either as full-time officials or part-time advisors. Some of the grosser forms of patronage endemic to Quebec politics were eliminated and in 1963 came legislation which both limited campaign expenditures and provided generous subsidies to candidates of recognized political parties. Through the Societé Générale de Financement private and public funds were channeled into Quebec industry and some attempts were made to rationalize such industry. A provincial Department of Education was established and a comprehensive programme of educational reform undertaken from the kindergarten to university levels. Health and welfare systems were rationalized and bureaucratized. Hydro-electric resources were brought under public ownership, significantly increasing the opportunities for French-speaking Quebecers, particularly in the professional and management categories. There was a new emphasis by the provincial authorities on linguistic and cultural matters, including contacts with the French-speaking world in Europe and Africa. Comprehensive programmes of provincial and regional economic planning were devised and some progress was made in their implementation.

Despite the speed and comprehensiveness of reform the changes being effected by the Lesage government were very much the same as those which had been undertaken in other parts of Canada but over a longer period of time. There were of course some differences. Understandably, these developments in Quebec had repercussions for the relations between the Francophone and Anglophone communities which were absent from modernizing trends elsewhere in the country. In the eastern part of Quebec the province sponsored the first large-scale programme of development through "animation sociale" which had ever been undertaken in Canada. The bureaucratization and rationalization of public services involved new relations between the religious and public authorities in Quebec much more than the other provinces. On the whole, however, the reforms undertaken in Quebec were in the direction of bringing its institutions in harmony with those of other western democracies. This circumstance created an essential sympathy for the province and its new leadership within the federal government and among Canadians throughout the country. For the first time in the history of Canada the source of change was coming from Quebec.

The Lesage programme can best be understood as a reflection of the interests of the emergent middle classes of Quebec. Guindon has said of the period just before and after the death of Duplessis, "The (provincial) Liberal party . . . became the political expression of the new middle class, the champion of its interests and aspirations. It heralded a bureaucratic revolution under the banner of modernization and was spontaneously acclaimed internally and externally. Its election in 1960 publicly consecrated the political dominance of the new middle class in French Canada."[15] In 1965 Charles Taylor evaluated the nationalism of the Lesage government in terms of socialist objectives:

> . . . a nationalist policy distinguishes itself from a traditional policy of the left partly by its aims and partly by the transformations it is capable of undergoing. In the first respect, it concentrates on a policy of development with an eye more to national greatness than to welfare benefits. Thus what are known as welfare measures have a relatively low priority, although they are not actively opposed. If we compare the present Quebec government with the recently defeated CCF government in Saskatchewan, we can see the difference: the latter left a monument of pioneer measures in the field of welfare: first hospitalization scheme on the continent, first medicare scheme,

and so on. The Lesage government has applied hospitalization belatedly to Quebec when it came to office, and has recently announced its intention to institute a pension scheme. Characteristically, though, this was seen more as a means of acquiring development funds than as a social security measure. This exhausts the present concern of the government in this field. Secondly, the concentration on francizing the economy can conflict with traditional left policies, which have been concerned above all with employment-creation, whatever the source. This conflict has not yet shaped up here, and one can only guess at the nationalist reaction should it arise.[16]

Writing from the very different ideological perspective of economic liberalism, Albert Breton argued that the effect of nationalist policies in Quebec as elsewhere was to make the total income of a community smaller than if purely economic criteria were used and to redistribute that income in favour of the more prosperous members of the preferred national group to the disadvantage of less prosperous citizens.[17] Breton applied this analysis specifically to the nationalization of hydro-electric resources in Quebec and the purchase by the Societé Générale de Financement of certain Quebec industries.

The Quiet Revolution in Quebec led the government of that province to impose very heavy demands on the federal authorities and in large part those demands were met, particularly after the coming to power of the Pearson administration as a result of the general election of April, 1963.[18] Prime Minister Pearson and perhaps most of his cabinet colleagues were in essential sympathy with the new Quebec. The federal government was in a minority position in the House of Commons as a result of the 1963 and 1965 elections. Just as significantly as these circumstances, the highly centralized federal system which had been established during the Second World War and perpetuated afterward was being subjected to other strains apart from those emanating from the new Quebec.[19] Beginning in the mid-1950s national fiscal and monetary policies proved incapable of securing full employment and price stability and in the face of these difficulties the provinces assumed a more important role than before in economic development. In several of the provinces able civil services had developed and the balance of bureaucratic competence had shifted away from Ottawa. Many of the objectives in social and economic policy formulated by the federal government at the end of the Second World War had been achieved in whole or in part and no new national policies had been devised to replace them, while several of the provinces, including of course Quebec, had committed themselves to fairly comprehensive and fairly precise aims. The new social priorities — particularly in health, welfare and education — were for the most part within provincial rather than federal jurisdiction and the proportion of total public expenditures made by the provinces and local authorities combined was increasing while that of the national government declined. Thus Quebec's demands for autonomy in the first half of the 1960s were in basic harmony with other circumstances making for an enhancement of provincial power.

The Lesage government made very specific demands on Ottawa and pressed these demands in a very effective way through the elected leadership and their extraordinarily sophisticated senior advisers. I have said elsewhere of these developments, "Such pressures (toward enhanced provincial discretion) arose as much from the requirements of particular Quebec policies as from a generalized disposition toward autonomy on ideological grounds ... The provincial administration was motivated to increase its range of effective discretion because it had very ambitious plans for reform and, to a greater or lesser degree, specific activities of the federal government stood in its path."[20] There were three classes of demands on Ottawa:

1. *For financial autonomy.* The reforms undertaken by the Lesage administration were understandably expensive and the Quebec authorities, with of course support from other provinces, pressed successfully both for higher unconditional subsidies from Ottawa and decreases in federal income tax rates so that the province could increase its revenues without increasing the burden on its taxpayers.

2. *For a withdrawal of federal involvement from matters within provincial legislative jurisdiction.* Particularly in the period between 1945 and 1960 the federal government had come to involve itself in a very large number of matters within provincial jurisdiction, largely through the exercise of the spending power. The Lesage government demanded that such encroachments cease on the double grounds that they threatened the integrity of the French-Canadian community and interfered with provincial objectives and priorities. In particular, Quebec demanded that in respect to existing and future shared-cost programmes the province be allowed to contract out without either itself or its citizens being subjected to financial penalties. As we saw in Chapter 5, by the enactment in 1965 of the Established Programs (Interim Arrangements) Act this demand was in part met. Under the British North America Act as amended in 1951, Parliament and the provinces were permitted to legislate concurrently in respect to old age pensions and Quebec established its own system of contributory public retirement pensions and after hard bargaining with Ottawa the federal Canada Pension Plan did not apply in the province. Quebec was also successful in establishing certain programmes which elsewhere in Canada were administered by the federal authorities — student loans and youth allowances.

3. *For more institutionalized procedures of intergovernmental collaboration.* In its quest for autonomy the Lesage administration showed a basic distrust for the informal and segmented pattern of relations between the provinces and the federal government. As we saw in Chapter 3, the Quebec government centralized the control of its relations with outside jurisdiction

in a Department created for that purpose and under the direct supervision of the Premier. One of the basic elements of Quebec's formulation of cooperative federalism was a fastidious respect by Ottawa for matters within provincial jurisdiction. However, because most federal economic policies had direct and immediate implications for the provinces Quebec demanded that there be established regularized patterns of federal-provincial consultation in respect to these policies.[21] There was also the desire to institutionalize procedures of interprovincial cooperation.

By the time the Lesage government left office, as a result of the Quebec general election of 1966, the province had attained very considerable elements of a *de facto* special status in the Canadian federal system. Alone of the provinces Quebec had chosen to contract out of several of the established shared-cost programmes thereby both ending federal control in these matters and increasing its own share of personal and corporate income taxes. Alone of the provinces, Quebec had its own machinery for collecting these taxes. As we have seen, Quebec established several programmes in the field of social policy which elsewhere in Canada were carried out by the federal authorities. In all of these situations, each of the provinces had precisely the same options to go its own way but only Quebec used these options.

Despite the positive responses of the federal government to the demands of Quebec for autonomy, these demands were seemingly insatiable. In the period just prior to its defeat in 1966 the Lesage administration was pressing on several fronts: toward more extensive and autonomous provincial participation in international affairs, for provincial jurisdiction over old age security and family allowances, toward confining federal jurisdiction over agriculture to extraprovincial trade, for direct provincial participation in federal cultural programmes, toward restricting the federal role in manpower development and regional economic development. All these pressures for autonomy assumed complementary policies by Ottawa to enhance the revenues that the Quebec government would have at its disposal.

Throughout its six years in office the Lesage government failed to evolve a coherent constitutional policy and in particular failed to formulate an unequivocal answer to the question as to whether Quebec required explicit constitutional changes to give it a wider jurisdiction than that wanted or needed by the other provinces. In his last year in power Premier Lesage and his chief constitutional advisor, Paul Gérin-Lajoie, the Minister of Education, came to speak in a specific way about a *statut particulier* for Quebec.[22] However, these statements could be read either as a rationalization of the existing contracting-out arrangements, and their future application to other federal-provincial activities, or a rather generalized demand for explicit constitutional change. The specific demands of Quebec for autonomy had been spectacularly successful and because of this — and perhaps because of conflicting pressures operating within and on the government — the Premier and his colleagues chose to proceed in a piecemeal way rather than directing their activities toward comprehensive constitutional reform.

THE 1966-1970 PERIOD

There were two events in 1966 which were crucial in the evolving relations of Quebec within the Canadian federal system. The first was the replacement of the Lesage Liberals by the Union Nationale government as a result of the Quebec general election in June of that year. The second new influence was a new firmness in federal policies toward the provinces attendant, it may reasonably be conjectured, on the growing influence of Pierre Elliott Trudeau and his formulation of Canadian federalism in the government of Canada. These circumstances taken together led to a polarization between Quebec and Ottawa sharper than in the immediate past, and a polarization based on somewhat abstract formulation of the place of Quebec in the Canadian Confederation.

For most observers, the defeat of the Lesage Liberals in 1966 was unexpected. The anomalies of the Quebec electoral system allowed the Union Nationale to win a one-seat majority in the Legislative Assembly with 40.8 per cent of the popular vote as against 47.4 per cent for the Liberals. (The Liberals had failed when in power to effect a comprehensive electoral redistribution because, so Mr. Lesage claimed after the election, Section 80 of the BNA Act precluded the legislature from altering the boundaries of twelve electoral districts which in 1867 had English-speaking majorities without the consent of a majority of members of the Assembly from those districts.) So far as the federal authorities and those of the other provinces were concerned, not much was known of the new Quebec leadership and what was known gave cause for apprehension. In particular, the incoming Premier, Daniel Johnson, had been a supporter of the Duplessis tradition before and after 1959 and had won the leadership of the Union Nationale over Jean-Jacques Bertrand with the support of the old guard of the party.

With the coming to power of the Union Nationale, the focus of conflict between Quebec and Ottawa shifted somewhat from the specific demands for provincial autonomy which had characterized the Lesage period to broader and more symbolic matters of constitutional reform and of the role of the province in international affairs. By reason of ideology and the basis of its electoral support the Union Nationale was less interventionist than its predecessor and thus felt less urgency about effecting specific changes which would have brought it into conflict with federal policies. Further, a continuation of reform at the pace set by the Lesage government was impossible without imposing intolerable burdens on the Quebec taxpayer.

While in opposition, the Union Nationale had been persistently critical of what it claimed to be the pragmatism and opportunism of the Lesage government in constitutional affairs. The party was instrumental in having the Legislative Assembly establish a committee on the constitution in 1963 to hear interested and expert opinion and to stimulate debate on these matters. The U.N. led the struggle against the Fulton-Favreau formula for constitutional amendment and challenged the Lesage government to fight the forthcoming general election on its acceptance of this proposal. Daniel Johnson in 1965 had published his *Egalité ou Indépendance*[23] which called for a radical reform of the Canadian constitution on binational lines. After coming to power the Union Nationale continued to place a high priority on comprehensive constitutional change. In retrospect, this may be explained as an attempt to reconcile conflicts within the cabinet and the party — as well as the wider Quebec society — on the place of Quebec in Confederation. There were undoubtedly many traditional U.N. politicians whose basic commitment was to the continuation of federalism in a revised form. Other and younger members of the party espoused even the more thoroughgoing variants of Quebec nationalism. All could be brought to at least transient agreement on the desirability of constitutional change on binational lines but the successive Premiers, Johnson and Bertrand, resorted to exquisite equivocation on the urgency of change. On some occasions, such changes were pressed stridently in terms that suggested their almost immediate acceptance was necessary if separation was to be avoided. At other times, the tone if not the substance of Quebec's position was moderate.

The major policy issue on which the federal and Quebec governments came into conflict in the 1966-70 period involved the province's role in international affairs.[24] Under the Lesage administration Quebec had extended its economic and cultural contacts abroad with the opening of several quasi-diplomatic offices in Europe and the United States. The government had asserted its right to participate independently in international relations in respect to matters within provincial legislative jurisdiction but a major conflict with Ottawa over this issue had been avoided. After the Union Nationale came to power there was a series of incidents involving Quebec's participation in international affairs and both federal and provincial governments were disposed toward carrying on this struggle in doctrinaire and symbolic terms. Ottawa came to believe that France with the connivance of its African allies was engaged in a deliberate policy of encouraging Quebec's international pretensions in an attempt to destroy the Canadian federation, or at the very least to challenge its stability by involving themselves in domestic Canadian affairs. In waging this conflict Ottawa put great emphasis on the abstract principle that foreign policy was indivisible and that in both law and practice there was a vast gulf between sovereign states and other governments.[25] The Quebec authorities on their part were disposed to assert in a symbolic way their right to independent participation in external affairs within the broad but indeterminate limits set by France and the French-speaking nations of Africa.

From his appointment as Parliamentary Secretary to Prime Minister Pearson in January, 1966, Pierre Elliott Trudeau and his formulation of Canadian federalism became increasingly influential in federal policies toward Quebec and the other provinces. The new directions in fiscal policy announced by Ottawa in the fall of 1966 were in harmony with Trudeau's formulation. Those policies, which were discussed in Chapter 5, were in part directed toward reducing those elements of special status which Quebec had in fact acquired and in facilitating the withdrawal of direct federal intervention in several matters within provincial legislative jurisdiction. Trudeau became Minister of Justice in January, 1967, and played an important role in federal-provincial relations before and during the first Constitutional Conference of February, 1968. He became Prime Minister as a result of the Liberal national leadership convention two months later and in the general election June 25, 1968, he led his party to a majority in the House of Commons. During the election campaign the Liberal party made few specific promises except to commit itself to the Prime Minister's view of Canadian federalism. This view as he expounded it both before and after entering elective politics in 1965 can be summarized in five propositions.[26]

1. *The distribution of legislative powers between Ottawa and the provinces under the British North America Act corresponds with the needs of the French-Canadian community in Quebec.* During the Duplessis period Trudeau had supported the secularization and democratization of Quebec society. According to his view then and subsequently the powers conferred on the provinces by the constitution are those necessary to the integrity and survival of French-Canadian society in Quebec.

2. *The federal authorities must respect provincial jurisdiction.* In American terms, Trudeau was and is a "strict constructionist." During the 1950s he broke with other liberals and socialists in Quebec by defending Duplessis' defence of provincial autonomy. For Trudeau, Quebec's interests rest not only on the effective and imaginative exercise of provincial powers but also on a fastidious respect by Ottawa for provincial jurisdiction.

3. *A special status for Quebec is unacceptable.* In Trudeau's view, Quebec is well served by the existing distribution of legislative powers. If Quebec had more extensive powers than the other provinces Quebekers would not be able to participate as influentially in the affairs of the federal government as did other Canadians.

4. *There must be an enhanced recognition of the French fact in Canada as such.* From 1964 onward Trudeau has supported the further constitutional entrenchment of the rights of the French language in Canada. So far as individuals are concerned, he has argued that French Canadians have failed to play as influential a role as they should have in Canadian affairs largely through choice rather than because of the resistance of the Anglophone community. Canadian society and government must be reformed so that Francophones feel that the whole of Canada is their

country and be ready to assume their rightful place in participating in this wider framework rather than Quebec alone.

5. *Liberal and nationalist values are diametrically opposed and the latter are incompatible with Canadian federalism.* The major philosophical axis of Trudeau's political views is the clash between liberalism and nationalism. The enemy is the nationalist state, i.e. the sovereign political community embodying the interests and values of only one cultural and linguistic group. In Canada according to Trudeau nationalism can only result in the destruction of the federal system — as well as liberal and humane values — in the clash between Quebec and Canadian nationalisms.

Pierre Elliott Trudeau has thus formulated a coherent view of Canadian federalism and as Prime Minister he has lost no opportunity to try to polarize politics within Quebec and throughout Canada on this issue. In pressing this polarization Trudeau has defined as unacceptable the views of some of those whose allegiances are basically federalist. For example, during the 1968 election campaign the Prime Minister attacked the Progressive-Conservative party as supporting the "two nations" solution because of the views of the Quebec Conservative leader, Marcel Faribault, although Faribault had spoken and written extensively in support of federalism. Within his own party Trudeau had previously taken a very strong position against the very cautious special status position elaborated by Maurice Lamontagne in 1966, although Lamontagne was like Trudeau both a federalist Liberal and a distinguished student of Canadian federalism.

During the 1966-70 period the national question assumed a higher salience in the politics of both Quebec and Canada as a whole than in any previous period of Canadian history. The national question involves two sets of relations, (a) between Quebec and the rest of Canada, (b) between Francophones and Anglophones in Quebec. Despite the profound redefinition of Quebec in the Lesage period, both elements of the national question had been somewhat muted. As we have seen, Quebec's extensive demands for autonomy could be — and after, were — pressed in terms of the requirements of a community undergoing modernization. Further, the reforms of the Lesage government did not suggest in any explicit way a redefinition of the relations between Anglophones and Francophones in Quebec itself. To take a crucial example, the comprehensive reform of Quebec education embodied in an enactment of the Legislature in 1964, Bill 60, involved profound changes in the relations in education between the Church and the public authorities and the preceding conflict was almost entirely within the French-Canadian community.[27] On the other hand, the struggle over Bill 63 enacted in 1969 engaged the interests of Anglophones in Quebec directly and polarized French Canadians more clearly in terms of their response to the national question. This legislation attempted a compromise by protecting the rights of parents to have their children educated in the English language in publicly-supported schools with the proviso that such curricula and examinations would ensure a working knowledge of French.

The increasing salience of the national question in the late 1960s can be explained partly by the disposition of both the federal and Quebec governments to state this issue in doctrinaire and symbolic terms. Another element in this polarization occurred in the union in October, 1968, of the major separatist groups in the province to form the Parti Québécois under the leadership of René Lévesque. To the extent that the P.Q. became a major force in Quebec politics, it was inevitable that the salience of the national question in Quebec politics would be enhanced and that each subsequent Quebec election would be essentially a plebiscite on the Canadian Confederation.

In the latter 1960s there was a renewed emphasis on the relations between Francophones and Anglophones within Quebec itself. A report published by the Royal Commission on Bilingualism and Biculturalism in 1969 concluded:

> Our examination of the social and economic aspects of Canadian life (based on the 1961 census figures) shows that there is inequality in the partnership between Canadians of French origin and those of British origin. By every statistical measurement which we used, Canadians of French origin are considerably lower on the socio-economic scale. They are not as well represented in the decision-making positions and in the ownership of industrial enterprises, and they do not have the same access to the fruits of modern technology. The positions they occupy are less prestigious and do not command as high incomes; across Canada their average annual earnings are $980 less than those of the British. Furthermore, they have two years less formal education. Quebec manufacturing firms owned by Francophones produce only 15 per cent of the provincial output.[28]

Although this conclusion refered to disparities in Canada as a whole, the most politically significant inequalities related to Anglophones and Francophones within Quebec.

The demographic situation occasioned by a declining birth-rate among French Canadians in Quebec gave new urgency to the national question in the province. Three University of Montreal demographers — Hubert Charbonneau, Jacques Henripin and Jacques Légaré — examined these circumstances in a study published in 1969.[29]For a century before 1960 the proportion of Francophones in Quebec had been relatively constant at about 80 per cent, with the higher birth-rate of this group overcoming the effects of immigration and other "mouvements migratoires" favouring the Anglophone group. During the period 1956-1961 the Francophone birth-rate was about 30 per cent higher than that of other Quebecers. The study estimated that the decline of this birth-rate would continue until Francophones and Anglophones would be equal in this respect by 1985. On this basis two alternative hypotheses about the composition of the Quebec population in 2000 were made, (a) the hypothesis more favourable to the Francophones assumed a net immigration of 13,000 per year, of which 30 per cent were Francophones. This would reduce the proportion of that group in the province from 82.3 percent in 1961 to 79.2 per cent in 2000. (b) The hypothesis less favourable to the Francophones assumed a net immigration of 30,000 per year, of which 15 per cent were Francophones. This would reduce the Francophone proportion to 71.6 per cent in 2000. The projections for the metropolitan region of Montreal were also striking — a projected decline of the proportion of Francophones from 66.4 per cent in 1961 to 60.0 per cent or 52.7 per cent, depending on the hypothesis accepted. The authors concluded that what was urgent was the "francisation des immigrants" along with broader demographic, social and economic policies to further the "francisation du Québec."

The 1966-70 period was a stalemate in the relations between Quebec and the rest of Canada. The polarization between the federalist and separatist alternatives has seen the most articulate defenders of each position in Pierre Elliot Trudeau and Marcel Rioux respectively. In a bitterly polemical essay, published in 1964, Trudeau spoke of the betrayal by nationalist intellectuals of the possibilities of a liberal revolution opened up in 1960. "Quebec's revolution, if it had taken place, would first have consisted in freeing men from collective coercions: freeing the citizens brutalized by reactionary and arbitrary governments; freeing consciences bullied by a clericalized and obscurantist Church; freeing workers exploited by an oligarchic capitalism; freeing men crushed by authoritarian and outdated traditions. Quebec's revolution would have consisted in the triumphs of the human being as inalienable rights, over and above capital, the nation, tradition, the Church, and even the State."[30] According to Trudeau, the intelligentsia of Quebec had turned away from these possibilities to separatism which was inherently exploitive and authoritarian. "The truth is that the separatists counter-revolution is the work of a powerful petit-bourgeois minority afraid of being left behind by the twentieth-century revolution. Rather than carving themselves out a place in it by ability, they want to make the whole tribe return to the wigwams by declaring its independence."[31] Rioux writing in 1969 saw the two conflicting ideologies of contemporary Quebec as "catching up" and "surpassing."[32] The former is federalist and suggests that Quebec society should be reformed to embody more completely the liberal and individualist values prevailing elsewhere in North America. Although Rioux does not use this phrase, what is sometimes recommended is "North American technology in the French language." But, he asserts, "a culture and a nation whose only distinctive trait was language would soon cease to be a culture and a nation."[33] The formula for survival is in the emerging conjuncture of the national and the social questions in which an independent and distinctive Quebec society would be established.

QUEBEC AND CANADIAN FEDERALISM AFTER THE ELECTION
OF APRIL, 1970

In the general election of April 29, 1970, the Liberals were returned to power in Quebec under their new leader, Robert Bourassa.[34] The Parti Québecois contested all 108 seats in the National Assembly and for the first time the Ralliement Créditistes entered provincial politics. The results were as follows:

	Seats	Percentage of popular vote
Liberals	72	45
Parti Québécois	7	23
Union Nationale	17	20
Creditistes	12	11

The 1970 election and its results saw a much more clear-cut polarization on the issue of the relations between Quebec and the rest of Canada than had occurred in previous provincial contests. Throughout the previous decade the major provincial parties, the Liberals and the Union Nationale, had comprehended both federalist and nationalist influences. The Bourassa Liberals, on the other hand, won the 1970 election on a straightforwardly federalist programme emphasizing economic reform and the adverse material consequences of the separation of Quebec from Canada. The new Liberal leadership was less inclined to indulge in nationalist rhetoric than had been successive Quebec governments in the 1960s. The Parti Québécois of course represented the separatist alternative. The rout of the Union Nationale can be explained in terms of its equivocation on the national issue as well as a widespread disposition among the electorate to perceive the party as incapable of dealing effectively with the social and economic problems confronting the province. These factors combined with the dominance of federal politics by the Trudeau Liberals opened a period in which the polarization on the relation between Quebec and the rest of Canada would increasingly dominate Quebec political life.

Since coming to power the Bourassa government has worked toward enhancing the province's scope of discretion in particular fields of jurisdiction. As we saw in Chapter 2, the government has put a very high priority on social security. Unlike its predecessor in the 1960-66 period the new Liberal administration, as a matter of personal style or deliberate policy, or both, has pressed its demands almost exclusively in terms of efficiency rather than cultural and nationalistic values. Writing at the beginning of the Constitutional Conference of June, 1971, in which the Quebec government made a major attempt to win priority for the province over social policy Michel Roy of *Le Devoir* said of the Quebec strategy:

Pour la première fois depuis début du processus de la révision, les revendications du Québec ne sont pas principalement fondées sur des arguments exclusivement culturels ou nationalistes. L'aspect culturel n'est pas absent, mais les raisons les plus martelées par M. Castonguay sont d'un autre ordre: c'est la cohérence, c'est l'efficacité, c'est le fonctionnalisme, c'est la logique, c'est l'économie, c'est le bon sens, c'est l'équité, c'est le couci de coordination, c'est la connaissance parfaite des véritables besoins des citoyens moins fortunés qui militent en faveur de sa thèse.[35]

Significantly, the Bourassa and Trudeau governments were able to effect a reconciliation of the conflict about the role of the province in international affairs and in October, 1971, Quebec was admitted as a member of the French Cultural and Technical Cooperation agency composed of thirty nations whose first or second language was French. The formula agreed to by the federal and provincial authorities allowed such Quebec participation "with the permission of the Canadian government."

THE OPTIONS: I. THE BILINGUAL AND BICULTURAL ALTERNATIVE

The response to the circumstances of post-1960 Quebec by people and governments in Canda outside the province and by Quebecers like Pierre Elliot Trudeau who support federalism has in the main been in terms of what one may call the bilingual and bicultural alternative. This alternative suggests that to survive Canada must become in some fuller sense than at present a genuinely bilingual and bicultural country. Such reforms, it is argued, or hoped, will attenuate the pressures toward autonomism in Quebec as Francophones develop allegiances and interests within the broader Canadian framework. Specifically, there must be an enhanced recognition of the French language and culture both within federal institutions and in those regions and provinces outside Quebec where there are large enough members and concentrations of Francophones to make this practical.[36]

During the 1960s relatively rapid progress was made in implementing the bilingual and bicultural alternative. From the coming to power of the Pearson government in 1963 there was a policy of bilingualization of the federal public service with the double objectives of facilitating communication between the federal governemnt and French-speaking citizens and of making it possible for Francophones within the federal bureaucracy to work wholly or partly in their mother tongue. In 1969 Parliament enacted the Official Languages Act giving formal recognition to the equality of the two official languages in operations of the national government. Under the Act a Bilingual Districts Advisory Board was set up and this Board in its 1970 Report delineated bilingual areas in Canada where federal services would be provided in both French and English. A federal programme of grants-in-aid to the provinces has been established to encourage facilities and services in the minority official language. In all of the provinces outside Quebec there was an enhanced official recognition of the French language and culture, with the most extensive changes in those provinces with the highest proportion of Francophones. The New Brunswick Legislative Assembly in 1969 enacted its own Official Languages Act along similar lines to the federal legislation of the same year. Ontario also moved rapidly toward a vastly extended recognition of French, most importantly in establishing in areas of the province where there was a concentration of Francophones a system of French-language educational institutions, including two bilingual universities. Even in provinces like British Columbia and Newfoundland where the Francophone population was small there was some symbolic recognition of French by the public authorities.

Certain doubts may be raised about the efficacy of the bilingual and bicultural solution as an instrument for maintaining Canadian federalism.

1. This alternative has assumed the relative stability in the relations between Francophones and Anglophones in Quebec during a period when these relations were changing rapidly. The Royal Commission on Bilingualism and Biculturalism in its Report on Official Languages, published in 1967, declared:

> At the moment Quebec is the only province in which the official language minority receives full recognition. No matter what the historical or economic justification for this situation may be, it appears more and more of an anomaly. What is less and less acceptable is not so much that Quebec, with its large English-speaking minority, is officially bilingual, but that despite their sizable French communities, Ontario and New Brunswick are not. This flagrant inequality must be corrected as soon as possible if we are really to achieve equal partnership in Canada.[37]

According to this formulation, the bench-mark for the treatment of Francophones outside Quebec is to be the treatment of Anglophones within that province and in its "Consensus on Language Rights" reached at the first Constitutional Conference in February, 1968, it was declared that "as a matter of equity, French-speaking Canadians outside of Quebec should have the same rights as English-speaking Canadians in Quebec."[38] However, as we have seen, the respective position of the two languages in Quebec is changing rapidly and in the same year as Parliament and the New Brunswick legislature enacted their respective Official Languages Acts the Quebec National Assembly took steps to ensure that all students in the public schools of the province whose major language of instruction was English would become proficient in French. This latter solution was subjected to vigorous attack by various unilingualist groups in Quebec. The traditional privileges of the English language is that province are very much on the defensive, and some Quebekers have seen in certain moves of Ottawa toward the bilingual and bicultural alternative an unacceptable attempt to stabilize Quebec's traditional linguistic duality.[39]

2. To the extent that it is founded on official-language minorities, the bilingual and bicultural alternative is founded on groups whose size relative to that of the total Canadian population is probably in decline and whose patterns of development are bringing about a situation where there are fewer parts of the country than before in which large concentrations of Anglophones and Francophones live together. In a study published in 1967 Richard J. Joy traced these patterns of linguistic segregation.[40] Within Quebec he predicted that English would almost disappear outside the Montreal region and that Anglophones would be a declining proportion of the population there. Outside Quebec, "French will continue to be spoken in the border counties of Ontario and New Brunswick but will virtually disappear from Southern Ontario, the Atlantic Region and the Western Provinces."[41] It is of course possible, although it seems to me unlikely, that the new and more generous policies of the federal, provincial and local authorities to the French language outside Quebec will arrest these trends in some areas and regions. On the whole, however, official-language minorities continue to be increasingly concentrated in a very few parts of Canada.

3. While the bilingual and bicultural alternative was in process of being implemented, Quebec nationalism grew in strength. It is of course possible that nationalism would be much stronger than it now is if those linguistic policies had not been undertaken. However, since at least the rise of the Union Nationale in the 1930s the dominant forces in Quebec provincial affairs have been relatively little concerned with the recognition of the French fact elsewhere in Canada. During the period since 1960 successive governments of Quebec have not placed a high priority on the bilingual and bicultural alternative. Under some conditions this alternative has been regarded as a diversion from what is regarded as the more essential problem of a new distribution of legislative and financial powers. In the context of changing French-English relations in Quebec, even some Francophones whose basic allegiance is federalist see in Ottawa's policies toward official-language equality an illegitimate attempt to sustain the position of the Anglophone community in the province.

The alternative assumption to that underlying the bilingual and bicultural alternative argues that future relations between Quebec and the rest of Canada will be decisively determined by developments within Quebec itself rather than through changes outside the province. This latter hypothesis appears the more reasonable one.

THE OPTIONS: II, THE SPECIAL STATUS SOLUTION

There has been a great deal of discussion in the past decade of the practicality and desirability of a special status for Quebec in the Canadian federal system in the sense that Quebec will have a more extensive range of powers than those possessed by other provinces. The then Quebec Minister of Education put the case in hypothetical terms in 1965:

From now on, the question which must be faced is this: do the other nine Canadian provinces consider themselves to be "nations" or "societies" sufficiently distinct from one another to want the same measure or the same form of autonomy as does Quebec? If, on the contrary, they desire to preserve a unity of action between themselves in the areas where Quebec deems it essential to be able to act freely and autonomously, what is there to hinder us from translating this desire into a constitutional form?[42]

Writing from the perspective of an English-Canadian nationalist, Gad Horowitz said in 1967:

There is no way of avoiding an autonomous Quebec. Quebec demands and deserves a far larger degree of autonomy than that required by the other provinces. It will have this autonomy within Confederation, or there will be no more Confederation. The danger to English Canada arises out of the fact that the inevitable transfer of power to Quebec has been and is being carried out as part of a *general* transfer of power from the federal to the provincial governments. . . It becomes possible to foresee the breaking up of *English* Canada into nine autonomous units loosely coordinated by the central government. . . The obvious solution to Canada's difficulties would appear to be a federal government which is weak in relation to Quebec but strong in relation to the other provinces: in other words, a special status for Quebec within Confederation. This does not *necessarily* mean very much more autonomy for Quebec than it already has, but it does mean less autonomy for the provinces than they already have.[43]

Those observers who support a particular status for Quebec have never agreed on the extent of such particularity. For some in English Canada, the chief objective of special status is to allow a higher degree of centralization in respect to the provinces other than Quebec and from this perspective Quebec's present range of power is generally satisfactory. From another viewpoint Senator Maurice Lamontagne in 1967 propounded his theory of a limited special status for Quebec, a status whose extent would be defined from time to time as circumstances arose.[44] Essentially, Lamontagne's argument was that in specific circumstances where federal policies affected Quebec's interests adversely there should be an attempt by the province to have such policies changed before a demand was made that Quebec assume jurisdiction in such matters. This approach was in refutation of federalists, presumably Pierre Elliott Trudeau and his supporters, who rejected special status on what the Senator regarded as *a priori* grounds and of Claude Ryan's attempts some months before to specify Quebec's requirements for autonomy. Ryan's schema advanced in a somewhat tentative way suggested a very extensive transfer of constitutional powers from Ottawa to Quebec.[45] This transfer would include family allowances, old age pensions, social assistance, housing, scholarships and bursaries to students, scientific research in the universities, urban and regional development, marriage and divorce and the control of financial institutions other than banks. According to Ryan's formulation, a new constitution should spell out precisely both federal and extended provincial powers in respect to international relations, immigration and broadcasting. There should also be a constitutional definition of general federal powers and provisions whereby Quebec might dissociate itself and its people from the exercise of such powers except under emergency conditions without thereby incurring financial or other penalties.

Pierre Elliott Trudeau has been the most consistent opponent of special status. Undoubtedly he has seen embodied in these solutions the Quebec nationalism he abhors. However, he wrote in 1967 of pragmatic objections to particular status:

> All the various kinds of "special status" which have been discussed until now . . . lead to the following logical problem: how can a constitution be devised to give Quebec greater powers than the other provinces, without reducing Quebec's powers in Ottawa? How can citizens of other provinces be made to accept the fact that they would have less powers over Quebec at the federal level than Quebec would have over them? . . . How can Quebec be made the national state of French Canadians, with really *special* powers, without abandoning at the same time demands for the parity of French and English in Canada and throughout the rest of the country?
>
> These questions remain unanswered because they are unanswerable.[46]

In my view, it is imprudent either to dismiss a special status for Quebec on *a priori* grounds or to regard it as a panacea for saving the Canadian Confederation. Much of the discussion surrounding this solution has taken place in terms of somewhat abstract logic. The design for a new Canadian constitution made by Marcel Faribault and Robert M. Fowler in 1965 asserted, "There is no place in a truly federal system for different classes of regional governments or a special status for any one of them. They must all have the same constitutional powers and jurisdiction."[47] Contrariwise, one of the most distinguished students of comparative federalism, Carl J. Friedrich, sees in the principle of "federal association" one of the most hopeful devices for making the federal "process" capable of uniting areas with varying degrees of desire for union.[48] Unlike the Constitution of the United States, the British North America Act of 1867 provided several instances in which the provinces were to be in a different position and this device was followed subsequently when other provinces entered the Dominion.[49] In other than constitutional terms, the federal government in its current policies for regional economic development wields more extensive powers in the Atlantic provinces than elsewhere in Canada but this differentiation does not and need not mean that citizens of, say, Ontario and Alberta are thereby precluded from roles they might otherwise play in national affairs. On the other hand, there is surely some point at which Trudeau's pragmatic case against special status would become valid. If Ryan's scheme were followed it seems likely that relations between citizens of Quebec and the Canadian nation would become so few and tangential — and so much mediated by the provincial authorities — that membership in the Canadian political community would cease to have meaning for Quebekers. Further, under such circumstances Quebekers as such would be precluded from involvement in those aspects of national affairs impinging directly only on other Canadians. It might also be true, as Trudeau has suggested, that the scope of Quebec autonomy suggested by proponents of special status would cause other Canadians to be less willing than otherwise to provide funds for inter-personal and inter-regional equalization ion in that province.[50] In broad terms, it appears to me that a broadly equivalent distribution of legislative powers for all the provinces is the price of the continuance of Confederation.

THE OPTIONS: III, THE SEPARATE-STATES AND ECONOMIC UNION ALTERNATIVE

Apart from revolutionaries, most separatists in Quebec suggest that this new political community be associated with what remains of Canada in some form or other of economic union. The programme of the Parti Québécois adopted at its founding convention in October, 1968, suggested that at the time of attaining independence Quebec would negotiate a monetary union and a common market with Canada. Despite the presumed advantages of such a union to both parties, agreement on it is not to be a precondition of Quebec's independence and the P.Q.'s election programme of April, 1970, stated, ". . . agreement on details of an (economic) association with Canada is not an essential condition of Quebec's accession to its sovereignty. In fact, if negotiations were to fail, or if the agreement was not really to Quebec's advantage, a sovereign government would negotiate a fair distribution of federal institutions, forge its own monetary tools and, eventually, enter into economic agreements with other countries."[51]

The P.Q. position, so far as economic union is central to it, appears to be based on two assumptions. The first is that the political tie between Quebec and the rest of Canada can be severed while something like the existing level of economic integration is sustained. The second assumption is based on the continuing existence of Canada as a viable community after the secession of Quebec and the willingness of this community to enter into such an economic association. Both of these assumptions are in my view questionable.

Marcel Faribault wrote in 1964, "Today Canada is held together less by geography, natural resources, and nationality than by the very efficient composite network of communications, circulation and transfer of wealth, income, profits, and welfare."[52] While it is unclear just what Faribault meant by "efficient", he was perceptive in his recognition of the interdependence and integration of Canada. From the first the political and economic elements of the Canadian community have been closely related and it seems improbable that one of these elements can pass out of existence without the other being altered in a radical way. Prime Minister Pearson remarked at the first Constitutional Conference in February 1968 in commenting on the suggestion that ". . . if Quebec were to secede, it could then enter into negotiations with Ottawa in order to work out a *modus vivendi* with the rest of Canada while acquiring its own independent sovereignty,"

> . . . any such proposal rests on an illusion: indeed on a whole set of illusions. Surely it is an illusion to think that a declared intention . . . to seek a disputed divorce can be the basis of amicable and productive negotiations, especially when the parties concerned would still be living in the same house or as next-door neighbours. It may even be an illusion to think that in such circumstances there would necessarily be an "Ottawa" that could speak for the whole of English-speaking Canada. The proposal in short as I see it merely disguises the fact that separation could not be carried out without rupture and pain and loss.[53]

It is questionable that it would be to Canada's advantage to negotiate an economic union with a politically independent Quebec. The P.Q. position is based on the assumption that it would be to Canada's interest to maintain the previous levels of economic integration. However, it is unlikely that such integration would in fact survive independence or if it did that it would be in the interests of Canada and Quebec to sustain it. Thus from a material point of view it might well prove more rational for the two new states to take deliberate steps to *decrease* their levels of interdependence and integration because these were incapable of being effectively regulated by the common market authorities. Members of the Parti Québécois point to the Europe Economic Community as a model. However, steps taken to integrate national economies which were previously less interdependent are unlikely to be directly relevant to precisely the opposite circumstances. Rational nations do not enter into economic unions indiscriminately, and outside the frame-work of the Canadian Confederation it is by no means obvious that the Quebec and Canadian economies should be forced to complement each other — or so it might appear to western Canadians accustomed to restiveness under the previous national economic policies. Further, the most sophisticated observers of the E.C.M. regard these arrangements as a prelude to closer political union — something precluded by the formulations of the Parti Québécois.

The position of the Canadian government in economic policy-making under the alternatives proposed by the P.Q. would be intolerable. Both new nations would operate under external constraints, particularly those imposed by the government of the United States. Beyond these limitations, the Canadian government would be required to work within the framework of federal institutions, and in the new Canada the disproportionate size and strength of Ontario would impose even more severe difficulties than at present. Within this system of constraints, it would be highly irrational for Canada to contemplate seriously giving an independent Quebec a veto over national economic policies.

In general, the dismemberment of Canadian federalism by negotiation and the subsequent creation of a Canada-Quebec economic union is the least available alternative. Pursuing this alternative would in my view do much to create more bitterness among Canadians and Quebekers than there need be. It is impossible even to conjecture reasonably the substance of relations between Canada and an independent Quebec. However, it is plausible at least to assume that those relations would be much more constructive if they took place within the normal procedures of inter-national law and diplomacy in the absence of the frustrations of economic union.

NOTES

[1]See Brown's speech in *Parliamentary Debates on the Subject of Confederation of the British North American Provinces*, 1865, pp. 84-115, particularly p. 96.

[2]*(Transl.)* In Pierre Elliott Trudeau (editeur), *La Grève de l'Amiante*, Laval University Press, 1954, p. 12. I am very much indebted to Trudeau's remarkable analysis of Duplessis' Quebec. See also his essay "Some Obstacles to Democracy in Quebec" in Pierre Elliott Trudeau, *Federalism and the French Canadians*, Macmillan of Canada, Toronto, 1968, pp. 103-123.

[3]"Trois dominantes de la pensée canadienne-française; l'agriculturisme, l'anti-étatisme, et la messianisme" in *La présence anglaise et les canadiens*, Montréal, 1958, pp. 113-166.

[4]See generally *Cabinet Formation and Bicultural Relations: Seven Case Studies*, Frederick W. Gibson, Editor, Studies of the Royal Commission on Bilingualism and Biculturalism, Queen's Printer, Ottawa, 1970, and more particularly Gibson's conclusions "Co-Prime Minister, Chief Lieutenant or Provincial Spokesman," pp. 155-159 and ff.

[5]*Trudeau, Some Obstacles to Democracy in Quebec*, "regardless of how liberal were the conqueror's political institutions, they had no intrinsic value in the minds of the people who had not desired them, never learned to use them and finally only accepted them as a means of loosening the conqueror's grip," p. 106.

[6]For a history of the compact theories see Ramsay Cook, *Provincial Autonomy, Minority Rights and the Compact Theory, 1867-1921*, Studies of the Royal Commission on Bilingualism and Biculturalism, Queen's Printer, Ottawa, 1969. See also R. Arès S. J., *Dossier sur le pacte fédératif de 1867*, Les Éditions Bellarmin, Montréal, 1967.

[7]See Léon Dion "The Origin and Character of the Nationalism of Growth," *Canadian Forum*, Vol. XIII, No. 516, January 1964, pp. 229-233 and H. Guindon "Social Unrest, Social Class and Quebec's Bureaucratic Revolution," *Queen's Quarterly* LXXXI (Summer 1964), 155.

[8]"Two Cultures: An Essay on Nationalism, Class and Ethnic Tension" in *The Canadian Political Process*, Orest Kruhlak, Richard Schulz and Sidney Pobihuschy, Editors, Holt, Rinehart and Winston of Canada, Toronto, 1970, pp. 75-93.

[9]Fernand Ouellett in *Quebec: Year Eight*, Glendon College Forum, C.B.C. Publications, Toronto, 1968, p. 80.

[10]For accounts of the failure of Prime Minister Diefenbaker in respect to Quebec by two former Conservative M.P.s from that province see Pierre Sevigny, *This Game of Politics*, McClelland and Stewart, Toronto, 1965 and Vincent Brassard, *Les insolences d'un exdeputé*, Montréal, n.d.(1963).

[11]Maurice Pinard, *The Rise of a Third Party: A Study in Crisis Politics*, Prentice-Hall, Inc., Englewood Cliffs, N.J., 1971.

[12]*Le Devoir*, 29 Octobre, 1966.

[13]*Egalité ou Indépendance*, Éditions Renaissance, Montréal, p. 35. Emphasis in text.

[14]"un droit naturel, une vocation normale à l'autodétermination," p. 42.

[15]*Two Cultures, op. cit.*, p. 83.

[16]"Nationalism and Political Intelligentsia. A Case Study," LXXII, *Queen's Quarterly*, (Spring 1965), p. 166. By permission of the author and *Queen's Quarterly*.

[17]"The Economics of Nationalism", *Journal of Political Economy*, Vol. LXXII, No. 4, August 1964, pp. 376-386.

[18]For an outline and analysis of Quebec-Ottawa relations in this period see Donald V. Smiley, *The Canadian Political Nationality*, Methuen, Toronto, 1967, pp. 56-86.

[19]For a more extensive analysis see Donald V. Smiley, *Constitutional Adaptation and Canadian Federalism since 1945*, Documents of the Royal Commission on Bilingualism and Biculturalism, Queen's Printer, Ottawa, 1970, Chapter III "Postwar Canadian Federalism: The Attenuation of Federal Dominance."

[20]*The Canadian Political Nationality*, pp. 66-67.

[21]For Quebec's formulation of the institutional requirements of cooperative federalism see Premier Lesage's statements at the Federal-Provincial Conference of November 1963, *Proceedings*, Queen's Printer, Ottawa, 1964, pp. 44-46.

[22]For the Premier's statement see his Ste. Foy speech reprinted in *Le Devoir*, 23 et 24 décembre 1965. Mr. Gérin-Lajoie spoke along similar lines to the 1965 Couchiching Conference, Gordon Hawkins, Editor, *Concepts of Federalism*, Canadian Institute on Public Affairs, Toronto, 1965, pp. 62-68.

[23]Éditions Renaissance, Montreal.

[24]For an account of those incidents see Edward McWhinney, "Canadian Federalism: Foreign Affairs and Treaty Power" in *The Confederation Challenge*, Ontario Advisory Committee on Confederation, *Background Papers and Reports*, Volume 2, Queen's Printer, Toronto, 1970, p. 115-152.

[25]For the federal position see the Honourable Paul Martin, *Federalism and International Relations*, Queen's Printer, Ottawa, 1968; and the Honourable Mitchell Sharp, *Federalism and International Conferences on Education*, Queen's Printer, Ottawa, 1968. The best analysis of the Quebec position came from Paul Gérin-Lajoie, Chapter I, n. 91. See also Jacques Brossard, André Patry et Elisabeth Weiser, *Les pouvoirs extérieurs du Quebec*, les Presses de l'Université de Montréal, 1967.

[26]See the collection of his essays written between 1954 and 1967, *Federalism and the French Canadians*, Introduction by John T. Saywell, Macmillan of Canada, Toronto, 1968. The best academic defense of Trudeau's view of Canadian federalism is in Ramsay

Cook's writings. See *Canada and the French-Canadian Question*, Macmillan of Canada, 1966 and *The Maple Leaf Forever*, Macmillan of Canada, 1971. For critiques see Marcel Rioux, *Quebec in Question*, James Lewis and Samuel, Toronto, 1971 and Denis Smith, *Bleeding Hearts . . . Bleeding Country*, M. G. Hurtig Publishers, Edmonton, 1971, particularly Chapter 6, "The Federalist Dogma".

[27]Léon Dion, *Le bill 60 et le public*, les Cahiers de l'I.C.E.A., No. 1, Montréal, 1966.

[28]Book III, *The Work World*, Queen's Printer, p. 61. Reproduced by permission of Information Canada.

[29]*Le Devoir*, 4 novembre 1969.

[30]*Federalism and the French Canadians*, p. 205. By permission of The Macmillan Company of Canada Limited.

[31]p. 211. By permission of The Macmillan Company of Canada Limited.

[32]*Quebec in Question*, pp. 131-136.

[33]p. 132.

[34]For an analysis of the election see Vincent Lemieux, Marcel Gilbert et Andre Blais, *Une élection de réalignment*, Editions du jour, Montréal, 1970.

[35]*Le Devoir*.

[36]In general see the *Report on the Official Languages* of the Royal Commission on Bilingualism and Biculturalism, Queen's Printer, Ottawa, 1967.

[37]p. 96. By permission of Information Canada.

[38]*Proceedings*, Queen's Printer, Ottawa, 1968, p. 545.

[39]For an expression of this view see Albert Tremblay, "Faut-il aider les anglais du Québec?', *Le Magazine Maclean*, Avril 1971, p. 48f.

[40]*Languages in Conflict: The Canadian Experience*, Published by the author, Ottawa, 1967.

[41]pp. 135-136. Joy's study is based on the 1961 and previous census statistics and thus does not take into account the more recent decline in the Francophone birth rate in Quebec. However, this does not affect his conclusions about the Francophone minority outside Quebec. See also Frank G. Vallee and Norman Shulman, "The Viability of French Groupings outside Quebec," in *Regionalism in the Canadian Community*, Mason Wade, Editor, University of Toronto Press, 1969, pp. 82-99.

[42]1965 Couchiching Conference, *Concepts of Federalism*, Gordon Hawkins, Editor, Canadian Institute on Public Affairs, Toronto, 1965, p. 66.

[43]"Special Status: The Only Way to Assure the Free Development of the Two Founding Peoples," *Quebec in the Canada of Tomorrow*, Translated from *Le Devoir* Special Supplement, June 30, 1967, Ontario Advisory Committee on Confederation, Toronto, 1967, G-2. This supplement contained several articles on the special status option. By permission of Department of Economics and Treasury, Government of Ontario. Emphasis in Text

[44]Senator Lamontagne's speech was mimeographed and has not as far as I know been printed.

[45]"The Possible Contents of a Special Status for Quebec" in *Quebec in the Canada of Tomorrow*, E-1.

[46]*Federalism and the French Canadians*, pp. XXIV-XXV. By permission of the Macmillan Company of Canada Limited.

[47]*Ten to One: The Confederation Wager*, McClelland and Stewart, Toronto and Montreal, p. 13.

[48]*Trends of Federalism in Theory and Practice*, Praeger, New York, 1968, Chapter 11 "The Issue of Federal Association".

[49]Donald V. Smiley, *Constitutional Adaptation and Canadian Federalism since 1945*, Documents of the Royal Commission on Bilingualism and Biculturalism, Queen's Printer, Ottawa, 1970, pp. 46-49.

[50]This is one of the points the Prime Minister has made against the current demands of Quebec for priority in social policy. See his *Opening Statement* at the Victoria Constitutional Conference of June, 1971 (mimeo), p. 4.

[51]Reprinted in Paul Fox, Editor, *Politics: Canada*, Third Edition, McGraw-Hill of Canada, Toronto, p. 55. See also Le Parti Québécois, *Programme*, Edition 1969, as adapted by the Founding Convention of the P.Q. in 1968, Montreal, pp. 22-24. There is a notable lack of precision in P.Q. statements on just what cooperative activities would be carried on with Canada. On an interview with Harry Reich and Peter Shezgal of *Otherstand* in November 1969 René Levesque suggested joint operation of an international airline. *Otherstand*, Montreal, Nov. 12, 1969.

[52]"Can French Canada Stand Alone?", *Atlantic Monthly*, November, 1964, p. 137.

[53]*Proceedings*, Queen's Printer, Ottawa, 1968, p. 9. Reproduced by permission of Information Canada.

7

The Compounded Crisis in Canadian Federalism

This study thus far has been focused almost exclusively on ongoing structures and processes. The last chapter shifts emphasis by dealing in a tentative way with what appear to me to be the underlying crises of the Canadian federation. This federal system has shown considerable powers of adaptability to new circumstances without decisive breaks with the past and continues to be a great deal more durable than those contemporary observers who assert the end is near through the double onslaughts of provincialism and continentalism tell us.[1] These resources for adaptation are, however, being subjected to dangerous stresses.

For purposes of analysis, the challenges confronting the Canadian political community might be divided into those common to western democracies and those specific to Canadian history and geography. Everyone might contrive his own list in the first category, but mine would include the protection and prudent development of the natural environment; the effective management of the national economy to secure acceptable levels of price stability, employment and growth; the elimination of poverty; intelligent responses to the demands of hitherto relatively quiescent groups in some cases for equality within the present system and in others for radical change; the creation of consensus and the minimization of coercion in the face of the progressive erosion of shared values. All these matters of public concern must be dealt with through the intricacies of federal institutions and processes. However, Canada, like other nations, is confronted with challenges specific to its geographical environment and historical experience. Wryly but perceptively Marcel Rioux has said, "We might briefly define Canada as a collection of North American territories whose major problem is not the Black problem."[2] To Rioux, as to others,[3] *the* Canadian problem is the relation of English and French.

As I see it, the three specific and continuing problems of Canadian nationhood have each a jurisdictional-territorial dimension, (a) the relations between Canada and the United States, (b) the relation between English and French communities, (c) the relations between the central heartland of Ontario and Quebec and those Canadian regions to the east and the west of this heartland. Crises exist in each set of these interactions, and each set is inextricably connected with the other two.

CANADIAN FEDERALISM AND AMERICAN POWER

In the early 1970s the preoccupations of English-Canada came decreasingly to focus on Quebec and more and more to be concerned with the various dimensions of American power. Despite the attention of some to the military, diplomatic and cultural dimensions of this power, most of the public debate came to be centred on the implications of direct foreign investment in Canada and, after the announcement of President Nixon's new economic policies in August, 1971, on the relations between the Canadian and American governments in respect to economic policy.

The impact on federal institutions of the increasing control of the Canadian economy by American economic and political power deserves more careful investigation than anyone has recently given it. The so-called "Gray Report" as published in part by the *Canadian Forum* in 1971 made many strictures against foreign control of the Canadian economy but concluded that this control "does not seem to have had any direct bearing upon the Canadian political system."[4] This judgment appears hasty and superficial. Writing in 1948 Harold Innis spoke of the Canadian constitution as having been "specially designed for an economy built up in relation to Great Britain and Europe" and traced strains in this constitutional system largely to conflicts between those parts of central Canada still primarily dependent on British and European markets and the outlying regions of the country, particularly of western Canada, increasingly integrated into the continental economy.[5] Innis' magisterial insights into the relations between nationalism, imperialism and structures of government cry out for systematic application to the contemporary Canadian federation. On a much more restricted scale we saw in Chapter 4 that Khayyam Paltiel has argued that the Liberal and Conservative parties have declined as forces for national integration because their provincial wings have become decreasingly independent of funds collected by the federal parties from corporations in Toronto and Montreal concerned with influencing national economic policies; the natural resources industries on which the provincial parties, according to Paltiel, have come largely to depend for funds are overwhelmingly American-owned. From another perspective Kari Levitt in her sophisticated argument related to the American economic domination of Canada has written:

> The effect of the American corporate presence on relations between central and provincial governments is clear; the linear trans-continental axis, which once integrated the nation under an active and strong central government, has largely disintegrated. The new pattern of north-south trade and investment based on resource-development and branch-plant manufacturing, does not require a strong central government. The central government is left to manage the old infra-structure of communications and commercial institutions carried over from the previous era. However, new public expenditures are typically regional — hydroelectric schemes, highways, schools, hospitals and the like. The system of fiscal redistribution conflicts with the economic interests of the richer and more fortunate provinces. The federal function of providing for the defence of the nation is not sufficiently urgent to offset the shift of so many other functions to the regional level. Furthermore, a considerable part of the prosperity of defence work originates from the United States government, and is strongly regional in its impact on employment and income.[6]

Any comprehensive federal measures to restrict direct foreign investment in Canada or to subject foreign capital to controls in harmony with Canadian national objectives is almost certain to bring Ottawa into conflict with most if not all of the provincial governments. In the present environment of provincial aggressiveness those governments will almost certainly demand a voice in the devising and implementing of federal policies in this direction and can be expected to work toward the emasculation of these policies. The relative failure of national fiscal and economic measures from the mid-1950s onward to provide for growth and full employment projected all the provinces in varying degrees into a search for capital investment.[7] In these efforts the provinces were character-istically unconcerned from whence such capital came and, according to some of the case studies presented by Philip Mathias, unwilling or unable to exercise even elementary prudence in conferring generous concessions on foreign corporations.[8] This "development psychology" as Mathias calls it still prevails in most if not all of the provincial governments. Only in Ontario has Canadian economic nationalism become an important issue in provincial politics, and in the Ontario general election of October, 1971, the party measurably less disposed toward nationalism than its two competitors received a decisive mandate. Thus to the extent that Ottawa responds positively to pressures against the Americanization of the Canadian economy, a new issue of federal-provincial conflict emerges.

Up until this was written in December, 1971, the reaction of the federal government to the new economic directions taken by the Nixon administration from mid-August onward had been hesitant and confused. The first response from Ottawa was an attempt to gain an exemption from the American policies on the apparent assumption that in dealing with its balance-of-payments problems the United States government had inadvertently failed to take into account the extent of integration between the two countries and the adverse effect of the new measures on Canada. It soon became evident, however, that the United States had a number of specific economic grievances against Canada and was determined to use the 10 per cent surcharge on certain imports as a bargaining lever to have these grievances removed. It is interesting to speculate why neither Canadian policy-makers nor influential commentators on Canadian economic matters had given serious consideration to the possibility that the Americans might embark on a programme of economic nationalism. Perhaps the federal government proceeded on the assumption that Canadians would be able to gain exemptions from such measures as had proved possible in the past. Canadian economic nationalists on the other hand had become so preoccupied with direct foreign investment as to ignore almost completely the eventuality that some of the most crucial American decisions affecting Canada might come to be made not by the managers of multinational corporations but by the government of the United States.

In the absence of a decisive response from Ottawa to the new directions of American policy, the provinces were left to a large extent on their own to adjust to the emerging circumstances. Facing the prospects of unduly high winter unemployment some if not most of the provinces devised their own winter-works programmes before Ottawa announced to them its plans in mid-October.[9] During the middle of the election campaign in October, 1971, Premier Davis of Ontario announced he would recommend to the provincial Parliament a 3 per cent reduction in the personal income tax following a similar move in the recent federal budget. The Ontario authorities also announced that they would establish an office in Washington to protect the province's interests and convene a conference of Ontario exporters to try to develop a strategy for the emergent circumstances. The newly-elected Conservative government in Alberta declared its intention to create a Washington office, although it later appeared that the province would prefer to safeguard its interests by institutionalized machinery by which it might participate in the making of federal policies concerning natural resources.

It seems likely that some process of bargaining on a broad range of Canadian-American relations is in the offing. The Gray Report asserts ". . . the weight of evidence suggests that there has been little overt tendency on the part of the U.S. (Government) to whipsaw, i.e. to use pressure in one area to gain advantage in another."[10] The fragmentary reports available suggest that this piecemeal approach of the Americans to economic relations with Canada may be coming to an end, although the range of matters to be negotiated will itself be an important element of the bargaining.[11] Further, the approach of at least the thoroughgoing of Canadian economic nationalists is toward an integrated strategy to deal with American power and to the extent that Canada proceeds in this way the United States is pushed toward broad counter-strategies. Whatever the comprehensiveness of these negotiations, Ottawa faces strong pressures from the provinces to be directly involved in this Canadian-American bargaining. As we have seen, Alberta has made such a demand in respect to natural resource matters. Similarly, Premier Davis of Ontario announced in late November, 1971, that his government would resist any move by Ottawa to bargain away any existing Canadian advantages under the automobile agreement to gain relief from the 10 per cent surcharge on imports into the United States.

It seems almost certain that the challenges posed by American political and economic power will do nothing to resolve the differences between Quebec and the rest of Canada and may exacerbate those differences. Quebec like the other provinces is "capital hungry" and its government may resist federal measures to restrict or restrain foreign capital even more aggressively than do other provincial administrations because in Quebec economic deprivations may be perceived to lead more directly to uncontrollable civil disorder. The present Quebec government appears somewhat insensitive to the implications of American economic power and is unlikely to support any challenges from the federal government to that power.[12] Economic nationalism thus remains almost entirely an English-Canadian cause.

In general then, Ottawa is challenged by the need to devise and implement comprehensive new policies in Canada's international economic relations under circumstances where the provinces are more aggressive than ever before in demanding a strong and institutionalized influence over national economic policies. To the extent that the federal government yields to such pressures, its position in dealing both with the United States administration and the multinational corporation is weakened.

Quebec and the Canadian Federation in the 1970s

The refusal of Quebec to accept the Victoria Charter ended any early possibility of a comprehensive accommodation between that province and the rest of Canada through a new constitutional settlement. Even if the Charter as it emerged from the Conference of June, 1971, had been accepted, it would not have altered the place of Quebec in the Canadian federation in any decisive way. The major significance of the breakdown of the constitutional discussions appears to be that it was a turning away of Ottawa and the other provinces from an attempt at an over-all accommodation with Quebec. Unless some crisis like that of October, 1970, intervened, it was unlikely that political leaders whose major constituency was English-Canadian would give their urgent concern to relations with Quebec.

In the post-Victoria period the only new initiative in the relations between Quebec and the rest of Canada was a renewed pressure in some quarters that there should be an explicit recognition of Quebec's right to self-determination. The Editor of the *Canadian Forum*, Abraham Rotstein, declared his support of the "*symbolic* right to independence" contained in a formula asserting that "Quebec has the right to self-determination up to and including independence."[13] This proposition if construed literally recognizes not only Quebec's right to become a sovereign state but, short of that, Quebec's right to determine unilaterally its pattern of relations with the rest of Canada — a patently absurd suggestion. In his appearance before the Special Joint Committee of the Senate and House of Commons on the Constitution of Canada on March 30, 1971, Léon Dion of Laval University recommended that explicit recognition be given to the right of any province to leave Confederation after a referendum whose procedures should now be negotiated and presumably embodied in the Canadian constitution.[14] Dion believed that such recognition would decrease the virulence of political conflict both within Quebec and between Quebec and Ottawa. In the province federalists do not now recognize the separatist option as legitimate and separatists are fearful that their political opponents would not accede to a majority verdict of the Quebec electorate for independence. Within the context of federal-provincial relations, successive Quebec premiers have used separatism in an attempt to "blackmail" Ottawa to accede to their demands. The explicit recognition of the right of the Quebec majority to choose either federalism or independence would, according to Dion, diminish the intensity of those conflicts. Dion is an articulate federalist, who has supported the bilingual and bicultural alternative and his judgment appears to be that separatism would be less likely than otherwise if his proposal were accepted.

Those like Dion and Rotstein who press for the recognition of Quebec's right to self-determination do so in apparent anticipation of a situation in which a separatist party like the Parti Québécois came to power as the result of a free election. There are other and perhaps even more likely possibilities. Because the most fundamental of vested interests and political allegiances are engaged in the conflict between federalists and separatists, such a democratic electoral verdict might be impossible. In circumstances involving widespread repression and intimidation what responsibilities, if any, has Ottawa either for taking whatever means were available to try to ensure a democratic verdict or for giving *post hoc* scrutiny to the way in which the Quebec electorate made its collective judgment for or against national independence? From the point of view of English-Canada, the explicit recognition of Quebec's right to independence would in all probability be widely regarded as a prelude to separatism. Many English Canadians might believe too subtle the proposition that granting Quebec the "symbolic right to self-determination" makes actual separatism less likely than otherwise and might also conclude that the relations between the two historic communities might better be carried on through the processes of politics rather than group psychotherapy. Also many English Canadians seem to fear that recognizing the right of self-determination would be a self-fulfilling prophesy in hastening separation. On a more mundane level, Canadian federalism can be carried on only in terms of one of two contradictory assumptions, either that Confederation will survive or it will not. It is impossible to develop policies for dealing with both possibilities together.

Within Quebec, the federalist-separatist cleavage is coming increasingly to range against each other those who support the existing social and economic system and those who press for radical change. The radicalization of Quebec nationalism and the polarization of Quebec society on these compound axes of conflict makes violence and repression likely. As was the case in the crisis of October, 1970, such internecine conflicts within Quebec are likely to involve other Canadians and the federal government in domestic Quebec politics and to a greater or lesser degree polarize Canadian sentiment outside the province on the Quebec issue.

In the absence of such dramatic events as those in the fall of 1970, the relations between the federal and Quebec governments are likely to be abrasive. The immediate challenge is that Quebec is participating with the other provinces to deprive Ottawa of a significant scope of independent discretion to a dangerous degree; in the last months of 1971 Premier Davis of Ontario was in fact waging the struggle for provincial power more aggressively than his Quebec counterpart. Although the style of the Bourassa administration is to press the case for provincial autonomy in less provocative terms than did the Lesage government, the same strategy prevails of attempting to roll back Ottawa's power in specific fields of public responsibility such as social policy and communications. In two perceptive articles on Quebec policy with respect to communications, and in particular to the regulation of cablevision, William Johnson of the *Globe and Mail* reported:

> Quebec's strategy is to start with an area of communications where the federal jurisdiction is not evident, namely cable broadcasting. By passing legislation in this area, then issuing regulations under the legislation, Quebec will provoke a confrontation with Ottawa to force a re-examination of the whole communications field.[15]

Significantly, the Quebec Minister of Education "rejects any reference to the Constitution in attempting to solve the jurisdictional problem involved." Rather he argues:

> It is essential that Quebec, as a Government and as a collective, (*sic*) take every means to ensure that its personality is protected, that it

develops according to its own priorities. New communications, just as social policy, just as manpower policy, just as a cultural and education policy, are an essential element in the protection and development of Quebec.[16]

THE CENTRAL HEARTLAND AND THE CANADIAN PERIPHERIES

From the first the Canadian federal system has had to manage an ongoing conflict between the aspirations and interests of the central heartland provinces of Ontario and Quebec and those of the regions to the east and west of this heartland. During the past decade successive federal governments have gone further than ever before in efforts to mitigate regional economic disparities and thus to deal with the more urgent economic difficulties of the Atlantic provinces. It is in the West where since the return to power of the federal Liberals in 1963 a smouldering resistance to national policies has burst into flame. It may seem an exaggeration to consider the recrudescence of western regionalism as a challenge to Canadian federalism of the same magnitude as the more obvious problems of Canadian-American or English-French relations. However, in the period between the two World Wars the West submitted Confederation to very dangerous stresses and in the existing circumstances of instability western grievances must no longer be overlooked.

Perhaps the most lucid and coherent recent statement of the western Canadian case was made by Premier Harry Strom of Alberta in his speech to the Federal-Provincial Constitutional Conference of February 1969.[17] Premier Strom drew a parallel between existing western grievances in Confederation and those which Quebec had previously experienced and suggested that the West's alienation was a similar threat to national unity. He criticized Ottawa's priorities in economic development which he claimed were "the manufacturing industries in Eastern and Central Canada, the raw resource industries of Eastern and Central Canada, then, the raw resource industries of Western Canada, and finally, the manufacturing industries of Western Canada." The Premier reiterated the traditional western position on tariffs and freight-rates and suggested a royal commission to inquire into these matters analogous to the attempt to meet French-Canadian grievances through the establishment of the Royal Commission on Bilingualism and Biculturalism. He recommended more emphasis on the Pacific community in Canadian trade and diplomatic policies and the inclusion of Canadian personnel who knew the West in these aspects of Canada's international relations. He criticized the lack of aggressiveness in Ottawa's policies for northern development and suggested that if the federal government was unwilling or unable to act more effectively the jurisdiction, and presumably the boundaries, of the provinces might be extended. He cautioned against restraints on foreign investment. There was the suggestion of the autonomy of regional branches of the Bank of Canada so that monetary policies might be better adjusted to regional needs. In its regional economic policies Ottawa should invest and encourage investment in "high potential as well as depressed areas." There was thus here a root-and-branch attack of the whole framework of national economic policy. It is a measure of the insensitivity of the Central Canadian news media to the West that Premier Strom's remarkable analysis, whose main outlines would have been acceptable to all western provincial leaders, received almost no public attention.

Beyond the specific grievances of the western provinces in economic matters, residents of that region have come to feel outside the mainstream of national life by the acceptance in Ottawa and among the elites of the central heartland of an orthodox formulation of Canada and of the Canadian experience which has little relevance to western life and traditions. This emergent orthodoxy is perhaps most fully embodied in the Reports of the Royal Commission on Bilingualism and Biculturalism. The Commission's specific recommendations involved relatively few changes in the West as such. However in its general perspectives — as well as those prevailing within the federal government and the universities and media of central Canada — there is the assertion that cultural duality is *the* central element of Canadian life and that all responsible Canadians must put aside other preoccupations and other conflicts to deal with English-French relations. On the basis of its history and problems, western Canada never accepted this orthodoxy and at the 1967 Confederation for Tomorrow Conference the then Attorney-General of British Columbia enunciated an alternative view which undoubtedly was widely accepted in the West:

> There are other philosophies for looking to Confederation tomorrow than the duality of cultures or languages... And I am not saying that the view which I offer on behalf of British Columbia would be the same in a hundred years if our population were different at that time. What I do say is that in relation to our population at this moment we have a responsibility not only to the ancient culture and language which is the foundation of our nation. We have a responsibility in percentages and in numbers to other cultures and languages and I suggest that there is room in the diversity of this nation for a province or region or any grouping you might imagine, to embrace the continuation of what can only be described as the egalitarian point of view with respect to both language and culture... [18]

As was the case with John Diefenbaker's "unhyphenated Canadianism" and "one Canada" point of view, this western analysis conflicted with the dominant orthodoxy of the central heartland.

From the 1963 election onward the Western Provinces, and in particular the Prairies, have been sparsely represented on the government side of the House of Commons. Weak popular support for the Liberals has been compounded by the working of the electoral system denying the party seats in proportion to its votes:

	Total seats	Liberal seats	Liberal percentage of popular vote
1963 election			
Manitoba	14	2	33.8
Saskatchewan	17	0	24.1
Alberta	17	1	22.1
1965 election			
Manitoba	14	1	30.9
Saskatchewan	17	0	24.0
Alberta	17	0	22.4
1968 election			
Manitoba	13	5	41.5
Saskatchewan	13	2	27.1
Alberta	19	4	35.7

Despite the Liberal practice of co-opting leaders into the senior elective ranks of the party, neither Prime Minister Pearson nor Prime Minister Trudeau showed a disposition to so strengthen the party on the prairies. This is in marked contrast to the party's strategy under the leadership of Laurier, King and St. Laurent where a succession of able western leaders with support in their respective provinces was brought into the top ranks of the federal Liberal party. In his study of the formation of federal cabinets, F. W. Gibson states that it has been very rare for prospective ministers to exact policy commitments from the Prime Minister as a condition of joining his administration, but of the only instances in the twentieth century where such bargaining was successful westerners were involved (T. A. Hudson and T. A. Crerar in 1921, James G. Gardiner in 1935 and Stuart Garson in 1948).[19] Later Liberal administrations have felt no such urgency about the West.

The recrudescence of regionalism in western Canada is contributing along with other influences to the fragmentation of the federal system and the inability of the national government to deal effectively with the challenges of American power and of Quebec. The Trudeau government has shown a remarkable and regrettable insensitivity to this western challenge to national unity.

CONCLUSION

Only the reassertion of power and purpose by the national government can roll back the influences of what Donald Creighton has called "American continentalism and Canadian particularism."[20] By the time of the First World War the nation-building policies of the Confederation settlement and the national policy of 1878 had been in the main achieved and the decade of the 1920s saw the provinces more dominant than ever before in the federal system. At the end of the Second World War the federal government committed Canada to a new set of national purposes in domestic and international affairs.[21] The provincialism which developed from the late 1950s onward is a complex phenomenon of which a partial explanation is that the objectives of the new national policy of the previous decade had been in large measure achieved without new purposes being adopted.

As Creighton points out, none of the political parties in Canada has devised or accepted a strategy for national survival. In his almost unrelieved pessimism he sees, however, some hope in the recrudescence of Canadian nationalism and in an apolitical nationalist movement which operates under the prospects that "if it cannot capture one party, it can influence them all."[22] On the other hand, the nationalist movement, if it can be called that, is almost entirely confined to English Canada and is deeply divided. A minority of nationalists asserts that Canada can survive only if it is socialist, the majority denies this assumption. More fundamentally, few nationalists with the possible exception of Creighton himself have formulated a strategy which deals simultaneously both with continentalism and with provincial particularisms, particularly as this latter is manifested in Quebec nationalism. The kind of non-socialist Canadian nationalism manifested in the Gray Report has almost nothing to say about Quebec or more generally about the federal-provincial implications of the recommended policies to roll back American economic power. Left-wing nationalists espouse the kind of two-nations formulation which accepts Quebec separatism as a necessary if not desirable development and in the ablest version of this current of thought available Kari Levitt states ". . . national equality for Quebec requires that economic decisions affecting Quebec must be made by French-Canadians, not by English-Canadians or American corporations"[23] and later "What is in question today is the will of *English-Canada* to survive as a distinct national community on the North American continent."[24]

What is the influence of the structures and processes of Canadian federalism on the attenuation of federal power? Canada cannot effectively be governed under circumstances in which the most important of public policies are made by processes of joint federal-provincial decision: yet Canada is in the most elemental way a federal country in that crucial interests and attitudes are specific to its particular provinces and regions. From this perspective the central government can commit the country to important objectives only if these territorial particularisms are effectively represented *within* the national government itself. When this condition is not met, those interests find an almost exclusive outlet through the provinces.[25]

The Canadian admixture of British parliamentary institutions with a federal division of legislative powers between two levels of government has developed into a somewhat unstable political compound. During recent decades parliamentary institutions at the federal level have worked in the direction of denying important regionally-based interests a permanent influence in Ottawa and such interests have come overwhelmingly to find an outlet through the provincial governments. Several circumstances may be mentioned in this connection:

1. The federal cabinet has become a less effective body representing provincial interests than it was in the earlier years of Confederation. One recent observer has written, "The governing party does not pick a Cabinet in order to resolve federal conflicts. It seeks to have ministers from every province to demonstrate its truly national character and to sustain as widespread an allegiance as possible."[26] This appears to be an exaggeration, although what we know about the regional role of cabinet ministers comes only from deduction and from fragmentary and often anecdotal information. Donald Gow has pointed out that ministers have virtually no staffs involved with the regions the ministers reputedly represent and the departments "are oriented to stress values associated with industries and social structures and aggregates" rather than particular cultures and regions.[27] I have said elsewhere, "Since the departure of the late James G. Gardiner and of Jack Pickersgill it is difficult to think of any minister who has had an independent base of provincial or regional political support independent of the head of government."[28]

2. The dominance by the Prime Minister of his cabinet and his parliamentary party[29] deprives important regional groups of an effective outlet through the governing party. The increasingly presidential nature of the prime ministerial office has been the subject of much recent discussion in Canada. For the first time in Canadian political history, the head of government has at his direct disposal a considerable reservoir of specialized expertise independent of the cabinet and permanent civil service.[30] The fragmentary evidence of the development of this office under Prime Minister Trudeau does not indicate that its most influential officials are oriented toward particular provinces or regions.[31] The processes by which national party leaders are chosen by conventions do not result in the aggregation of provincial interests.[32] The secret ballot, along with the assumption in recent conventions that more than one ballot would be necessary to elect a leader, encourages all serious candidates to seek the votes of individual delegates wherever those may be found rather than as in the United States to construct coalitions of state leaders.

3. The senior federal bureaucracy appears not to be effectively representative of regional and provincial interests. In the early period of Confederation where cabinet patronage prevailed the bureaucracy was broadly representative of provincial and regional interests through appointments by their respective ministers. From the reforms of 1918 onward this has ceased to be so. The developments of the 1960s had as their objective to introduce a much higher proportion of Francophones than before in the senior ranges of the federal bureaucracy. However, this policy in itself was

not directed toward correcting imbalances in other dimensions of provincial and regional representation and, although the evidence to this effect is not available, may work in the direction of lowering the proportion of middle-level and senior civil servants from those parts of Canada where the Francophone proportion of the population is small.

The developments I have outlined above contribute together to a circumstance in which certain provinces and regions can be and are left out of the critical centres of decision-making in Ottawa. Under such circumstances those territorial particularisms are channeled through the provinces and even after the influence of the formerly deprived area is restored in the central government as the result, for example, of a general election provincialism has been more or less permanently strengthened. The first three years of the Quiet Revolution in Quebec occurred under circumstances where the incumbent federal government reflected the new aspirations of Quebec very weakly and the growing sectionalism in the prairie provinces can be explained largely in terms of the failure of the Pearson-Trudeau Liberals to comprehend prairie attitudes and interests.

The electoral system works in the direction also of weakening the territorial representivity of federal institutions.[33] At certain times important regions and large provinces are almost totally unrepresented in the governing party, although that party has gained the support of a significant proportion of the electorate in those provinces and regions. The electoral system also encourages the parties to adopt electoral strategies which almost write off in advance parts of the country in which the party is perceived to have little chance of success. As Alan Cairns explains in his brilliant analysis, the electoral system contributes significantly to sectionalism in Canadian national politics. Since the general election of 1963 the Liberals have emerged as predominantly the party of Ontario and Quebec and the Conservatives of the Atlantic and prairie provinces. The electoral system has deepened this cleavage between what Peter Newman once called "Inner Canada" and "Outer Canada."

This diagnosis of the structural defect of Canadian federalism does not lead me to any confidence that steps to remedy the deficiency will be taken. If the diagnosis is broadly accurate, the directions of required change are clear — measures to attenuate the dominance of the Prime Minister over his cabinet and parliamentary party and to increase regional influences in the government caucus and the extra-parliamentary government party; to increase the influence of the Opposition parties in the House of Commons in public decision; to make the senior ranks of the federal bureaucracy more representative of all regions and provinces; to reform the electoral system so that provinces and regions receive party representation in the House of Commons more nearly proportionately than now to popular votes. Such a system of checks-and-balances in Ottawa need not mean the adoption of the American system of the separation of executive and legislative powers. Although the Fathers of Confederation established a

TABLE 1

Percentages of popular votes and seats from "Inner Canada" and "Outer Canada" in recent federal elections

	Liberals				Progressive Conservatives			
	% votes Ont./Que.	% seats Ont./Que.	% votes "outer Canada"	% seats "outer Canada"	% votes Ont./Que.	% seats Ont./Que.	% votes "outer Canada"	% seats "outer Canada"
1963	46.0	61.9	34.7	28.6	28.5	21.9	40.0	57.1
1965	44.4	66.9	33.2	22.9	28.6	20.6	38.6	62.9
1968	49.6	74.1	38.5	34.3	25.5	13.0	35.0	50.0

("outer Canada" includes the two seats allocated to the Yukon and Northwest Territories respectively)

highly centralized federal system, there appears to have been the expectation that provincial interests would find an effective outlet through the central government as well as the provinces — through the relations between the Senate and House of Commons, through a cabinet composed of ministers with regional and provincial bases of political power, through a civil service where regional representation was safeguarded by means of patronage, through a House of Commons in which M.P.s acted without the subsequent constraints of party discipline. The expectations were in the main fulfilled in the first years of Confederation within the framework of British parliamentary institutions.

The structural crisis of Canadian federalism is that in the most direct way the provincial governments have challenged the ability of governing parties in Ottawa to speak authoritatively for all Canadians so far as matters within the constitutional jurisdiction of Parliament are concerned. This challenge has been in large part effective because the representivity of federal institutions has been highly attenuated. Only a constitutional solution which gives each province and region a permanent influence in the structures of central decision-making can roll back the excesses of provincialism which now challenge the stability if not the existence of the federal system.

The analysis of the structural deficiencies of Canadian federalism which was outlined above should not be taken to imply either that these deficiencies were by themselves responsible for the current crisis in Confederation or that changes in these structures could in themselves resolve the existing difficulties. For the time being, these are the institutional arrangements with which Canadians are endowed and within this framework a national consensus must be sought.

Elements of an emergent national consensus were beginning to appear in the late 1960s. The key dimensions of this consensus were a more thorough going attempt than before to narrow regional economic disparities and a new attempt to make Canada in a fuller sense than ever before a bilingual and bicultural community. The "have" provinces accepted, albeit grudgingly, the significant extension of revenue equalization contained in the tax arrangements which came into effect in 1967. Even more remarkably, there was a relatively high degree of acceptance of the plan for reform contained in the Report on Official Languages issuing from the Royal Commission on Bilingualism and Biculturalism in 1967. In partisan-political terms, the Progressive Conservative party at its 1967 convention came under the leadership of a man much more committed to accommodation between Canada's two historic communities than had been his predecessor. Finally, of course, the electoral victory of the federal Liberal party in the 1968 election appeared to commit Canada to Prime Minister Trudeau's formulation of federalism.

In early 1972 there was disturbing evidence that the tenuous elements of a Canadian consensus which had seemed before to be emerging were breaking down. The "have" provinces were more openly aggressive than ever before in challenging federal policies toward interprovincial equalization and were demanding measures directed toward reducing federal discretion in these and other economic matters to insignificance. New tensions appeared in Anglophone-Francophone relations. In Moncton ugly quarrels came to the surface in a province in which, by ways not understandable to other Canadians, the two historic communities had over the generations developed patterns of mutual accommodation. The smouldering resentments of Anglophones in the federal civil service against the government's policies of bilingualization came into the open and Conservative M.P.s expressed the kinds of anti-French sentiments that had not been heard since the Second World War. The sullen sense of westerners grew that they were outside the mainstream of Canadian influence. There were no signs that Quebec nationalism was being weakened.

If a new national consensus was to be established, some clear sense of direction in Canada's external policies was essential. Yet in the early 1970s both people and government seemed more preoccupied than at any time since the Great Depression with domestic concerns and, so far as there was public interest in external relations at all, with American influence on Canada. In the St. Laurent-Pearson period it is undoubtedly true that Canadians somewhat overrated their country's actual and potential role in world affairs. However, to the extent that this pride contributed to national unity and Canadian policies to international stability, this was a harmless if not beneficent illusion. The incoherence, ambiguity and seeming aimlessness of current Canadian policies both toward the United States and the wider international community contribute heavily to the low state of Canadian morale.

This book would be projected into the field of partisan-political controversy if it attempted to assign the primary responsibility for the weakening of the consensus which had begun to emerge in 1967 and 1968. The leaders of the three major national parties are all personally committed to a formulation of Confederation based on the narrowing of regional economic disparities and the establishment of Canada as a genuine partnership of its two historic communities. These leaders, however, have failed, either alone or together, to commit to such purposes large numbers of Canadians whose traditions and circumstances do not easily predispose them to support these national policies. Yet this support is clearly essential for the stability if not the survival of the federal system.

NOTES

[1]See George Grant, *Lament for a Nation: The Defeat of Canadian Nationalism*, McClelland and Stewart, Toronto, 1965, and the recent writings of Donald Creighton, particularly "Watching the Sun Quietly Set on Canada," *Maclean's Magazine*, Novem-

ber, 1971. Denis Smith has written that in Quebec "the draining away of the commitment to the Canadian state is chronic, strongly motivated and irreversible by democratic means." *Bleeding Hearts . . . Bleeding Country: Canada and the Quebec Crisis*, M. G. Hurtig, Edmonton, 1971, p. 140.

[2]*Quebec in Question*, Translated by James Doake, James Lewis and Samuel, Toronto, 1971, p. 123.

[3]At the other end of the ideological spectrum from Rioux, see the assertion of Ramsay Cook, "Canada and the French-Canadian question is really the Canadian question." *Canada and the French-Canadian Question*, Macmillan of Canada, Toronto, 1966, p. 2. For a trenchant criticism of the revisionism of Canadian historiography in the 1960s see Donald Creighton, "Confederation: The Use and Abuse of History," I *Journal of Canadian Studies*, 1 May 1966, pp. 3-11.

[4]*Canadian Forum*, December 1971, p. 34.

[5]"Great Britain, the United States and Canada," in Harold A. Innis, *Essays in Canadian Economic History*, Edited by Mary Q. Innis, University of Toronto Press, 1956, pp. 396-402.

[6]*Silent Surrender: The Multinational Corporation in Canada*, The Macmillan Company of Canada Limited, Toronto, 1970, p. 145. By permission of the publishers.

[7]For an analysis of the postwar "new national policy" and its attenuation see Donald V. Smiley, *Constitutional Adaptation and Canadian Federalism since 1945*, Documents of the Royal Commission on Bilingualism and Biculturalism, Queen's Printer, Ottawa, 1970, Chapters II and III.

[8]*Forced Growth*, James Lewis and Samuel, Toronto, 1971.

[9]See the statement by Premier Davis of Ontario to the Federal-Provincial Conference of November 15-16, 1971, "Questions in Federal-Provincial Cooperation" (mimeo), p. 5.

[10]p. 36.

[11]For example in an interview with Jack Cahill published in the *Toronto Star* of December 2, 1971, the Honourable Mitchell Sharp declared that foreign ownership was a matter of domestic Canadian policy and thus not to be negotiated with the Americans but one which in both a constitutional and political sense involved the provinces.

[12]So far as the moderate elements of Quebec nationalism are concerned the chief economic strategist of the Parti Québécois, Jacques Parizeau, claims that immediately after Quebec attains independence the nation will have a "once-in-a-lifetime chance" of laying down rules for foreign investment in a way that Canada cannot now do. These directions as outlined by Parizeau do not seem any more stringent than those recommended by non-socialist economic nationalists in English-Canada. The *Toronto Star*, Nov. 11, 1971. Despite the affinity that the English-Canadian left, and particularly the Waffle movement of the N.D.P., feels for the Parti Québécois, René Lévesque has recently asserted that the P.Q. is not socialist. *The Varsity*, Toronto, November 20, 1971.

[13]*Power Corrupted, The October Crisis and the Repression of Quebec*, Abraham Rotstein, Editor, New Press, Toronto, 1971, *Postscript*. Emphasis in original.

[14]*Minutes of Proceedings and Evidence*, the Special Joint Committee of the Senate and House of Commons on the Constitution of Canada, March 30, 1971.

[15]*The Globe and Mail*, November 27, 1971.

[16]*op.cit*. The first article was in the edition of November 26, 1971.

[17]*Proceedings*, Queen's Printer, Ottawa, 1969, pp. 121-136. For other statements of western views from a group of young Albertans see *The Unfinished Revolt, Some Views on Western Independence*, Edited by John Barr and Owen Anderson, McClelland and Stewart, Toronto, 1971. This book seems almost unknown in Toronto, although every new expression of Quebec nationalism is quickly brought into public prominence there.

[19]*Cabinet Formation and Bicultural Relations*, Frederick W. Gibson, Editor, Studies of the Royal Commision on Bilingualism and Biculturalism, Queen's Printer, Ottawa, 1970, pp. 172-173.

[20]*Watching the Sun Quietly Set on Canada, op. cit.*

[21]*Smiley, Constitutional Adaptation and Canadian Federalism since 1945, op. cit.,* Chapter 2.

[22]*Watching the Sun Quietly Set on Canada.*

[23]*Silent Surrender, op. cit.,* p. 147.

[24]p. 149. Emphasis mine.

[25]The analysis of these pages is elaborated at more length in my article "The Structural Problem of Canadian Federalism," *Canadian Public Administration,* Feb. 1971, pp. 326-343.

[26]Steven Muller, "Federalism and the Party System in Canada" in *Canadian Federalism: Myth or Reality,* J. Peter Meekison, Editor, Methuen of Canada, Toronto, 1968, p. 126. The Prime Minister, of course, rather than the "governing party" chooses the cabinet.

[27]*Canadian Federal Administrative and Political Institutions: A Role Analysis,* unpublished Ph.D. thesis, Queen's University, 1967, p. 114.

[28]*The Structural Problem of Canadian Federalism, op. cit.,* p. 336.

[29]There is a rapidly growing literature of analysis on the office of the Canadian Prime Minister. See the valuable book *Apex of Power: The Prime Minister and Political Leadership in Canada,* Thomas A. Hockin, Editor, Prentice-Hall of Canada, Toronto, 1971.

[30]Fred Schindeler "The Prime Minister and the Cabinet: History and Development," in *Apex of Power, op.cit.,* pp. 22-48 and other articles by G. Bruce Doern, Joseph Wearing and Denis Smith in the same book.

[31]The so-called "regional desks" in the Prime Minister's Office are at a relatively junior level in the hierarchy and appear to be designed exclusively to provide surveillance over regional and provincial attitudes.

[32]See Donald V. Smiley, "The National Party Leadership Convention in Canada: A Preliminary Analysis" in *Canadian Journal of Political Science* I (December, 1968), pp. 373-397 and Lawrence Leduc, Jr., "Party Decision-Making: Some Empirical Observations on the Leadership Selection Process," IV *Canadian Journal of Political Science* (March 1971), pp. 97-117.

[33]For a masterly account of the impact of the electoral system on Canadian politics see Alan C. Cairns, "The Electoral System and the Party System in Canada, 1921-1965", in *Canadian Journal of Political Science* (March, 1968), pp. 55-80.

Index